# CHALLENGES IN MENTAL RETARDATION:
## Progressive Ideology and Services

# CHALLENGES IN MENTAL RETARDATION:
## Progressive Ideology and Services

FRANK J. MENOLASCINO, M.D.

**HUMAN SCIENCES PRESS**
Formerly **BEHAVIORAL PUBLICATIONS INC.**
72 FIFTH AVENUE, NEW YORK, N.Y. 10011

Library of Congress Catalog Number 76-6947

ISBN: 0-87705-295-6

Copyright © 1977 by Human Sciences Press
72 Fifth Avenue, New York, New York 10011

Printed in the United States of America
6789   987654321

**Library of Congress Cataloging in Publication Data**

Menolascino, Frank J
 Challenges in mental retardation.
  Bibliography: p.
  Includes index.
   1.   Mental retardation services.   2.   Mentally
handicapped—Rehabilitation.   3.   Mentally handicapped.
I.   Title.   [DNLM:   1.   Mental retardation.   WM300 M547m]
HV3004.M36          362.3          76-6947
ISBN 0-87705-295-6

# Contents

# Preface

The field of mental retardation is not new. The work of the pioneers in the field—Itard, Seguin and Howe—is, by now, over 150 years old.

Yet, because the mentally retarded have for so long in this country been buried in institutions, it is only in the last 25 years that we have really gone beyond the findings of the first investigators.

Today the field of mental retardation is lit with hope, a striking contrast to the gloomy and despairing attitudes that prevailed for the first half of this century. Today we have a great deal of data and proof of the learning capacities of retarded people. Many young and idealistic persons work at all levels in the field; their efforts and empathy have helped to demonstrate that not only can retarded persons learn—they can live independently, work, support themselves, and, in short, live a normal life.

Community service programs have liberated many retarded persons from the confines of institutions to strive for that life of independence, work, and community. In the process, the questions we psychiatrists, administrators, teachers, counselors and behavior trainers must grapple with in the field of mental retardation have changed. For we, as well as retarded persons, have traded the dreary repetition and security of the old institutional life for the risks and challenges of growth and learning. We now ask ourselves:

1. Are the drugs we prescribe for retarded persons prescribed for their medical needs or for our convenience?
2. In devising community service programs, does our expertise sometimes blind us to the common sense dictates of organizing our services?
3. Are we letting complex diagnoses, such as infantile autism, blind us to the possibilities of changing that retarded person's behavior?
4. What risks can and should we permit retarded persons if the risk-taking promises to enhance their social growth and learning?
5. Can effective programming be designed to enable severely handicapped persons to live more normal lives?

I have tried to deal with these questions and others in this book in hope of helping other people to avoid the pitfalls, stumbling blocks, and easy but incorrect answers I have encountered in my own work in the field. The problem in the field of mental retardation is not knowledge, of which there is a wealth, but refinement of those diagnoses, judgments, decisions, and services that may well determine a retarded person's future.

When parents of retarded persons bonded together in 1950 to form the National Association for Retarded Citizens—NARC—there were few markers to guide them in obtaining and creating better services for the retarded. Nevertheless the changes they inaugurated have, in the last 25 years, constituted a revolution in the field. Today, we have the knowledge; what we need is the compassion and insight to use it wisely. If we do, who knows what changes today or 25 years from today can bring to bettering the lot of retarded citizens.

This book, I hope, is a step toward that better day.

I would like to thank Robert Coleman for his outstanding help in the preparation of this book. His work, interests, and overriding concern for the quality of the book is hereby acknowledged with deep thanks.

FJM

# A CRITICAL LOOK AT THE DEFINITIONS AND TREATMENT OF MENTAL RETARDATION

Among those medically defined conditions which are labeled developmental disorders, mental retardation is America's most prevalent, occuring during the developmental stages of infancy and childhood.

The term "mental retardation" refers to impaired mental ability. It is both a symptom of an underlying developmental disorder and an assessment of potential ability to learn. The retarded individual learns slowly, and at physical maturity his capacity to understand will be, to varying degrees, less than average. Mental retardation has often been measured by degrees, in terms of an intelligence quotient, or IQ, as gauged by psychological testing. However, the accuracy of the IQ score has been grossly overvalued in assessing an individual's actual ability—or projecting his potential with appropriate help and services. IQ scores have been overused to prophesy failure for children with disorders that inhibit or delay development.

## GENERAL DEFINITIONS OF THE PAST

Over the years, there have been many definitions of mental retardation that have attempted to differentiate between the intellectually subaverage and those persons with "normal" intelligence. Unfortunately, past definitions of mental retardation have been couched in extremely negative terms. Early definitions have included the following:

> Mental deficiency is a state of social incompetence obtained at maturity or likely to obtain at maturity, resulting from developmental arrest of constitutional origin; the condition is essentially incurable through treatment and unremediable through training except as a treatment or training instills habits which superficially or temporarily compensate for the limitations of the person so affected while under favorable circumstances and for more or less limited periods of time. (1)

> A mentally defective person is a person who is incapable of managing himself and his affairs, or being taught to do so, and who requires supervision, control, and care for his own welfare and the welfare of the community. (2)

> Mental retardation refers to a condition of intellectual inadequacy which renders an individual incapable of performing at the level required for acceptable adjustment within his cultural environment. (3)

In addition to these past definitions, a number of terms have been coined to distinguish among persons with varying degrees of mental retardation. Such unfortunate misnomers as "idiot," "imbecile," "moron," "low-grade," "custodial," "trainable," and "educable," were once—and in some cases still are—used to describe the retarded. These terms not only set the mentally retarded apart from other members of society but also convey to most people the visions of subhuman status, a seriously restricted ability to develop or learn, and prolonged dependency—all of which may be used as justifications for isolation from the community, custodial care, and overprotection.

One of the most undesirable effects of past definitions and related terminology has been their negative impact upon the attitudes and expectations of persons who are directly or indirectly responsible for the care, education, and training of the mentally retarded. Self-fulfilling prophecies have been generated which have operated against successfully maximizing the retarded person's level of functioning. For example, once he is labeled as "custodial," a retarded person's living and learning environments are likely to be so structured as to reflect the predictions implied by that label, thereby precluding his developmental progress to a more advanced level of functioning. That is, the statement that a person is incapable of benefiting from anything other than custodial care clearly implies that he is incapable of learning and development. It follows, then, that education and training programs are unnecessary.

On the basis of this type of reasoning, retarded persons are frequently denied access to appropriate educational and social development programs, thereby preventing further learning and development and thus confirming the original prediction.

This not to say that *labeling* is in itself necessarily destructive. The process of categorization and classification is basic to scientific inquiry and, as such, is fully legitimate. However, in the case of human beings, it is too often assumed that once the label ("diabetic," "mildly retarded," or whatever) has been assigned, it will result in the delivery of appropriate services; and in theory, at least, it should. Unfortunately, in the case of the mentally retarded labels have too often been used as a rationale for exclusion from benefits and services that are ordinarily available to non-retarded persons.

## A Widely Used Current Definition

A definition of mental retardation that is generally accepted in the United States was adopted by the American Association of Mental Deficiency (AAMD) in 1961 and reaffirmed in 1973. This definition states, "Mental retardation refers to significantly subaverage general intellectual functioning existing concurrently with deficits in adaptive behavior, and is manifested during the developmental period" (4). The terms used in this definition may be explained as follows:

> *Subaverage General Intellectual Functioning:* Falling below 97% of the population on standardized tests of global intelligence (i.e., tests which attempt to measure vocabulary, comprehension, memory, reasoning, judgment, and visual-motor functions).
> *Adaptive Behavior:* The ability to adapt to and control one's environment, usually defined in terms of maturation, learning, and social skills.
> *Developmental Period:* From conception to about 16 years of age. (5)

It should be noted that the AAMD definition addresses a dual concept of mental retardation; mental retardation is defined in terms of reduced intellectual functioning which, in turn, is associated with deficits in maturation, learning, and the development of social skills. Even though this definition is more general than earlier statements and does not emphasize the deficiencies and the inabilities of the mentally retarded, it still does not adequately stress the learning, growth, and developmental potentials that do exist for mentally retarded persons.

## The Difficulties of Diagnosis

No person should be classified as mentally retarded until he has been evaluated by a team of qualified professionals, including representatives from the social, educational, psychological, and medical disciplines. Moreover, the assessment should not be considered complete unless parents or relatives have been involved in the evaluation process as significant observers, and unless the person's adaptive behavior has been assessed in relation to his community and family situation, taking into account the cultural norms of his environment.

As indicated above, the diagnosis of mental retardation is made on the basis of two dimensions: (1) measured intelligence and (2) adaptive behavior.

*Measured Intelligence*

A primary tool in the diagnostic process is the standardized intelligence test. Tests of this type are used to sample a wide range of knowledge and skills with the intention of comparing a person's test performance to a standard established for his age level. A person exhibiting knowledge and skills similar to the standard for his age group is considered average. Below- and above-average performance, therefore, mean that a person's test performance is comparable to persons either younger or older than himself. This relationship of "mental age" or "test age" to actual chronological age is usually expressed as an intelligence quotient (IQ), with an IQ of 100 assigned to represent the average, or mean, performance. Intelligence quotients are computed according to the following basic formula:

$$\frac{\text{Mental Age}}{\text{Chronological Age}} \times 100 = IQ$$

Thus, if Mary is 10 years old and has achieved a mental age of 6 years on a standardized intelligence test, her IQ would be computed as follows:

$$\frac{\text{Mary's Mental Age } = 6 \text{ years}}{\text{Mary's Chronological Age } = 10 \text{ years}} \times 100 = IQ \text{ of } 60$$

The expected (that is, theoretical) distribution of intelligence quotients is depicted in Figure 1.1.

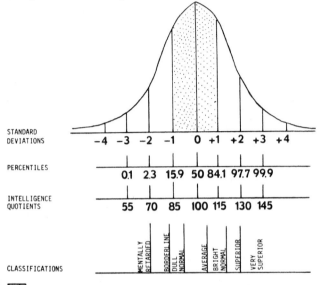

STANDARD
DEVIATIONS        −4  −3  −2  −1   0  +1  +2  +3  +4

PERCENTILES
                 0.1  2.3  15.9  50  84.1  97.7  99.9

INTELLIGENCE
QUOTIENTS         55   70   85  100  115  130  145

CLASSIFICATIONS    MENTALLY RETARDED | BORDERLINE DULL NORMAL | AVERAGE | BRIGHT NORMAL | SUPERIOR | VERY SUPERIOR

▨ = The normal range of intelligence; almost 70% of the general adult population is within this range.

*  Adapted from figures given in:
   Wechsler, D. Wechsler Adult Intelligence Scale (Manual).
   New York: Psychological Corporation 1955, pp 19-20.

   Robinson, N.M. & Robinson, HB. The Mentally Retarded Child (2nd Ed).
   New York: McGraw-Hill, 1967, pp 35-42.

**Figure 1.1   Normal Distribution Curve of Intelligence:
Classification According to Wechsler Deviation Standard
Cumulative Percentiles and IQ's**

Several tests are commonly used to measure general intellectual functioning in children and adults. The most frequently used tests of general intelligence are the *Stanford-Binet Scale,* the *Wechsler Intelligence Scale for Children,* and the *Wechsler Adult Intelligence Scale.* The Stanford-Binet measures a wide range of abilities ςorresponding to the various mental ages, whereas the Wechsler Scales for Children and Adults are separated into specific skill areas with performance compared to the average abilities of persons at different chronological ages.

## Adaptive Behavior

The second criterion used in the diagnosis of mental retardation is social-adaptive behavior. It refers primarily to an objective assessment of how well the individual copes with the educational, vocational and social demands of his environment. The major facets of social-adaptive behavior are (1) the degree to which the individual is able to function and maintain himself independently and (2) the degree to which he satisfactorily meets the culturally imposed demands of personal and social responsibility.

As in the case of measured intelligence, social-adaptive behavior is evaluated by comparing an individual with members of his own age group. Accordingly, adaptive behavior is always measured in terms of the degree to which the individual meets the standards of personal independence and social responsibility expected of his chronological age. (See Fig 1.2)

Thus, maturation would be emphasized in the early childhood years, during which such skills as sitting, stand-

**Figure 1.2  Adaptive Behavior**

| Components | Age focus | Assessment |
|---|---|---|
| 1. Maturation<br>   a.  Motor<br>   b.  Socialization<br>   c.  Communication<br>   d.  Self-help (dressing<br>       toileting, feeding) | Infancy and<br>Early Childhood | 1.  Infant Development<br>   a.  Cattell<br>   b.  Gesell<br>   c.  Merrill-Palmer<br>2.  Social Maturity Scales<br>   a.  Vineland (doll) |
| 2. Learning | School Age | 1.  Achievement Tests<br>2.  Tests of Acquisition of<br>    Knowledge and Skills |
| 3. Social Adjustment<br>   a.  Interpersonal<br>      Relationships<br>   b.  Social Conformity<br>   c.  Socioeconomic<br>      Independence | Adulthood | 1.  History and Observation<br>2.  Personality Tests |

ing, walking, self-feeding, toileting, and speech are ordinarily developed. Academic performance would be stressed during the school-age years, while vocational and social effectiveness would be emphasized in adulthood.

Social-adaptive behavior is more difficult to assess than intellectual functioning, due to a lack of satisfactory measures. For example, the Vineland Social Maturity Scale, a common tool for evaluating adaptive behavior, must be supplemented by other sources of information regarding the individual's everyday behavior if an adequate assessment is to be made.

It is to be expected that a positive correlation will exist between measured intelligence and social-adaptive behavior. That is, an individual who ranks relatively high in one dimension would be expected to rank high in the other area as well. Figure 1.3 illustrates this interrelationship between the measurements of general intelligence and adaptive behavior. Marked discrepancies between measured intelligence and adaptive behavior, such as an intelligence

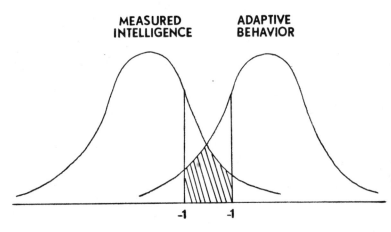

Figure 1.3  Measured Intelligence and Adaptive Behavior
Must Both Be Impaired Before a Person Is Considered
to be Retarded . . .

quotient within normal limits coupled with a subaverage adaptive behavioral level or vice versa, would cast serious doubt upon the diagnosis of mental retardation.

## LEVELS OF MENTAL RETARDATION

Mentally retarded persons attaining IQs significantly below 100 are usually classified according to levels of mental retardation as follows:

| Level of retardation | Standardized intelligence test | |
| --- | --- | --- |
| | Stanford-Binet | Wechsler |
| Mild | 52–67 | 55–69 |
| Moderate | 36–51 | 40–54 |
| Severe | 20–35 | 25–39 |
| Profound | Below 20 | Below 25 |

The classification of "borderline mental retardation" is also frequently employed (IQs of 68–83 and 70–84 on the Stanford-Binet and Wechsler Scales, respectively). It is felt, however, that persons falling within this group should not be considered as mentally retarded. Rather, they are individuals whose measured intelligence falls between the mentally retarded and the normal ranges.

Basic to the use of intelligence tests is the assumption that the person taking the test has had similar opportunities to learn, and shares a common language and culture with, those persons on whom the test was standardized. While this assumption may seem rather obvious, it is not necessarily true; the 1970 litigation *Dianna* v. *California Board of Education* was won by the plaintiff on the grounds that some 22,000 Mexican-American children had been "entrapped" in classes for the mentally retarded because they were given allegedly culturally unfair tests in English rather than in Spanish. It is also well known that a number of factors other than intelligence can significantly depress test scores; these include sensory impairments, motivation to perform well in a testing situation, anxiety associated with test-taking, and mental illness.

Therefore, the classification of retardation should be applied only to those persons who, after a comprehensive and appropriate evaluation, continue to function at a significantly subaverage level, even after various attempts at remediation have been made. Stated in another way, Figure 1.2 illustrates the principle that an individual probably should not be labeled as mentally retarded unless he is in need of special services.

## THE "ETERNAL CHILD"

In the diagnostic or evaluative process, there is a danger of approaching the mentally retarded person as an eternal child. Thus, diagnostic conclusions such as "this child will always have the mind of a five-year-old" have been common. This approach places unnecessary limitations on the development of the retarded person and assumes that he or she cannot be expected to progress beyond the dependent stage of childhood. The retarded individual may thus be treated as a child even during his adult years, thereby preventing development of the independence associated with adult maturity.

It must be remembered that a retarded person's mental age does not necessarily reflect his social interests and needs; while a 16-year-old mildly retarded adolescent may have a mental age of 10 years, it is likely that his social interests will be similar to those of non-retarded young people of 16.

## THE CAUSES OF MENTAL RETARDATION

Since the focus of this book is on the treatment-management approaches to the mentally retarded, the diagnostic aspects will be reviewed only in synoptic fashion. There are over 350 known causes for the symptom of mental retardation. The most commonly recognized ones are:

1. An imperfectly developed or damaged brain
2. Genetic disorders
3. Infections and other factors affecting the mother's health during pregnancy
4. Damage to the child during the birth process
5. Environmental-cultural deprivation
6. Inappropriate educational opportunities, or education which is at odds with cultural background.

Injuries and illness during infancy and childhood can sometimes injure the brain. Adverse living conditions, neglect, or mistreatment can interfere with the intellectual development of the infant or child. There is still a great deal of research to be done in discovering and dealing effectively with the multitudinous causes of mental retardation.

More specific information on diseases in which the symptom of mental retardation is noted have been described in recent excellent reviews (6, 7). The classification system of the American Association on Mental Deficiency (8) is an accepted standard wherein the many causes of the symptom of mental retardation are classified into eight distinct groupings on the basis of the known (or suspected) etiological factors and associated clinical manifestations. Table 1.1 presents a synopsis of this widely utilized classification.

The diagnostic approach to deciphering the possible cause of the symptom of mental retardation must stress:

1. A detailed medical history. What has been the evolution of the problem? The time and type of onset may tip you off to the diagnosis. For example, the onset of seizures in the first six months of life is commonly noted in

## Table 1.1    Causes of Mental Retardation

A.  Mental retardation associated with diseases due to infections: *prenatal* (syphilis, rubella); *postnatal* (after-effects of meningitis or encephalitis).

B.  Mental retardation associated with intoxication: *prenatal* (Rh blood incompatibility, toxemia of pregnancy); *postnatal* (postimmunization reactions, toxic substances such as lead).

C.  Mental retardation associated with trauma or physical agent: *prenatal* (injury or anoxia at birth); *postnatal* (physical injury).

D.  Mental retardation associated with disorders of metabolism: inborn (such as PKU); *growth* (such as arachnoidactyly), or *nutrition* (such as hypothyroidism).

E.  Mental retardation associated with new growths such as a brain tumor.

F.  Mental retardation associated with unknown causes (prenatal): malformations of the brain or skull (microcephaly and hydrocephaly) and Down's Syndrome.

G.  Mental retardation associated with unknown causes (postnatal): Slow destruction of the white or gray matter of the brain (Schilders disease).

H.  Mental retardation associated with social or emotional factors: cultural-familial, psycho-social-environmental deprivation, severe mental illness, etc.

hemorrhages within the brain and skull and malformations of the brain—with a high incidence of associated mental retardation. At the age of two years, these disorders become far less common as causative agents, and symptom entities such as convulsions associated with high body temperatures are more likely.

2.    Thorough physical, neurological, and psychiatric assessment should include measurement of head size and specific searching for major or minor body abnormalities and minimal signs of nervous system involvement such as a slight tremor or unequal balance. The testing should be supplemented by laboratory studies of the body fluids as clinically indicated. A developmental framework is most valuable in assessing both the child's intact and atypical

growth attainments. Psychiatric examination focuses on both the quality and quantity of responses in the interview and the nature of the parent-child interactional unit. Hyperactivity, distractibility, impulsivity, and emotional ability characterize the most frequent behavioral syndromes observed. The psychoses of childhood, which can be presented clinically as pseudoretardation, are also a differential diagnostic challenge.

    3.  The following factors are to be especially searched for in the evaluation of possible retardation:

        a.  Frequent history of prenatal, birth, neonatal, and postnatal disorders.

        b.  Growth and developmental slowness including seriously delayed physical size, slow language development (such as no words by two years, no sentences by 3½ years), motor slowness (such as no unsupported walking by 18 to 22 months), social-adaptive retardation (such as prolonged preference for play with younger children), and evidence of deficient global intelligence (primitive play patterns, inability to follow simple requests, etc.).

Although the complexity of the range of possible causes of the symptom of mental retardation is rather awesome, some general principles can provide clarity in the individual case. These clinical diagnostic challenges—the different levels of mental retardation as manifest at differing chronological ages—tend to translate into three types of diagnostic approaches by which the mentally retarded are usually identified:

    1.  Multidisciplinary diagnostic team assessments usually confirm the diagnoses of profound, severe, or moderate mental retardation in infancy and the preschool years.

These infants and children tend to have early histories of high "at risk" factors (9), body symptoms, and distinct signs of slow developmental progress.

2. School tests and general underachievement usually are the cardinal signs which prompt the identification —and subsequent referral for diagnostic evaluation—of the mildly retarded. Interestingly, the symptom of mental retardation is rarely suspected in mildly retarded youngsters before their initial school attendance and subsequent academic failure, which is the most frequent first sign of an adjustment difficulty in the mildly retarded.

3. At all chronological ages, the recognition of some degree of social inadaptability and vocational inadequacy becomes the major reason for diagnostic referral.

Elements of the diagnostic approach include a sequential personal-clinical history, followed by thorough physical and neurological examinations, laboratory testing as indicated, psychological assessment, and an evaluation of the family structure. Pearson (10) has provided an excellent overview of the diagnostic process in the mentally retarded, with special reference to translating the findings of such studies into an individualized treatment-management approach for each person so examined. He noted that the active implementation of habilitative programs must flow directly from the initial diagnostic assessment—lest the family request for help become a mere academic exercise that illuminates all but helps no one, and the family is sent on a shopping tour for help elsewhere. Wolfensberger (11) has succinctly summarized this same diagnostic exercise in futility, which is still all too frequently practiced.

In brief, a thorough diagnostic study which clearly outlines the treatment-management intervention that will be needed by the individual patient directly leads to a discussion of principles for bringing these treatment-management challenges to fruition.

No family is immune. An "accident of nature," a birth injury, or a disease in infancy can strike any home. Mental retardation affects families rich and poor, learned and ignorant. Mental retardation has no respect for social class or racial heritage.

## FREQUENCY OF MENTAL RETARDATION

The President's Committee on Mental Retardation has published the estimate that 3 percent of our nation's citizens are mentally retarded to some degree.* Translated into absolute numbers, the historically used 3 percent figure indicates that some 6½ million children and adults are afflicted with this "developmentally delaying" disorder. More than 125,000 infants are born each year—one every five minutes—who will at some time in their lives be diagnosed as mentally retarded. Further, one in every ten Americans has a direct involvement with this problem by virtue of having a mentally retarded person in his or her immediate family. It is a disorder which handicaps twice as many children as cerebral palsy, rheumatic heart disease, and blindness—combined.

## DEGREE OF RETARDATION

The degrees of retardation are usually discussed according to severity and potential to grow, learn, and develop. They are usually classified as follows:

1. *Mild.* Mildly retarded persons are almost always capable of learning to do productive work; nearly all can

*There is a substantial and wide spread use of this frequency figure in this country despite some conceptual and statistical problems with some. (Luckey, R. E. and Neman, R., Practices in estimating mental retardation prevalence. *Mental Retardation* 14 (1976): 16–18.)

learn academic school subjects to varying degrees; and they are capable, as adults, of living independently and becoming self-supporting—if they have received appropriate care, training and other services during childhood, adolescence, and early adulthood.

2. *Moderate.* Moderately retarded persons can almost always learn to care for themselves; profit to varying degrees from classroom instruction; and learn to do simple routine tasks. With an appropriate background of stimulation and training from early childhood, most are able to become at least partially self-supporting, and they are able to live in the community with some degree of supervision.

3. *Severe.* Severely retarded persons generally require intensive services at all stages of life. They generally are capable of learning to care for themselves, and many can become marginally productive as adults under supervision in a sheltered work setting.

4. *Profound.* The profoundly retarded person nearly always requires continuing medical or nursing supervision in order to remediate physical-medical disabilities and maintain life. Many who are ambulatory can be taught some degree of self-care skill, such as feeding, dressing, etc.

The President's Committee on Mental Retardation (12), in estimating the percentages, by the degree of mental retardation, among the total population of America's retarded citizens, used the information in Figure 1.4.

## CONTEMPORARY TREATMENT-MANAGEMENT APPROACHES

### Professional Attitudes

An overriding ingredient of any professional approach to meaningful treatment-management of the retarded is the need for a positive attitude and respect for the personal

Figure 1.4   Degree of Mental Retardation in
America's Retarded Citizens

| Mild | 89% |
|---|---|
| Moderate | 6% |
| Severe | 3.5% |
| Profound | 1.5% |
| TOTAL | 100% |

dignity of mentally retarded citizens. Although this principle may sound like a cliché, I strongly believe it must be at
the core of any professional's stated interest to be of service
to the mentally retarded. Professionals have for too long
viewed the retarded as eternal children or subhumans who
have limited developmental potentials; and these negative
self-fulfilling prophesies have come home to haunt professionals in the current wave of public concern, right-to-
treatment litigations, and the associated direct criticism of
the large congregate care models of our public institutions
for the retarded.

These current public demands are tragic indictments
of past and current myopic professional views of the retarded, and a firm reminder that our retarded citizens have
a God-given right to enjoy the opportunities of America.
For example, most of the current texts in mental retardation list the level of retardation of individuals with Down's
syndrome (mongolism) as being in the severely retarded
range. Yet many recent studies (13) have clearly shown that
this particular group of retarded citizens tends to function
in the moderate range of mental retardation. This is not a
matter of semantics, but one of the old views that must be
appreciated by the modern professional lest his attitude get
in the way of the children whom he is privileged to serve.
Similarly, as previously noted, the frequently distorted concept of mental age ("He is a 22-year-old man but has the
mental age of only a 10-year old boy") reflects a profound
underestimation of the dimension of social adaptive behavior and a resultant professional attitude of hopelessness.

A number of recent events—such as the film *Who Shall Survive,* produced by the Joseph P. Kennedy, Jr. foundation in 1972—have clearly addressed the issue of professional attitudes-value judgements which can literally destroy any effective treatment-management approach to the retarded citizen. These issues, as they directly impinge on the professional's approach to management and habilitative efforts, were succinctly presented in a recent article by Crocker and Cushna (14). These authors presented the following two case vignettes and then directly confronted the salient issues:

> Freddy is a child with Down's Syndrome, whose birth had engendered an agonizing period of adaptation for his parents. As the early months of life proceeded, however, a sincere and abiding-affection had developed which assured him of the necessary personal support. At 6 months of age this growing security was interrupted when he was suddenly found to be acutely ill with bacterial meningitis. After some days of troubled course in the hospital, he finally seemed returned to nearly the level of his pre-illness competency. At that time, as his mother sat with him on the ward, a resident covering for the evening paused to visit with her, and asked how he was. The mother replied, "Considering that only a few days ago we were afraid we would lose him, he seems to be doing really well." "That's good," the doctor commented, "but for a child like him, it really doesn't matter, does it?"
>
> Karen was born with a large myelomeningocele and hydrocephalus was already fully apparent. She was shown to her father once, on the first night, but her mother was never allowed to see her because the pediatrician felt that the mother could not accomodate such a distressing picture. No neurosurgical consultation was obtained to discuss shunting of spinal fluid or repair of the meningocele (which was leaking). Separation of family involvement was enforced, but as the number of days in the hospital increased the pediatrician came to realize that a long-term care program elsewhere would be necessary. He was very troubled to learn that transfer of the child to a public care facility was simply not

a practicable recourse and that the few possible private nursing homes were priced beyond the means of the family (who had no relevant health insurance). In his frustration regarding Karen's deposition and ultimate future, he declared "You know the whole situation is really just a matter of economics."

"It really doesn't matter." "It's all just economics." "What difference does it make?" These remarks and others like them emanating from well trained child-care specialists cry out for critical analysis.

Crocker and Cushna outlined four areas in which professional decisions should be recommended: (1) lifesaving issues; (2) support programs; (3) studying of available options; and (4) enrichment possibilities. They then noted that many professionals find the predicament of the mildly mentally retarded child to represent a manageable challenge, but in dealing with more severely handicapped children—for whom the rewards of conventional emotional response and identifiable educational progress become less evident—their treatment-management enthusiasm wanes rapidly. Major conflict exists regarding the justification of effortful or expensive training programs, in that they may represent excessive commitment of family resources and adaptive potential. Cushna and Crocker state:

> A litany exists in which vigorous programming for the seriously retarded child or conspicuous involvement of the family in obligations for the child's special care are decried as an imposed burden and disservice—the microcephalic, deaf-blind, severely spastic and overtly multi-handicapped become a sub-culture for whom disenfranchisement and automatic inferences are the rule. (p. 413–414)

These authors have clearly delineated the attitudinal hang-ups of professionals in this area and succinctly outlined what can be done if and when these blind spots are resolved.

## Interpretation of Diagnostic Findings and Family Counseling

Beyond obtaining evidence of impairment of function in one or more areas, the professional needs to develop special skills in evaluating the relative importance of these findings within the total clinical picture and then actively engaging the family in a plan of treatment. The interpretation of the clinical findings to the child's parents must encompass the sum total of the examination findings.

Since the condition is often most confusing to parents, one should initially empathize with their perplexity and then attempt to review the various examination findings carefully—and tactfully. The interpretation interview should review both the child's developmental assets and liabilities and then ask, How can his developmental adjustment be improved? To be effective, interpretive interviews must engage the family's interest and active participation. Frequently a number of interviews are needed to involve the family adequately. Without this, the parents may continue to shop for diagnostic services and thus further delaying treatment intervention.

Professionals must actively engage the family through active participation as early as possible, since the family is the key to any effective treatment program. Professional attitudes and level of interest are of paramount importance in this endeavor; future cooperation—or lack of it—may reflect one's unspoken, as well as spoken, attitudes at the time of first contact. The professional needs to convey to the family his willingness to share with its members the facts he learns; not as an end in itself, but as part of the first step in treatment. Treatment plans become a cooperative process which parents and professionals work out over the course of time. In an early contact, it is wise to indicate that treatment planning rarely results in a single recommendation but is something which may shift in focus and alter in course as the child grows and develops. Early implementation of this idea helps develop the concept of the professional who views the total child, referring to other special sources of help as indicated.

These children are different from other children, and some of these differences are subtle and perplexing to parents. Parental reaction frequently causes the child to realize he is different; but not in what way, or what he can do about it. If the child already perceives the world in a somewhat distorted way, this weakens his anchor to reality so that normal avenues of learning and reality testing undergo interference or even destruction. A feeling of estrangement may ensue, and increased disorganization of behavior to the point of a major behavioral disorder may occur (15).

Early interpretation to parents of these differences and related feelings of the child is a necessary part of the child's treatment. Because of lack of awareness of this dimension, many of these children are unprotected by well-meaning parents. Normal parental expectations for the average child may be too high in some areas for these children. Apparent inconsistencies baffle the parents, and mutual frustrations occur. These are compounded by similar reactions from the child's peers and by subsequent encounters with other adults in the child's world.

These children frequently need more structure than usual for good functioning. Thus, what would be viewed as overprotection for the normal child may be therapeutic for some of these children. An example of this is the need for reduction of the number of environmental stimuli which is frequently necessary so that the child does not become disorganized. Too many demands on their attention, whether they be number of people, objects, or sounds, may cause hyperactive retarded children to become so distractable that they are unable to do anything effectively. The wise mother learns to let such a child visit with one friend at a time and frequently also interposes temporal and spatial controls which would be unnecessary for the normal youngster. Special education teachers frequently use such environmental maneuvers so that the child may function better in his learning process.

Much has been written about the grief reactions of families who discover they have handicapped children. Such a reaction may occur in parents of children with mild retardation as they become aware their child is handicapped. Alertness to this dimension must be retained by professional evaluation of these children and not forgotten at the time of interpretation to parents or in subsequent interviews. Assessment of family interaction and strengths is a necessary part of the total evaluation, since these assets are essential to plan a comprehensive treatment program. Some of the psychopathology encountered in these families is reactive to their difficulties with the child in question. Interpretation of this may free parents from considerable guilt and permit more spontaneous involvement and active participation in treatment planning.

### Treatment-Management Considerations

Another basic consideration in the treatment and management of the mentally retarded is early descriptive diagnosis and early treatment based upon it. This includes clarification not only of what needs treatment but what can (and cannot) be treated actively. Full discussion of these facts can assist families in establishing realistic expectations so that mutual frustration is reduced and fewer secondary behavioral programs are encountered. A helpful professional posture when initiating treatment-management procedures for the mentally retarded is to take each patient where he is at the time of initial contact. He needs acceptance for what he is, not what he might have been without his problem nor what he might have been if therapy had been undertaken sooner. A corollary of this is awareness of the family's feelings and acceptance of the family as they are at this time. Increasing their guilt feelings is rarely, if ever, desirable in attempting to motivate them toward therapy.

One must focus in each case on the maximization of developmental potential, a natural outgrowth of the implementation of treatment following the descriptive diagnostic formulation. This involves a different type of goal-setting from the usual treatment expectation, since so often we must focus on what the child can do rather than anticipate a "cure." The goal then becomes how to go about providing him the necessary opportunity and support to develop maximally with a minimum of obstacles.

While some crisis situations will be encountered, a majority of them can be anticipated and either avoided or minimized. Knowing the child's developmental level, his handicaps and strengths, and his family situation, the professional can predict what types of developmental crises are most likely. After the initial contacts, when rapport with the family has been established, much of the work is preventive psychiatry.

An overriding challenge is the need to effectively coordinate the services needed for the child. This requires awareness of the various services available in a given community and an attitude that permits collaboration. It necessitates sharing of the overall treatment plan with the child (when appropriate), the family, and community resources, with special emphasis on the family doctor and the child's teacher. Close attention to the clarity and continuity of communication is essential.

A specific example of specialized service needs is noted in the mentally retarded individual who also has an emotional disorder. He will need services ranging from psychotherapy, in selected instances, through many types of specialized medical care, special education, vocational rehabilitation, residential services, and so on. Psychopharmacologic adjuncts to modify overt behavioral manifestations of dysfunction may be useful in some patients. The advent of a wide range of such agents (16) has materially increased the range of active treatment for many of these youngsters. The level of arousal, motor activity, convulsive threshold, and mood may be selectively altered. Since the children do not respond uniformly to these drugs, it is necessary that the clinician become familiar with a wide range. Some drugs appear to have specificity in symptom management, although the use of psychopharmacologic agents is but one part of the total treatment approach to any child.

Many of the retarded are in need of specialized special education approaches, which must often be modified for both the behavioral and integrative-cognitive problems which the children so often present. At times a psychiatric special education program has to be literally created for an individual. At other times the professional is faced with the dilemma of the need for a special education program for retarded individuals whose deficits, though grossly understood, are not able to be programmed with available educational techniques (as with retarded individuals with associated central language disorders).

Proper selection of appropriate therapeutic techniques for problems encountered at different developmental levels will effectively assist the child to reach his full potential; however, none of these principles operating alone is enough. Combine and incorporate them from the initial contact on, and a major treatment program can be successfully accomplished. In this way, professionals can assist the child and his family in the ultimate goal of helping each child who has mental retardation to develop to his maximum potential.

## General Challenges

Contrary to commonly held public opinion, the treatment and management of the mentally retarded is not a hopeless cause. Today, we speak of:

1. *Cure for a few,* such as special dietary management of children with inborn errors of metabolism (for example, phenylketonuria); early neurosurgical intervention in premature closing of the sutures of the skull; and early diagnosis and definitive treatment of hypothyroidism.

2. *Treatment for many,* such as active resolution of any accompanying emotional disturbance or a special sensory handicap; improving environmental and family living conditions; and amelioration of other factors which may sometimes make a child appear retarded—or a retarded child appear even more retarded than he really is.

3. *Habilitation for all!* This is most important. The need for a strong habilitation posture towards the retarded —initially as a child and then as an adult—is the major key to modern approaches for our retarded citizens. It is important to stress that 29 out of every 30 mentally retarded individuals can be helped to grow and develop into useful, productive, and happy members of the community, possessing a considerable degree of self-sufficiency. The retarded child and his family need early help from resource experts in understanding the nature of the handicap, and guidance as to how both the retarded child and his family can lead useful and happy lives in spite of this condition that delays normal development to varying degrees.

## THE CURRENTLY UNMET NEEDS

The mildly retarded—by far the most numerous group of retarded individuals—are among those to be found in such programs as: Head Start; public and parochial special education classes; workshop-school vocational training programs; federal-state vocational-evaluation and job-training programs; and among the ranks of the hard-core unemployed. Although often not labeled as retarded, this group of citizens has received a great deal of attention over the past decade in our nation's attempt to prepare these mildly retarded individuals to function more adequately as a part of our increasingly complex society. At the present time, there are not nearly enough public-school operated special education classrooms, community-based vocational training programs, or adequate social services available to assist this type of individual in making a positive adjustment to the community so that he can make his maximum contribution to our society in a constructive and regarding manner, as well as living as independently and self-sufficiently as he is capable of doing.

Contrasted with the mildly retarded are those citizens who are moderately retarded. They are the ones generally recognized by the public as representing the "mental retardate" in modern society. Most often, these retarded children do not fit into Head Start programs. When they reach school age, they are called "trainable;" and only in the past few years have such children been admitted to public school programs in significant numbers. As young adults, there has been an absolute absence—in most of our nation's communities—of habilitative programs to prepare them for appropriated jobs and adult life in the community.

For the moderately retarded and their families , the real crisis occurs with the advent of adolescence. Previously, the only alternatives available to parents of the moderatly retarded in most communities were institutionalization in large public institutions; placement in private institutions—for the very few who could afford them; or having the youngster sit, unproductively, at home. For the parents of such children, the prevailing unavailability of services, coupled with an increasing degree of turmoil within their own family and an overriding sense that they are not "doing the right thing" for their child, often leads to institutionalization by default, as the only available alternative. Those adolescents who are moderately retarded desperately need prevocational training services, workshop training programs, supervised living facilities within the community, and opportunities for employment as adults in a wide variety of service occupations and some industrial enterprises. The picture becomes slightly brighter with each passing year for preschool and school-aged moderately retarded children. Our current frontier is in the development of adequate and appropriate services for those of America's adolescents and adults who are moderately retarded.

The severely retarded now have access to virtually no community programs in most areas of our nation! If a severely retarded child or adult cannot be cared for in the family home, the only alternative now available in the overwhelming majority of cases is either public or private institutional care. Nationally, about 40 percent of the residents at public institutions for the mentally retarded are classified as severely retarded. Those who function at the severe level of mental retardation need, and can benefit from: developmental day-care services during their preschool and school-aged years, access to long-term sheltered workshop programs as adults, and supervised living facilities (such as group-living homes) within our nation's communities. Group-living homes or hostels for six to eight persons are greatly needed across our nation to serve the severely retarded who, for a variety of reasons, cannot remain in their family homes.

In general, the profoundly retarded are, at the present time, committed to institutions within a few months after their birth, or upon the diagnosis of the profound degree of their retardation. It is interesting to note the logic—or lack of logic—in our society's methods for dealing with the most unfortunate and multiply-handicapped of the developmentally disabled infants and children among us. The traditional logic has been that in order to serve those who need intensive medical and nursing supervision (the profoundly retarded), we must send them to relatively small communities—where most of America's large state institutions are located. The remote locations make it extremely difficult to attract qualified medical and nursing personnel; a recent assessment of the medical staff at a large Eastern institution for the retarded noted that the majority of its physicians were either foreign born with no state medical license, far past retirement age, or had had no training whatsoever in mental retardation.

We continue these practices rather than retain these profoundly retarded children in our metropolitan area centers, which are the focal points of the most sophisticated medical services now available within our nation. This logic is both myopic and appallingly inappropriate for the needs of such children. Many of the profoundly retarded, even those who are currently termed "bed-care cases," can develop a repertoire of self-help skills for daily living, with resultant improvement in their overall ability to function, if they are given adequate care, medical-habilitative services, training, and personal attention during these crucial early developmental years of their lives. Some of those now considered bed-care cases can become at least partially independent of the confines of a crib or hospital bed.

Lastly, it should be stressed that we, as a society, have not fully utilized the potentials of our retarded citizens who are of employable age. The U.S. Department of Labor, in a recent annual publication (17), endorsed the estimate that:

1.  87 percent, of our 6½ million mentally retarded citizens are potentially capable of entering the competitive labor market

2.  10 percent, or approximately 650,000, are capable of working gainfully in sheltered environments with adequate vocational habilitation training, assistance, and support
3.  Only 3 percent of these 6½ million are estimated to be incapable of some form of productive work-effort under present conditions

However, recent projects in Israel and Holland, as well as some progressive programs here in America, give evidence to challenge the validity of that last 3 percent, because more of those who are the most severely retarded, both in and out of institutions, will benefit from programming based on newly developed, innovative techniques. Truly we have quite a way to go in our efforts to provide modern treatment-management services for all of our mentally retarded citizens.

## SUMMARY

The definition, causes, frequency, and levels of mental retardation, as well as the general management and treatment goals for our mentally retarded citizens, have been reviewed as a background for our discussion of modern trends in helping the mentally retarded. The following chapters are intended to serve as a major introduction to the problems and issues relevant to understanding some of the factors which complicate the lives of the retarded, and the modern ideologies and techniques which can alleviate these roadblocks to their future developmental attainments as fellow citizens in our world.

# MODERN IDEOLOGICAL TRENDS AND NEEDS

*Chapter 1*

# MENTAL RETARDATION: ITS TREATMENT PAST AND PRESENT

For the past decade or so, enlightened citizens, government officials, and professional groups throughout the nation have come to recognize the need for substantial improvement in services for the mentally retarded and their families. Although mental retardation should be a concern for all health professions, it presents a variety of problems that invite the special participation of community psychiatrists.

Initially, this section reviews some historical data regarding the attitudes and practices of nineteenth-century psychiatry—the initiation and development of systems of diagnosis, training, and behavioral management for the mentally retarded. Then we consider some current perspectives and possible future guidelines for community psychiatry in promoting a renaissance in the treatment of mental retardation. Although psychiatry is the consistent focus of this section, the negative attitudes indicated and the future guidelines offered apply equally well to the other human service professions who work with the mentally retarded.

## THE REMOTE PAST

Except for Hippocrates and a few of his contemporaries, the physicians of antiquity and the first 17 or 18 centuries of the Christian era had little or no interest in mental illness and the forms in which it occurred. The nature of the mind was considered to be the province of philosophers, and the care and cure of "madmen" was delegated to the Church and its bishops and priests. The Church did inspire such benevolent approaches to the retarded as refuges and almshouses. For instance, the entire town of Geel, Belgium, was a religiously motivated, sheltered community setting for the mentally handicapped. Yet during the Middle Ages other extremes also occurred: the retarded were often used as objects of ridicule and were occasionally thought to be possessed and subjected to exorcism and torture.

Medicine had to wait hundreds of years, almost until the latter part of the eighteenth century, before it could realistically involve itself with mental illness without being considered an intruder by philosophers and theologians. Even near the end of the eighteenth century, Immanuel Kant violently opposed any move to involve medicine in the nature of psychopathology. The retarded apparently shared with the mentally ill the stigma of being regarded as social outcasts; they were indiscriminately segregated, along with criminals and other social misfits. While there were a number of perceptive observations about the retarded during the Middle Ages and the Enlightenment, they did not generate significant interest in mental retardation nor concern about the retardate and his needs as a human being. These matters lay dormant for another 125 years.

The first modern references to mental retardation as such appeared in medical writings of the early years of the seventeenth century, when Paracelsus described "cretinous idiocy" and its frequency in the Alps. This was some 2,000 years after Hippocrates had tried to dispel the belief that madness—and retardation—were mysterious manifestations of some supernatural phenomenon, such as demonological possession.

## AN ENLIGHTENED AWAKENING

At the dawn of the nineteenth century, Jean-Marc Gaspard Itard, a pupil of the famous Parisian psychiatrist Philippe Pinel, published a report on his five-year project of "educating the mind" of Victor, known as the Wild Boy of Aveyron. Victor was, in all probability, a severely retarded child who had been abandoned by his family. Itard's project arose out of his rewarding efforts in the education of the deaf, his commitment to the Cartesian theory of the mind as a tabula rasa, his dedication to John Locke's maxim that "nothing can produce that which it does not contain," and his conviction that Victor's mind could be educated by a system of sensory input and habit training. His work clearly illustrated what a highly structured and creative educational approach to the retarded could accomplish.

Itard's monograph *De l' Education d'un Homme Sauvage* (18) revealed his recognition of the significance of motivation, needs, and transference in his work with Victor. Much of his effort, too, was directed toward fostering what we could today call ego development and the strengthening of ego controls through the use of identification. Itard's monograph might also be called the first detailed published report on dynamic psychotherapy.

Edouard Séguin's book *The Moral Treatment, Hygiene, and Education of Idiots and Other Backward Children* (19) was a landmark in the literature of mental retardation and sparked widespread recognition of mental retardation and a systematic approach to the "education of the idiot." Under the leadership of Samuel G. Howe, a Boston neuropsychiatrist specializing in the education of deaf-mutes, Séguin's inspired system was introduced to American psychiatry in the mid-nineteenth century when Howe became director of the first state-supported school for the retarded in South Boston, Massachusetts.

The American Association on Mental Deficiency was founded in 1876. All of its charter members were psychiatrists; all were dedicated to the proposition that, through the application of psychotherapeutic principles and dynamically oriented education, "idiot" and "imbecile" children could be substantially improved—a fact that has been rediscovered only recently.

However, in the last half of the nineteenth century another fateful trend was developing. The Parisian School of Psychiatry and Neurology turned its attention to the basic nature of mental retardation, and, while describing mental illness and mental retardation in psychological and behavioristic terminology, firmly adhered to the thesis that the ultimate nature of these conditions lay in some form of brain pathology. Before the end of the nineteenth century, neurologists had seemingly established that most of mental retardation was an expression of some form of brain pathology or was associated with neurological disease. Unfortunately, this view predominates today and is expressed in a variety of "defect theories" which assume that the symptom of mental retardation is always a manifestation of distinct and fixed central nervous system pathology. This conceptualization implies a distinct limitation on the learning and adaptive ability of the retarded person which, because of damaged internal mechanisms, is seen as beyond the scope of extrinsic manipulation. This conceptualization played a dominant part in shifting the interests and role of the psychiatrist from one of positive therapeutic intervention to that of a custodial gatekeeper.

As the twentieth century approached, the discovery of brain pathology in mental retardation had a sobering effect upon the optimism and enthusiasm for "educating the minds of idiots." In only a few short years, custodial care for the mentally retarded had practically replaced all remedial efforts. While a spirit of benevolence and purpose continued to permeate professional approaches toward the retarded, the ascendency of the "defect position" dimmed hopes for the education of the retarded and drastically altered the emphasis from sheltering the retarded from society to protecting society from the retarded. The residue of benevolence toward the retarded slowly faded away.

In summary, borne along on the wave of a growing social conscience, the nineteenth century saw the discovery of mental retardation as a "condition in which the intellectual faculties have never developed sufficiently." It witnessed the introduction and vigorous pursuit of a rational plan for "educating the minds of idiots"; and for about 60 years psychiatry led the way in promoting the best interests of the mentally retarded. However, while the nature of many types of retardation were discovered and classified, this increasing concentration on brain pathology and its accompanying professional commitment to the "defect position" began to dim the previous therapeutic enthusiasm of the psychiatrist.

## THE TRAGIC INTERLUDE

At the end of the nineteenth century, societal trends created a tragic interlude that left a lasting imprint on psychiatric involvement in the field of mental retardation. This interlude lasted only about 20 years (1900–1920), but it produced a radical shift of psychiatric interest away from mental retardation. Changes in society's view of the retarded ushered in institutional models of care which protected society from the "deviant," who was isolated in a low-budget institution that placed a premium on his labor as a major means of support. Unfortunately, this new role not only lessened enthusiasm for treating the retarded but increasingly allied psychiatrists with penologists; the National Conference on Charities and Corrections became a major vehicle for the transaction of professional affairs in mental retardation. Thus began a half-century or more of bench-sitting and wheelchair ambulation for the retarded in most of our institutions, and the historical period of the "retarded as a menace."

Three crucial developments, operating in symbiotic relationship, administered the coup-de-grace to the challenge of mental retardation for the psychiatric profession: (1) the appearance of the Binet test; (2) the introduction of psychoanalysis to American psychiatry; and (3) Goddard's 1912 monograph on the Kallikak Family (20).

Almost overnight the Binet test and its subsequent modifications gained acceptance as a crucial diagnostic technique for mental retardation. It soon came to be utilized as the one and only guide for educational programs and even for the prognosis of social effectiveness. The psychiatric approach was replaced by the mental-test approach, and the professional services of the psychiatrist became expendable. Psychometric tests found vast numbers of "morons" in our midst. This discovery caused widespread concern, especially since so many morons appeared to be social misfits. No one seemed to notice it was mostly the social misfits that came under scrutiny. Obviously all morons were social problems, or potentially so. "The menace of the feebleminded" was upon us.

Goddard was not alone in sounding this eugenic alarm. Others, such as Davenport (21) and Fernald (22) also contributed to the consensus which, in time, included four distinct conclusions: (1) there were more retarded persons in our society than people realized; (2) the mentally retarded accounted for virtually all of the current social ills; (3) heredity was the major cause of mental retardation; and (4) since the "decadent" retarded appeared to reproduce faster than nonretarded citizens, society would soon be destroyed unless drastic measures were taken.

While these concepts were jelling, American psychiatry was rapidly assimilating the dynamic concepts of psychoanalysis into psychiatric evaluation and treatment. Psychotherapeutic efforts with the psychoneuroses served to lure psychiatrists away from "prosiac and purposeless activities" in mental retardation. Itard's psychopedagogical efforts with Victor were soon forgotten. The "menace of the feebleminded" and the sounding of the "eugenic alarm" together with the notion "once feebleminded, always feebleminded" led to the advocacy of immediate institutionalization for all mental retardates wherever and whenever identified. Thus the new policy: to isolate the retarded, at least for the duration of their reproductive years. This step alone was enough to repel most psychiatrists who had any thoughts about rehabilitating persons with mental handicaps.

The tragic interlude stimulated construction of larger institutions in which to incarcerate the "dangerous" retardate. From the early twentieth century until 1960, the institutional theme song was, "Protect society from the deviant." In rapid succession, restrictive marriage and sterilization laws were passed. Retardates were doomed to lifelong warehousing in inexpensive institutions. Vail (23) has aptly described these moves as "dehumanization." Psychiatrists became jailers. Modern professional-societal expectations left little room for the humane and supportive care models that had so typified the earlier role of the psychiatrist in mental retardation. At that time, the major journal in this field was entitled *The Journal of Psychoasthenics*, a title which implied the constitutional inferiority of the retarded.

A close review of this period (1900–1920), and its aftermath until 1960 clearly reveals that professionals literally led the field into a wilderness. Arguments supporting mass sterilization, enforced labor, and inexpensive warehousing could be viewed as unfortunate events. Hindsight, however, paints a different picture. During the period from 1920 to the present, the fruits of new knowledge could have been applied. There was no justification for the prevailing institutional practices. Momentum played a larger role than reason.

The pictorial overview entitled *Christmas in Purgatory* by Blatt and Kaplan (24), coupled with a special report of the President's Committee on Mental Retardation, documents this aimless continuity of momentum in pictures and words.

The institutional aspect of the psychiatrist's recent role in the field of mental retardation has been stressed here because it may hold the key to a new renaissance of psychiatric involvement. New rationales are direly needed. The wave of humanism that typifies society's current posture toward the handicapped can provide multiple challenges for the psychiatrist. It can impel him to invest— or reinvest—his skills in an area which genuinely needs him.

In summary, mental retardation attracted the interest and participation of the psychiatric profession throughout the nineteenth century and for the first decade or so of the twentieth century. But by 1920 the interests of psychiatry and other mental health disciplines began to deteriorate. Until the early sixties, mental retardation occupied only a peripheral position in psychiatric teaching, training, and practice.

## PRESENT STEREOTYPED PSYCHIATRIC VIEW

We have reviewed some of the extraordinary historical events that led to psychiatry's relative withdrawal from the field of mental retardation. This withdrawal has resulted in a number of blindspots psychiatrists characteristically exhibit in dealing with the retarded. Briefly, they are:

Uncritical acceptance of mental age as an adequate description of a person

Treatment nihilism usually based on lack of program knowledge

A myopic view of conceivable, or even available, program alternatives

Excessive focus on the severely retarded and their families, in contrast to the mildly retarded

### The Mental Age Myth

The psychometric mental age as an overall description is still too often used to pigeonhole mentally retarded persons. This stereotype can be altered by realistic study of individuals and how they actually experience the world around them. A number of recent works by professionals, laymen, parents and siblings of the retarded, and even the retarded themselves provide an insight into the phenomenological world of the retarded.

For example, a recent book by Edgerton (25) entitled *The Cloak of Competence* well illustrates the wide range of adjustment styles of the adult retardate and dispels the common professional stereotype of the passively compliant and socially/vocationally inept individual. Similarly, the recent autobiography of an adult with Down's syndrome, *The World of Nigel Hunt* (26) lets readers get under the skin of a human being who has an adaptive problem we choose to call mental retardation. Although the young Nigel employs grammatical contruction typical of a third or fourth grader, his word fluency and range of topics are quite beyond that. It is obvious that this young man has a rich interpersonal world. He has feeling, hopes, and aspirations that go beyond the usual stereotypes of "moderate mental retardation" or "mental age of seven years" of the young adult with Down's syndrome.

The mental age myth also comes to bear in another area. A mildly retarded child seen in the company of his low socioeconomic status parents is too often termed a cultural-familial mental retardate. Yet a similar youth from a higher socieconomic grouping is apt to be diagnosed as "minimal cerebral dysfunction," and his low mental age is ignored or interpreted as a spurious assessment in view of accompanying neurological findings. In these two instances, the myth of mental age reflects a negative bias on the part of the examiner toward the value system of the retardate from a low socioeconomic class. It also indicates strong professional conjectures as to the relative efficacy of psychotherapy for the retarded. This negative attitudinal bias is not limited to psychiatrists. Recent educational reports strongly suggest that the track system for educating the retarded from low socioeconomic groups may reflect the myth of fixed mental age and its associated low expectancy set for mentally retarded students.

Thus the mental age myth, with all of its trappings of fixed intellectual functioning and developmental expectancy, has given rise to a companion myth about the value of any psychiatric treatment for those declared "unchangeable." The myth that the intelligence quotient determines an individual's capabilities and ability to partake in, and benefit from, psychotherapy is often implicit in current psychiatric practice. Similarly, Bernstein (27) reports the surprise and subsequently changed attitudes on the part of psychiatric trainees who have been given an opportunity to relate to the retarded on a protracted basis.

All of these considerations strongly suggest that the mental age myth will only be destroyed when the professional is fully able to appreciate the recently rediscovered social-adaptive potential of the retardate. Such a view demands individual assessment of the retardate's function in the worlds of family, peer group, school, or work and a new look at him as a person in the world, in contrast to the mental age label that attempts to predict academic adjustment rather than life adjustment potentials. The mental age myth has permeated both professional and institutional postures toward the retarded. Interestingly, a re-examination of this topic may suggest that we return to the pre-IQ tester, with strong focus on individualized assessments in a variety of life settings.

## Preoccupation with Severe Retardation

There are eight times as many mildly retarded persons as there are moderately, severely, and profoundly retarded combined. Because their problems are more educational, psychological, and habilitative in nature than medical, the mildly retarded have less in common with the more severely retarded than with normal children. Nevertheless, the greatest part of psychiatric attention—especially that motivating institutional services—appears to focus on the more severely retarded. The majority of the mildly retarded will manage fairly well in our society, given some aid and guidance from other members of the family, neighbors and friends, and from society through its agencies and special services. The members of this large group will acquire sufficient reading, writing, and arithmetic, and, if provided with vocational training and guidance, will be able to obtain and hold unskilled, semiskilled, and even occasionally skilled jobs. If they have adequate emotional support and guidance, it is highly probable that they will not be social misfits. Most will marry, and most of these will bring up families. The long term follow-up studies of community-based mentally retarded individuals are forceful reminders of what the retarded can do!

A significant percentage of mildly retarded children have adjustment problems which contribute significantly to their learning difficulties. The primary psychopathological features of the retarded, their poor self-image, and their unfavorable competitive position in the world around them make them especially prone to anxiety. Interventive psychiatric care thus becomes a critical ingredient in providing adequate services for a large number of mentally retarded children. Without psychiatric care, secondary emotional disturbances may well prevent the inclusion of these children in developmental special education programs during childhood. In adults, emotional disturbance or personality dysfunction often disrupts vocational training and job placement. The importance of obtaining necessary psychiatric services for emotionally complicated instances of mental retardation again stresses the incongruent nihilistic posture adopted by many contemporary psychiatrists.

In this regard, it's important to note that the psychiatrist has usually viewed or treated a very select sample of retardates: those with emotional disturbances. What about the 70 percent who are not emotionally disturbed? Unfortunately, it is likely that the average psychiatrist's very limited training and clinical experiences lead him to expect disturbed behavior in all or most of the retarded. Similarly, the selected samples of severely retarded children usually seen by pediatricians has led to generalizations reflecting this selectivity.

Retarded children thrive in selected community settings. This is particularly true of those with problems in speech and language. These two skills develop earlier or more completely in retarded children when they live at home and attend developmental day-care centers and community schools, instead of residing in institutions. Similarly, these children display greater development when they reside in small residential units with high staffing ratios and flexible treatment regiments, in contrast to large, overcrowded, and understaffed facilities where care and training is institution-centered rather than child-centered.

In conclusion, the overemphasis on severe mental retardation has not only produced a distorted view of psychiatric dimensions of the mentally retarded but has also failed to focus psychiatric effort where it is quantitatively, socially, and programmatically most desperately needed: for the mildly retarded.

## Treatment Nihilism and Lack of Program Knowledge

Treatment nihilism stemming from sterotyped psychiatric concepts is reflected in the usual lack of knowledge among psychiatrists concerning therapeutic possibilities and the necessary components of meaningful programs for the retarded. The blunt fact is that few psychiatrists are conversant with the tremendous advances in vocational rehabilitation and residential programming that have been fully documented. The significance of the actual implementation of these programmatic components, as in the Scandinavian facilities for the retarded, are frequently not grasped or are totally ignored. A typical professional comment: "Vocational training successes occur in 'atypical' or undiagnosed retardates, and Tizard's Brooklands film (28) gave me the impression that it was a small pilot program which had ideal staffing patterns but, like so many pilot programs, it isn't really applicable to the problem at large." This lack of understanding is stressed because it has probably led directly to the psychiatrist's misdirected defense of the tragic models of care which have recently been so clearly condemned (29). To implement enlightened programming, we must actively utilize the new concepts and programs in the field of retardation.

However, we may have to cross another barrier first: admit that what we see is really there, that the large congregate care purgatories do exist. I have personally visited over one-half of the state-supported residential facilities for the retarded in the United States. Typically, what is most obvious is their failure to apply what is known in the treatment of mental retardation. Every large institution for the retarded I visited has units where ambulatory young adult and middle-aged moderately and severely retarded individuals regularly embark on a daily schedule of futility. We continually fail to stress the obvious: that use of currently available program knowledge can completely change these terrible patterns which perpetuate an environment devoid of respect for the human dignity of the retarded.

For example, a severely retarded ambulatory young adult who works on even the simplest industrial task in a sheltered workshop—on the institution grounds or, even better, off them—is constructively occupied, is preparing himself for placement in the community; is viewed by others more positively; has a more positive self-image than he did formerly; and contributes to society. Today, such an individual would most likely be found in one of the Scandinavian countries. The same retardate in a public institution in the United States probably would be wandering about in the play yard, exhibiting stereotypical hand movements, mumbling to himself, digging aimlessly at the ground, and performing little purposeful activity.

We must stress not only the vocational habilitation potentials that are available but also those very dimensions that are of such importance to politicians and state legislative budgetary committee members. Specifically, we are long overdue in reassessing the high rate of psychoactive drug usage in current institutional programs and the high rate of "autistic" primitive behaviors which are frequently and erroneously accepted as part and parcel of the syndrome of severe retardation (30). It is difficult to throw off this particular stereotype unless one sees widespread quality programming, as in Scandinavia, and finds how little autistic behavior is exhibited in such environments. Hardly any of this behavior is visible in Scandinavia and, as other visitors to that area have observed, the focus on a truly total therapeutic atmosphere—and isolation from which such behavior—commonly evolves into an atmosphere of normalization (31). Such programming also has major implications in parents' views of retarded children, and their role vis-à-vis an institutionalized child. Once their child has become behaviorally quiescent by learning a more purposeful role via meaningful education-vocational programming, parents are more eager to visit him regularly, to take him home for visits, and to assist him in the eventual transition to community placement and habilitation.

We cannot overemphasize the importance of seeking alternatives to current methods of handling programs and issues in mental retardation. The myopic professional view of treating the moderately and severely retarded ambulatory adult consists of high doses of tranquilizers, selective restraint, isolation, and an attitude that implies, "If he's quiet, we've done our job."

The present purveyor of institutional care for the severely retarded typically views any alternative programs as fads, not serious alternatives. The stereotyped views of what the retarded cannot do are more prevalent than convictions regarding what they can do. Low budgets are a chronic problem—and a scapegoat. There is a tragic lack of professional awareness concerning new program knowledge and competence. The "low budget" argument is rather embarrassing when one notes that daily costs at most of our inadequate public institutions are higher than the prorated daily costs of the Scandinavian facilities, or even of some outstanding private facilities in the United States. Also, the specter of "politics" and "national health systems" are commonly advanced to belittle the Scandinavian comparisons. Yet there is current data on a cost-service benefit ratio approach to assess realistically these differing programmatic approaches for the retarded.

Could it be that we do not want to look squarely at the national disgrace of our residential facilities for the retarded? Have we unconsciously or otherwise accepted the previously noted historical "loss of rationales" and acquiesced to an aimless continuity of momentum? Or can the psychiatrist come to grips with his historical heritage, learn, and then implement available alternatives of programmatic excellence both in institutional and community settings?

There are available treatment programs that disavow treatment nihilism. Embracing this future for the retarded is a major opportunity and challenge for the contemporary psychiatrist.

## IDENTITY CRISIS OF THE PSYCHIATRIST IN MENTAL RETARDATION

Today, when there is an urgent need for active participation of mental health personnel in the field of mental retardation, the United States has only a handful of psychiatrists, clinical psychologists, psychiatric social workers, and vocation rehabilitation experts prepared to respond to the demands and opportunities of implementing the mental health aspects of a national program of action for the mentally retarded. At both the community and institutional levels, there is an alarming gap between supply and demand for mental health personnel to work with the mentally retarded.

What, ideally, is the role of the psychiatrist in mental retardation? As noted, much of his historical role has been supplanted by changes in the fields of mental retardation and psychiatry. Stripped of his cherished professional standbys—the diagnostic interviews, assessment of intellectual function, etc.—he has apparently slipped into the uncomfortable role of clinical and institutional gatekeeper. Meanwhile, his clinical skills in mental retardation have not been enlarged by concurrent trends in general psychiatry. As far as mental retardation is concerned, he remains in a limbo of ideological perplexity and practical disengagement. He has adopted the mental model of management in retardation. Too frequently, he has become an administrator of a clinic or a gatekeeper at an institution.

This overemphasis on an administrative role is rather ironic in view of the great professional challenge to understand the entire psychobiological unit presented by the retarded individual. In other words, concern for control at all levels has gained precedence over the study of individual or collective dimensions of mental retardation.

With its nihilistic conceptual approach and physical disengagement from the field, it comes as no surprise that psychiatry has been relegated to diminishing roles in the planning and administration of both community programs and residential facilities for the retarded. The current trend toward more lay administrators has demanded a hard new look at the necessary training and individual personality variables that are needed to operate mental retardation programs or facilities. Despite the fact that administration of mental retardation programs was once the sole prerogative of the psychiatrist, this lingering bias is no longer tenable. What is tenable is a renaissance of the psychiatrist as an enlightened perveyor of human services. Potter's (32) guidelines for this professional role can be an excellent administrator's bible.

The psychiatrist's current identity crisis in mental retardation was thoroughly reviewed during a roundtable discussion at the 1969 national meeting of the American

Psychiatric Association (Miami Beach, Florida) entitled "The Psychiatrist and Mental Retardation: Divorce, Separation, or Re-Marriage?" It evaluated questions such as the following: Shall we continue to fight the movement toward increasing lay administration of mental retardation programs? Would such a professional posture be of any real value to the persons we are privileged to serve? When will we appreciate and accept that we are not needed in a central role in many current treatment approaches. This new role would have to more actively involve the consumers: the retardate, his parents, and the community (for example, the National Association for Retarded Citizens). Such reemphasis would require elimination of some cherished professional blindspots.

Psychiatry's medical role in mental retardation overlaps with that of administrators, mental health specialists, educators, pediatricians, practitioners in general medicine, neurologists, geneticists, and pharmacologists. The psychiatrist has functioned actively in all of these medical science roles in mental retardation except surgery. This kaleidoscopic involvement should serve to increase rather than limit the role of the psychiatrist in mental retardation. There are many roles in this field, both now and in the future, that can truly utilize his skills.

Since many of the diagnostic and treatment needs in mental retardation can be provided by others in the mental health, medical, and paramedical fields, we must broaden our discussion to include other human management personnel rather than pursuing the "psychiatrist alone" posture of the past. Such a shift recognizes the efforts of colleagues in the fields of child development, education, nursing, psychology, social work, and vocational rehabilitation. We must also realize that the attitudinal changes are necessary in virtually all professional fields. For example, though pediatrics has recently taken an active role in mental retardation (via the university-affiliated mental retardation centers), there are relatively few developmentally oriented pediatricians who are strongly identified with the field of mental retardation. Concentrating almost exclusively on the medical and neurological needs of the child, pediatrics has aimed at only a limited portion of the needed diagnostic-treatment-management services for the retarded. Just as the retarded do grow into adults, and thus limit the range of involvement of the pediatrician, so does the psychiatrist have built-in limits that delineate his role.

Virtually every professional group currently involved in mental retardation has had its heyday in the field. One wonders if this alternation of leadership does not reflect the attitudinal and social values of both society and of the professionals themselves. We could more profitably utilize our energies to explore current societal and professional benefits for the retarded and gear our professional training programs to erase a multitude of inherent blindspots.

*Chapter 2*

# MODERN IDEOLOGICAL TRENDS
# AND THEIR IMPLICATIONS

Twenty-six years ago the National Association for Retarded Citizens (NARC) was formed, and thus was inaugurated a courageous effort to enkindle hope for the lives of our retarded fellow citizens. In the middle 1950s NARC helped illuminate biomedical research in order to discover the causes of and possible treatments for mental retardation. Meanwhile, parents of the retarded and advocates of social justice spoke out to educate the public about the educational, cultural, and social plight of the retarded during the early 1960s. Now, in the 1970s NARC stands ready to bring the retarded out of the shadows of destructive folklore, to rescue them from their subhuman social status and their role of pawns to be maneuvered by the only temporarily interested cadre of planners, professionals, and politicians.

Today, we are on the threshold of providing truly normalizing programs for the mentally retarded. I recently attended the annual convention of a state association for retarded citizens which is pushing past this threshold of normalization on some of the major ideological and programmatic challenges of the seventies. On their convention program were such topics as:

1. Preschool education for the retarded child at home
2. Special education dropouts: multiply handicapped children
3. Work and recreation for the mentally retarded: programs for developing independence and facing risk
4. Sexual guidance
5. Community homes for the retarded: what should they offer?
6. The voice of the consumer: the National Association for Retarded Citizens and mentally retarded citizens
7. Advocacy: who will care and take care?

These challenges concerning future ideological directions and programming were discussed at the most important level of change: by the citizen advocates, representing the consumers of services for the retarded.

To bring the laser beam of developmental maximation and personal dignity to the retarded, there must be a commitment to support services in their behalf. Contemporary services for the mentally retarded during the 1970s will, in the author's opinion, embrace the ideological concept of normalization, wed it to the programmatic guidelines which flow from the developmental model, and permit our nation to really bring our retarded citizens out of the shadows. In this chapter, we will review the factors which can, and will, allow the provision of normalized services for our retarded citizens in the current decade and beyond.

## BACKGROUND

Contemporary Western society places high social value on the attributes of intelligent behavior, social adaptability, emotional independence, economic self-sufficiency, and physical attractiveness. Since the mentally retarded individual generally does not meet any of these expectations, he is in dire need of overall developmental programming to meet or approximate these attributes and thus fit into the world around him. Yet our future is deeply tainted by our past, and today's reactions to the mentally retarded still carry the imprint of negative and destructive definitions and labels. This section will initially review many of these current attitudes and practices, particularly as they relate to the provisions of residential services for retarded persons.

Today more than 150,000 mentally retarded persons live in approximately 175 public institutions, and an additional 60,000 persons reside in private residential facilities. Commenting on present-day conditions, the President's Committee on Mental Retardation (33) reported that institutions for retarded persons are usually located in remote areas and are characterized by inappropriately designed, overcrowded, and antiquated buildings. The problem is made worse by the fact that most residential personnel are underpaid, poorly trained, and often without hope of better working conditions or advancement.

## DEVELOPMENT OF TRADITIONAL SERVICE MODELS

The purpose of the first institution in the 1850s was to provide educational services for the mentally retarded. These facilities were actually schools in the true sense of the word, and long-term custodial care was not inherent in the plans for service. The schools were designed specifically to habilitate mentally retarded persons and return them to the community to live and work. In a few short years, however, the emphasis on services shifted from helping the mentally retarded to protecting society from them. There was a gradually increasing concern over the morality of the mentally retarded, their presumed criminal tendencies, inheritance of mental retardation, and eugenics. As these concerns increased, a cloud of pessimism and fear stifled the initial and brief period of progress initiated by the first facilities. Mentally retarded persons were moved from populated areas where they could best be served to isolated rural areas where they were rejected, abused, and subjected to inhuman treatment. By the turn of the century, mentally retarded persons were blamed for a wide array of social ills, and more and larger custodial institutions were endorsed by society.

The emphasis on protecting society from mentally retarded persons was at its height immediately after the turn of the century, and the needs of the retarded person were completely overshadowed by society's frantic attempt to protect itself. Mentally retarded individuals were slighted even more by society's unwillingness to provide any more than the essentials for survival in the institutional setting. Institutions had to be largely self-supporting in order for the inhabitants to survive; thus, mentally retarded persons were used as captive work force. Such conditions continued through the early 1920s.

By the end of the first quarter of the century, the treatment of, and the lack of services for, mentally retarded persons were subject to widespread criticism. However, due to a lack of readily apparent alternatives, the enormity of the established problems, and a general resistance to change, little or nothing of significance was done to improve conditions for institutionalized mentally retarded persons until the last decade.

## NEED FOR A MODERN SERVICE MODEL

The manner in which society perceives the mentally retarded has been a major factor in determining the location, design, and program orientation of residential facilities. These basic role perceptions may be thought of in terms of service models.

In this context a service model for mentally retarded persons is a set of premises (or predictions) from which services are structured. In most cases the total environmental setting reflects these predictions, and there is no allowance for behavior or development contrary to such predictions. Thus models generate self-fulfilling prophecies; the type of behavior or development predicted is encouraged and, generally, the expected results are achieved.

Seven models have, over the last century, been used as rationales for the services frequently found in institutions for the retarded in this country. The first six are destructive in nature and have resulted in inappropriate and dehumanizing approaches to residential care:

1.  *The sick person.* Mentally retarded persons are cared for in a hospital-like setting, as if they were ill or diseased. Dependency, safety, comfort, cleanliness, and emphasis on the physical aspects of the "patient" are typical.

2.  *The subhuman organism.* Mentally retarded persons are viewed as being deviant to the extent of not being completely human and are typically housed in an indestructible setting with locked doors. They are allowed minimum freedom and considered incapable of making decisions. Basic human rights are considered nonapplicable.

3.  *The menace.* Mentally retarded persons are viewed as a threat because of their differences. The setting in which they live resembles a prison. Few provisions for safety are

provided. Care techniques may bear overtones of persecution. There is an emphasis on segregating the sexes.

4. *The object of pity.* Mentally retarded persons are cared for as if they were suffering victims. Responsible functioning is de-emphasized. The retarded are sheltered, made comfortable, and emphasis is placed on making them happy and contented.

5. *The burden of charity.* Mentally retarded persons are viewed as being the responsibility of public charity—but services given them should not exceed minimum expectations. The retarded are expected to be duly grateful and suffer through intermittent hardships without complaint.

6. *The holy innocent.* Mentally retarded persons are viewed as childlike and harmless. Such an approach is dehumanizing because it encourages treating the adult as a child.

7. *The developing person.* All mentally retarded persons, regardless of the degree of retardation, are considered capable of growth and learning. The structure of the environment in which they live is also considered of prime importance in influencing the rate and direction of behavioral change.

## Momentum of Old Service Models

Despite the rather impressive growth of knowledge and technology in the field of mental retardation, three major factors have perpetuated destructive service models and have impeded the implementation of appropriate residential services. These three major factors are architectural factors, staff resistance, and financial considerations.

ARCHITECTURAL FACTORS.    The physical aspects of institutions have provided momentum for the continuation of long-outmoded service approaches. The appearance of the physical plant of most public institutions conveys an unspoken message to the employees and residents that greatly inhibits the adoption of service models which emphasize the humanity and dignity of mentally retarded persons. Large groups of people in massive, impersonal, and sterile settings promote loss of individual identity, regimentation, dependency, and child-care practices for the total group which tend to accommodate the least capable members.

STAFF RESISTANCE.    Discrepancies between potential and actual services have continued because of the threatening implications of change for the institutional staff. Implementing modern service models requires retraining of personnel, reorganization of staff, delegation of authority and responsibility, and, in many cases, a complete reversal of attitudes toward the residents. Since modern program service models require constant planning, change, and flexibility, such changes may be especially threatening to the institutional administrative and midmanagement staff. Change may also be viewed as threatening by staff members working directly with the institution's residents. That is, direct-care personnel may see intensive programming as resulting in increased supervision, more stringent work evaluation, and the assignment of greater and more specific responsibilities for the education, training, and supervision of residents.

In effect, the adoption of modern service models would increase the complexity of the total institutional picture, thus creating more responsibility for the institutional staff and eliminating the security which may emanate from an established, simple, custodial approach to mental retardation.

FINANCIAL CONSIDERATIONS.    Concern over increased budgets, modification of buildings, and supplementation of staff has also impeded progress and overshadowed the major issue (changing the mentally retarded residents). Modern buildings with homelike exteriors and interior furnishings would promote maximization of the humanity and dignity of mentally retarded persons. However, unless the attitude of the staff coincided with the message implied in the structure of the buildings, conditions would not be greatly improved.

Residential services have undergone little significant change since the first institutions were built, mainly because the general public, despite repeated exposés, has been essentially unaware of the plight of retarded persons. Unfortunately, there has also been an apparent lack of true concern for the welfare of the retarded.

Institutions and their services reflect public attitudes and respond to public pressures.

In summary, since the philosophies and attitudes of residential personnel regarding the capabilities and needs of retarded residents will directly affect the type and quality of training programs, they provide a rationale for continuing practices, whether they are appropriate or inappropriate. A recurrent theme throughout present-day concern with residential services is that former concepts of custodial care are no longer acceptable. Parents as well as professionals in the field of mental retardation are becoming increasingly vocal in their demands that every retarded resident be provided with a community-based program designed to optimize his developmental level, regardless of ultimate functional potential. There is, in this writer's opinion, a need for a viable residential service model, based on the premise of the developmental model—that mentally retarded persons are capable of growth, development, and learning—a topic to which we now turn.

The most exciting modern trends in the field of retardation have come with the embracing of the developmental model as the major prescriptive approach for treatment-management programs in this area, and the gradual acceptance of the ideological principle of normalization as an overall approach to the retarded. Each of these major ideological trends will be discussed in detail because they represent two key underpinnings of the current renaissance of community-based programs for the mentally retarded.

## THE DEVELOPMENTAL MODEL

In contrast to the image of the retardate as a sick person, use of the developmental model brings about habilitation of the mentally retarded through the application of positive programmatic principles. The developmental model is a means of bringing about normalization (see p. 66) and can be viewed as taking a positive view of the modifiability of human behavior. Further, all mentally retarded persons are perceived as capable of growth, development, and learning, as opposed to the old concept of negative reinforcement of difference from the norm.

Preliminary to development of program goals based upon the developmental model is the presentation of its three underlying fundamental concepts:

1. *Life as change.* To be living means that all human beings are in a constant state of change; to remain static is to cease to exist. A professional posture which focuses on the decreased psychological and physiological functioning of a mentally retarded individual, and which equates this with a negative state, denies the individual existence as a human being. Alternatively, professional consideration which concentrates on modifying both the developmental expectations and social/behavioral skills enables the individual to maintain the constant state of change necessary to life.

2. *Sequence of development.* Human beings develop through the various stages of life in a predictable sequence; the individual progresses from the dependency of infancy

to competent, independent functioning as an adult to (sometimes) decreased competency in old age. Development, whether physiological or psychological, is an orderly process.

3. *Flexibility of development.* While the general sequence of development is established, each individual is subjected to varying stimuli from the environment, from cultural differences, and from ongoing patterning by meaningful people; this accounts for variance in the rate and particulars of one's development. The complex interactions of genetic, internal, and external environmental factors are repeatedly demonstrated in different human beings; recent studies have shown that interactions begin prior to birth.

This last concept is particularly relevant to professionals involved with programming for the retarded. Here one can successfully demonstrate the interactions between environmental and inherited factors of retardation.

## SELECTING PROGRAM GOALS

Programs for retarded persons based on the developmental model are designed for the express purpose of modifying the rate of direction of behavioral change. Recognition of the fact that each retarded child or adult is in a continual state of flux, subject to the influence of dynamic encounters with the environment, is basic to the concept. Goals or programs based on this model consist of selecting some changes for acceleration, identifying others for deceleration, and selectively modifying the direction of these changes.

A critical issue revolves around the criteria to be used in selecting the rate and direction of changes sought. It might be argued that the most fundamental goal of all organisms is survival, and that developmental programs should thus be predicated upon goals which will insure continuity of the individual. It is important, however, to distinguish between survival as preservation of life and survival as effective coping with the environment. The former definition has often been interpreted as meaning that all possible steps should be taken to minimize risks to the individual. This action has resulted in programs which have significantly impeded development, induced regressive changes or fostered dependency, passivity, and related behaviors in the early stages of human life. A case in point is the use of gastric fistulae for feeding severely impaired children, on the premise that this procedure minimizes risk and increases the probability of adequate nutrition. Unfortunately, the technique is also likely to drastically decelerate (or prevent altogether) autonomy in feeding and related behavior.

In view of these considerations, it is felt that the definition of survival as effective coping with the environment is more appropriate to the developmental model. On the basis of this definition, three principles emerge as basic to the selection of program goals: increased control over environments, increased complexity of behavior, and maximization of human qualities.

## Increased Control Over Environments

An important aspect of coping is the ability to control the environment and to make choices among alternatives. Retarded persons should, therefore, be helped to develop behaviors that will extend their control over various environments, including other persons and themselves.

## Increased Complexity of Behavior

A second, directly related, principle is that goals should be selected which will lead to increasingly complex behavior.

The desirability of fostering complex patterns of behavior is based on the premise that such behaviors are in general more effective in coping with the environment than rudimentary activities.

## Maximization of Human Qualities

The third, and in some ways the most basic, principle for determining programmatic goals is the concept of maximizing the human qualities of each individual. In the present context, such qualities are defined as those which are culturally designated as "normal" or "human." Obviously, these characteristics differ from culture to culture and from era to era. Failure to comply with cultural standards may seriously impair, or totally vitiate, the individual's ability to cope with his environment, sometimes resulting in rejection, isolation, or even loss of his life. Indeed, the popular strategy of institutionalizing the retarded is a direct function of their failure to conform to cherished cultural values.

Maximizing the human qualities of deviant persons can be understood as "normalizing" them; as decreasing their deviancy from the cultural norm. Our culture defines relatively flexible parameters for behaviors considered acceptable during most stages of development—infancy, adolescence, and adulthood. The individual whose behavior consistently violates cultural expectations may be labeled as deviant and is in danger of social isolation. For retarded persons, then, this principle implies attempting to develop behaviors which are appropriate to the individual's stage in the life cycle.

Maximizing human qualities should not be interpreted as a sterile, mechanical procedure resulting in puppetlike individuals who vacuously mimic socially established patterns. On the contrary, human qualities include such attributes as the ability to determine one's goals and the strategies to accomplish them, spontaneity, enthusiasm, initiative in interpersonal relationships, and a myriad other behavioral characteristics judged desirable by contemporary society.

Developmental goals for retarded and nonretarded persons are basically identical. Indeed, although a truly developmental program should be individually conceived and designed, the underlying principles will hold, regardless of an individual's particular area of deviancy. At any stage of development, therefore, specific goals selected for the individual consist of target behaviors which would increase his "humanity"; that is, behaviors which would closely approximate the cultural norm.

## Programmatic Implications

Accepting the developmental approach to mental retardation implies adoption of certain basic program principles. Each individual is considered as a unique, changing human being. The program, whether it consist of biochemical intervention, socioeducational approaches, or other techniques, is designed to meet the individualized, dynamic goals of those being served. These goals are selected on the basis of fostering behavior which will enhance the individual's human qualities, increase the complexity of his behavior, and increase his ability to cope with the environment. Specific goals are based on the observed behavior of each individual and are determined by his current level of functioning.

Since each individual is in a constant state of change, goals are continually re-evaluated and revised in terms of observed behavior. Hence, goals may reflect increasingly complex behavior (in the case of progress) or increasingly simple behavior (as may be the case in senility or progressive neurological deterioration). Developmental programming is not limited, therefore, to the early phases of the life cycle but is applicable to all stages, including old age. During the latter stages of the life cycle, or in cases involving deterioration, goals are selected in terms of decelerating certain changes, while other goals may still be selected for acceleration. For example, a person afflicted with progressive paralysis of the legs may be helped to retain maximum muscle control (decelerating muscle atrophy and loss of functions) while learning new skills involving the use of mechanical devices, such as wheelchair and crutches (accelerating new behaviors).

As individual program goals are periodically re-evaluated, there will be some cases in which it becomes apparent that the rate of progress is so minimal as to render the long-range goal of integration into society unrealistic. In such instances, the principles of developing more complex behavior and increasing the individual's control over his environment may assume primary importance. Action may involve reliance on techniques which differ markedly from those typically employed in the teaching and socialization of non-retarded persons, although utilization of such unusual techniques may, in fact, hold little promise for equipping the individual to function effectively in society.

## Administrative Implications

The philosophy of programming basic to the developmental model contains a number of implications for the administration of mental retardation services. These implications pertain to:

1. Orientation of the program administrator
2. Structure of the service system and the manner in which resources are deployed within it
3. Use of modern management tools
4. Adoption of a systematic approach to change
5. Establishment of sound parent-staff relationships.

*Implications of the Developmental Model for Residential Programs*

Today, the developmental model is considered to be the most desirable approach to the mentally retarded, since it is the only one which does not result in a dehumanizing approach. The developmental model has recently been expanded to the extent that it can now serve as a basis for sound residential programming.

The primary implication of the developmental approach is that programs should be oriented toward the individual, and program goals should be dynamic and individually defined. Specific goals should be determined by observation of the individual resident's behavior and his current stage of development. Program goals for the group —increasing the complexity of behavior, increasing human qualities, increasing control over the environment—are appropriate, but the methods used to achieve these goals should be applied on an individual basis.

Equally important is the implication that the rate and direction of behavioral change in relation to specific goals will be constantly re-evaluated in order that the resident may progress at the maximum possible rate.

In summary, they are three basic elements of the developmental model. The first element is the concept of change; life means change, since nothing alive remains static—and professional consideration must be focused on factors, both within and without the retarded individual, which can be combined to direct this change. Secondly, development is sequential, since all organisms tend to grow from a simple state of structure and function to a more complex one. The third element underscores the recently noted series of findings that strongly suggests that development depends upon direct and continuing environmental stimulation and the patterning of stimulus. This appreciation of the complexity of factors which infringe on the quality and quantity of human development at any given point has opened new horizons for children whose developmental potentials at one time were viewed as inherently hopeless or genetically crippled. Increasingly, we are appreciating the fact that the interrelationships and interactions between inherited and environmental factors are crucial, and that the interface between these components is the point at which professional endeavors on behalf of the mentally retarded can be most successful.

Therefore, future developmentally oriented programs for the mentally retarded must focus on selected areas for accelerating, decelerating, or modifying both the direction and rate of learning and behavioral changes. The goal of the developmental model is to provide effective coping devices for the retarded citizen's interpersonal and physical environments. Reflect for a moment on how many of the current lost generation of the retarded have primitive behavioral repertoires because they are untutored rather than "autistic," "psychotic," or simply "odd."

Full utilization of the developmental model will produce programs that allow the retarded individual to increasingly develop control over his environment, increase the complexity of his behavior, extend his repertoire of interpersonal skills, and maximize his humanization. This developmental maximization of the retardate's human qualities leads to another basic component of current ideological trends in mental retardation: the concept of normalization.

## NORMALIZATION

Since the fostering of culturally appropriate behaviors is a prime objective of developmental programming, the "normalization principle" as enunciated by Nirje (34) is a useful strategy for achieving developmental goals. The normalization principle refers specifically to a technology for achieving the goal of maximizing culturally acceptable behavior. It advocates that retarded individuals should, to the greatest degree possible, be treated as if they were of normal intelligence. The implication is that this approach is more likely to yield socially appropriate behavior, an assumption which appears generally acceptable both on theoretical and empirical grounds.

In his 1972 book, Wolfensberger reaffirmed the following definition of normalization: "Utilization of means which are as culturally normative as possible, in order to establish and/or maintain personal behaviors and characteristics which are as culturally normative as possible" (35).

This concept embodies a philosophical position concerning the personal dignity and human rights of the individual, as well as encompassing a series of specialized program services whose direct application demands that we utilize services that are located in the mainstream of society. Accordingly, the concept of normalization, when applied to the mentally retarded, refers to both an attitude and an approach to the retardate which stresses his right to live a life as close to the norm as possible. It implies his equal right to maximal developmental opportunities along with his fellow citizens.

The retarded are not to be considered "vegetables," "mongolian idiots," or "low level retardates," but rather fellow human beings who have a variety of special problems in coping with the world around them. The normalization approach encompasses a positive posture of hope, challenge, and honesty about what can, must, and will be done to help the retarded. For example, the National Association for Retarded Citizens has already moved from illustrating what the retarded can do (as in the earlier parent-sponsored educational programs or "opportunity centers," which became the spur for developing and extending day-training programs for young moderately to severely retarded children), to obtaining legislation for establishing and implementing trainable classes for their chronologically older, developmentally delayed counterparts. Now NARC is pushing professionals to refocus their treatment-management goals to encompass the need for total rehabilitation programs for all retarded citizens.

The principle of normalization has been interpreted to mean the use of management techniques that are as culturally normative as possible in an effort to elicit and maintain behavior which is consistent with local and subcultural differences in the mainstream of society. In essence, the principle reflects the professional posture that when a retarded person lives as normal a life as he possibly can, within as normal a setting as possible, he will tend to live up to the normal expectations of the normal environment in which he has been placed.

The principle of normalization demands that the retarded citizen should have a normal rhythm of day, normal rhythm of seasons, be permitted to experience the normal developmental challenges of the life cycle of growth, the right to make decisions and choices for one's self, the right to experience living in a bisexual world, the right to normal economic standards in his vocational endeavors, and, finally, the right to live, work, and play in a manner that is deemed normal and humane for that society.

The above noted ramifications of the principle of normalization, because of their impact on current and future programmatic efforts in mental retardation, will now be enlarged on in some detail.

The application of the normalization principle in contemporary programs for the mentally retarded asserts that:

1.   Programs and facilities for the mentally retarded should be physically and socially integrated into the community. This implies that service facilities must not be

placed in physical or social isolation. The large institutions for the retarded which are geographically located out in the sticks or out on the hill obviously do violence to the normalization principle.

2.   No more retardates should be congregated in one service facility than the surrounding neighborhood can readily integrate into its resources, community social life, etc. Placing or continuing to maintain an institution for 3,000 retarded patients in a rural town of 10,000 population does not permit integration of the retarded; indeed, it continues the tragic historical model of isolating deviants from general society. International trends and findings strongly suggest that the population in such an institutional setting should be dispersed and then integrated into local schools so that the retarded child can go to school with children who have other handicaps, as well as children who are not handicapped.

We are doing a disservice to normal children in not allowing them to experience handicapped children in classroom settings. In the primary community the retarded youngster should attend the neighborhood school with his brothers and sisters, and not be assigned to a large central facility devoted to educating the social deviant.

3.   Integration of the mentally retarded—and, therefore, normalization—can best be attained if the location of services follows population density and distribution patterns. This rather obvious dimension was ignored during the era of institution building in the first, second, and third decades of this century; and it is being ignored during the eighth decade as well. Services for the mentally retarded not only need to be dispersed across the communities of a state but also across a single community. Such intracommunity dispersal is virtually mandatory if integration is to be attained in urban population centers. Dispersal suggests the need for multiplicity of services and facilities in dense population areas, and clustering of these services—for ex-

ample, a developmental training center and a children's hostel in close geographical proximity to each other so as to serve natural neighborhoods within a community.

4.    Services and facilities for the retarded, if they are to be normalizing in their intent, must meet the same standards as other comparable services and facilities for the nonretarded, not be stricter nor more lenient. For example, developmental training centers must focus on scientifically sound curricular approaches such as prescriptive teaching rather than babysitting. Similarly, residential facilities for the retarded should have fire, safety, and sanitary standards comparable to those of a transient residential facility such as a motel.

If you mention a residential option for the mentally retarded to the average program/facility planner, a valve seems to close in his mind, and he demands the fire and sanitary code standards of institutional occupancy rather than the dormitory living standards of the mainstream of our society, and then wants to design non-normalizing group home (or hostel) settings. However, the recently completed institutional and community-based residential standards are clear examples of the active incorporation of the normalization principle; they will bring about a totally new era of residential care for the retarded if they are consistently enforced.

5.    Staff personnel working with retarded persons must meet at least the same standards as those working with comparable non-retarded individuals. This aspect of normalization has long been ignored through the continued employment of unlicensed physicians, uncertified teachers, and similar borderline or troubled individuals who have not done well in community or institutional positions yet still are permitted to provide quasi-help for the retarded. Again, if the personnel do not meet the professional or personal qualifications of equivalent job descriptions in other service agencies, they should not be

permitted to dispense their tarnished wares upon the retarded.

6.    In order to accomplish maximal normalization, either by encouraging the retarded to emulate the behavior of the non-retarded or by endeavoring to improve public perception of the mentally retarded, the retarded must have maximal exposure to the non-retarded population in the community. The physical isolation of some community-based residential facilities at the edge of town, and the commonly noted self-imposed isolation of members of their professional staffs, are not consistent with this need. It is amazing how many purportedly community-based programs are located in the most isolated parts of town—against a mountain, near the city dump, etc.

7.    Daily routines for the mentally retarded should be comparable to those of non-retarded persons of the same age. How many institutionalized severely retarded persons are never permitted to spend time out-of-doors? How many of the moderately retarded leave their buildings only for walks to the central dining room? The lack of daily normalizing routines for these retarded citizens is predicted upon outmoded institutional policies and not on developmental realities. On the contrary, school attendance, recreational activity, and bedtime schedules should be made as normal as possible. Seasonal changes, including vacations, also should be programmed as a portion of the normalization experience.

8.    Services for children and adults should be physically separated, both in order to reduce the probability that children will imitate the deviant behavior of their elders and because services to adults and children tend to be separated in the mainstream of our society. Residential services for the retarded should be specialized for specific types of problems or groups, because only with such specialization can age separation be attained and congregation and dehumanization avoided. This approach is in sharp

contrast to the omnibus nature of the treatment programs of many of the current large public facilities for the retarded.

9.   The retarded should be dressed and groomed like other persons their age; they should be taught a normal gait, normal movements, and normal expressive behavior patterns; and their diet should be adjusted so as to assure normal weight. In other words, probabilities of the non-retarded individual identifying a retardate individual on sight should be minimized. The sloppily dressed retarded child with a bowl haircut is a frequent negative testimonial to our current professional-programmatic concept of retardation and the concurrent lack of caring.

10.   As much as possible, the adult retardate, even if severely handicapped, should be provided the opportunity to engage in work that is culturally normal in type, quantity, and setting. Even if performed in sheltered settings, work for adult retardates should approximate typically adult work; sheltered workshops should resemble industrial work stations rather than activities and settings that are commonly associated with children, with play, with recration and leisure-time pursuits.

This dimension demands serious reconceptualization of the occupational and recreational therapy activities that embody the arts-and-crafts, fun-and-games approaches that keep the retarded from "being a nuisance"—all of which are based upon wasting time rather than focusing upon meaningful work activity. In other words, diversional therapy too often masquerades as recreational or vocational programming!

Accordingly, normalization refers to concepts which are composed of a cluster of attitudes and programmatic methods toward the retarded, encompassing: high standards of excellence in providing necessary human services; specialized programs which are integrated into the community;

high expectations of and from the retarded, in keeping with behavior standards expected from all of us in the mainstream of society; and utilization of available social-family generic service whenever possible, so as not to have the retarded stand out as being in need of an exotic or overly unique type of service.

## GENERAL CONSIDERATIONS- NORMALIZATION AND THE DEVELOPMENTAL MODEL

The fact that a given approach has become culturally normative does not insure that it is the most effective procedure for modifying the rate and direction of individual change in retarded persons or, for that matter, in persons of normal intelligence. For example, the pattern of formal education in our society has been that of a teacher using primarily a didactic or expository approach to a classroom of students. However, recent research suggests that other approaches such as programmed instruction and discovery learning may be more effective.

Adoption of the developmental model suggests that the effectiveness of programs is determined by the degree to which developmental goals are achieved, rather than by the conformity of program strategies to culturally normative patterns. In those cases where non-normative techniques prove more effective than normative approaches in accomplishing developmental goals, the former would be preferable. It is conceivable that for certain individuals, particularly those whose behavior is widely divergent from the cultural norm, normative patterns may prove to decelerate desirable changes while accelerating undesirable behaviors. Some profoundly retarded children, for example, though raised in their parent's home under highly normative conditions, may manifest disturbingly little developmental progress.

## "Contentment" and the Developmental Model

In some instances developmental goals have been used to condone the retention of persons in institutions in spite of their potential capacity to function in the broader community.

If retarded children and adults are to be granted the same basic rights as their non-retarded peers, it is clear that developmental goals must take priority over the retarded person's contentment, for this is precisely the situation which prevails with individuals of normal intelligence. That is, in the socialization of the non-retarded, "happiness" or "contentment" is sacrificed in favor of developing behavior which is adaptive and culturally sanctioned.

Many retarded individuals will eventually attain a level of behavioral competency which meets the standards of culturally acceptable behavior and enables them to function independently in society. At this point, the individual should be accorded the same status and privileges as a non-retarded adult; he should have the freedom to continue to press toward his "physiological limit" of competency or to continue to function at an acceptable level below his maximum potential.

In a provocative article, Perske (36) clearly delineated the role of risk-taking behavior as a prerequisite for all human psychosocial development, whether in retarded or non-retarded individuals. He notes that the *dignity of risk* has been traditionally avoided for the retarded and replaced by a protective-dependent approach which tends to stunt their personality and learning potentials.

The professional person or organization working with the mentally retarded child or adult assumes certain responsibilities to and for the individual. Among these are the responsibility to protect the individual from accident, injury, or from undertaking courses of action that would be harmful to his well-being. However, the degree of protection must be at a optimum level; overprotection is as harmful as underprotection. Too great a degree of protection leads to an overly restrictive environment, deprives the individual of freedom and pleasure, and inhibits opportunities for growth and development.

On the other hand, the foregoing cannot be used as a rationalization for underprotection or for a laissez-faire attitude toward possible risks. One must strike a balance, and in doing so recognize that a limited—but only a limited—number of accidents are bound to occur. In establishing the level of protection needed by each individual, general rules or policies are of considerable help. However, whatever these policies may be they do not substitute for the individual evaluation of the needs of the particular person and the common sense and professional judgment of the person responsible for his care. For example, the open group home in the community does add some risks but these are more than outweighed by the advantages. What risks there are are minimized, though not eliminated, by individual attention to the needs of each patient.

Rather than become obsessed with whether or not restrictions are a major focal point in the management of the retarded, we are noting that guidelines and regulations are not substitutes for evaluation, judgment, and responsibility on the part of the attending professional(s). This very openness of an increasing number of professionals to accept a portion of the necessary risk-taking behaviors which are necessary for the retarded in their ongoing efforts to learn and develop personal dignity is a major current trend. Rather than acting as the official societal diagnostician of the past or the custodial gatekeeper, professionals are sharing risks with retarded citizens in a mutual effort to further understand what can be accomplished if negative attitudes are replaced with actual transactions, and destructive labels exchanged for acceptance as a fellow-citizen.

In certain rare instances (for example, cases involving gross neurological deterioration) the goals of the developmental model—increased humanness, control over the environment, and increased complexity of behavior—may appear to be unattainable in view of technological limitations. In these instances, it may be appropriate to design programs with the primary goal of maximizing the individual's quality of existence while remaining sensitive to future developmental possibilities.

## Implications for Service Delivery

In reference to actual service delivery, we must devote more attention to a retardate's current stage of development than his past etiology. For example, a retarded individual with a wide-based gait who is able to walk with the help of one-hand support is ready for ambulation whether he is two or ten years of age. Similarly, the retarded youngster with overnight dry diapers and regularity of bowel evacuation is ready for toilet training irrespective of his developmental-chronological age. In other words, the underlying cause of an individual's delay is not as relevant as is his readiness for developmental programming.

An alternative to the past approach, in which the supposed causes were instantaneously related to future expectations, replete with a rather hopeless view of how much the retarded could develop, the modern approach is to correctly assess current developmental status and then provide full stimulation and activation. I recently undertook a project to assess the developmental attainments of mature individuals with Down's syndrome, utilizing an institution-based population, ages 12 to 30 years. One of the first challenges noted in this study was the uncertain information in the literature concerning the expected developmental achievement of mature individuals with Down's syndrome. (We tend to subsume the social-adaptive range of behaviors to be found in these individuals.) In the study, the schedule for developmental assessment focused primarily on the areas of feeding, dressing, ambulation, grooming, and basic work skills. Utilizing these criteria, it was noted that the actual level of social-adaptive skills within this study group was far above that usually subsumed for those who "need custodial care." Accordingly, the study suggested that the "hopelessness" of the etiology of Down's syndrome tends to be carried over into a prognosis that initially sent these human beings to an institution to fulfill a dire professional prophecy of nondevelopment.

Assessment, via developmental specificity of the social-adaptive level, must focus particularly on language, motor, and personal-social skills rather than on the loose or implied diagnoses such as "autism." Without such assessment one easily falls back on subjective treatment approaches to subjective diagnoses, from which a specific treatment-management set of goals cannot be outlined, or by which administrative havoc is caused due to the lack of a cost-service/benefit-ratio approach to nonspecific treatment needs. This results in rather loose financial concerns which are defended by statements such as, "Who can withhold treatment from anyone in need? . . ." This type of reasoning is not realistic in today's cost-conscious approach to the provision of all human services.

Normalization also demands that the professional's attitude must be one of dignity and high expectations from the retarded, versus our current approach of gatekeeping and dehumanization.

Similarly, we have to help the retarded make more free choices, take risks, and make decisions. As we increase the complexity of their behavior, we thus help them maximize their humanness in regards to the types of risk-taking behavior and decision-making which occur in the real world.

The normalization approach also emphasizes identification. Most specifically, we must continue to stress that caretakers of the retarded, regardless of their role, must be *positive* identification figures. We know that, to learn, a person must first have a positive (passive) identification with his teachers. Without this relationship, learning cannot progress adequately either in scope or extent. However, we have so often handicapped the educators of the retarded, we have made it difficult for them to function, let alone provide an adequate identification model for the retarded whom they are privileged to serve.

In summary, we must actively move towards treatment-management approaches which speak, support, and help evolve models or developmentally oriented programs that focus on maximizing the social-adaptive levels of the retarded.

## FOUR NATIONAL TRENDS

There are four national trends which will have a major impact on the future delivery of services to retarded individuals. These trends are in the areas of (1) epidemiology, (2) residential services, (3) research, and (4) legal rights. Since they will have a profound effect on how we will serve our retarded citizens in the immediate future, each will be separately discussed.

### Epidemiological Trends

The epidemiological approach to mental retardation has traditionally embraced the concepts of incidence (the number of new cases of a disorder over a specific period of time) and prevalence (the total number of cases over a specific period of time) as rather firm indices of demonstrated need

for both services and research. However, recent considerations strongly suggest that the incidence and prevalence
of mental retardation tends to vary widely with a variety of
conditions—psychosocial, biological, socioeconomic, etc.
—and we note a shift away from "confirmed" incidence and
prevalence figures toward a broader view of the complex
causative mechanisms which can and do interact to produce
the symptom of mental retardation.

This change in epidemiological perspective has
brought with it a fresh new look at the current trends which
have altered and can further alter the epidemiology in mental retardation. For example, we are noting a continuing
reduction in birth rates among high-risk groups of mothers
—those in the poor and disadvantaged social-economic
groups, very young and older mothers in poor medical
health, mothers with a history of reproductive difficulty,
etc. As we have been able to elucidate causes of high-risk
pregnancies, more and more innovative approaches have
come forth to resolve these problems. Similarly, there has
been a rapid increase in the amount of preventive health
services that are provided for the high-risk groups. In this
regard, it has been noted that the newborn infant mortality
rates in the U.S. have dropped rather consistently since the
second decade of this century.

The increased liberalization and legalization of the
practice of abortion will also have a major impact on the
epidemiology of mental retardation. Although this particular topic remains a highly emotional one across our country, it should be noted that with the advent of techniques
such as amniocentesis and automated medical monitoring
of high-risk pregnancies, the potential parents of such children now have a rational basis for assessing the risks of
their unborn child and the allied opportunity to reconcile
these data with their religious and personal beliefs.

Lastly, there has been improvement of both health and
developmental services generally in our population, and

some advances in the improvement of our physical environment.

A wide variety of other phenomenon have a direct impact of the epidemiology in mental retardation. In particular, growing acceptance of early childhood education programs has literally exploded across our country. Early education programs such as day-care centers and Operation Headstart, the lowering of school entrance age for many types of handicapped children, and the evolving national pattern of mandatory education for the severely retarded are all examples of this national educational trend which has had and will have a direct impact on the epidemiology in mental retardation.

In brief, current epidemiology trends suggest that we now have the information to make further dramatic changes in the incidence and prevalence of mental retardation and that these epidemiology trends will have a marked impact on both the future pattern of need and types of residential care models for the mentally retarded.

## A Fresh Look at Residential Services for the Retarded

THE LARGE PUBLIC INSTITUTION MODEL.    As previously noted, serious deficiencies currently exist in the number and quality of community-based programs. Thus most communities are not fulfilling their responsibilities to the retarded in such basic areas as day care, special education, vocational training, and competitive and sheltered work opportunities. While the concept of a full spectrum of community services has remained largely unrealized, the general lack of sound community-based programs that include group homes, hostels, and apartments is particularly evident. The need for increased services at the community level is further dramatized by the fact that traditional institutional programs serve only about 4 percent, or some

240,000, of America's over 6 million mentally retarded citizens.

The establishment of adequate community services has been severely hampered by a long-standing emphasis on institutionalization for persons who cannot easily acquire independent living skills. One of the common reasons for stressing institutional placement has been the belief that the presence of a mentally retarded child or adult represents a serious threat to family harmony and community well-being. It was thus common in the not too distant past for professionals to advise parents to remove a mentally retarded child from the hospital or home and to sever all emotional ties with the retarded family member. In the face of such attitudes, which encourage separation and isolation of the mentally retarded, it has been extremely difficult to establish alternatives to institutionalization within the community setting.

The institution has traditionally served to isolate and protect the retarded from the community or to protect the community from the retarded. In order to achieve this end, most institutions have been built far from populated areas, and it has proven expedient for them to provide all needed services to their residents, making the institution a multipurpose, self-contained and dependent pseudo-community. Many new institutions, although built near population centers, continue to follow tradition by providing the full array of basic services—medical department, hospitals, schools, parks and playgrounds, on-campus stores, etc.—even though the same facilities and services may be available in the community. The expense of this unnecessary duplication of services is staggering and has made it more costly to serve the 5 percent of the retarded who are institutionalized than the remaining 95 percent who are badly in need of services at the community level.

Many of the inadequacies in traditional institutional programs have resulted from the dehumanizing manner in which services have been conceived and delivered. Approaches to programming within residential facilities have attempted to make the retarded person fit into predetermined programs. Until only recently there have been few efforts to provide for the needs of individual residents. Instead, programs have been designed to meet the needs of large groups, or the majority of the group members. Under such an approach, residents functioning at the lower limits of a group have made little progress, while inappropriately low ceilings of development have been forced upon the group's more capable members.

The large group living concept is a product of past attempts to provide only custodial care—minimal levels of cleanliness and safety, prevention of injury to self or others, and provision of basic life needs. Large-group living has generally resulted in a life of inactivity or activities without apparent purpose. There has not been sufficient personnel assigned to groups to provide adequate levels of stimulation and to encourage growth and development on an individual basis.

Perhaps the most unfortunate result of group living has been the assembly-line method of providing services to residents. Speed and efficiency of direct-care personnel are emphasized when staff-to-resident ratios are based on custodial approaches. When the bulk of the direct-care personnel's time is devoted to feeding, dressing, and bathing, time and efficiency become critical factors. As a result, residents are treated as though they were products on an assembly-line belt in a factory, each part being handled or inspected by a different and highly specialized person. It is not uncommon, for example, to find that total groups, especially groups of young or physically handicapped residents, are subjected to highly mechanized and impersonal bathing procedures in which staff members are assigned specific tasks such as one removing clothing, another applying soap and water and rinsing, another drying and dressing, while another may control lines of traffic to and from a central living area. Very similar approaches are frequently used during meals and toileting.

In such an environment, there is little, if any encouragement for a resident to develop his individual skills and abilities. In some cases, assembly-line approaches are geared toward the needs of the least capable members of the group. The remainder of the group is thus not allowed to develop; or even worse, is denied the right to use the skills which it has previously learned.

DEINSTITUTIONALIZATION.    The President's Committee on Mental Retardation is continuing its efforts to implement President Nixon's formal statement on November 16, 1971, which has been called the deinstitutionalization statement. He invited all Americans to help implement the following two major goals: (1) reduce by one-half the occurrence of mental retardation and (2) enable one-third of the retarded persons in public institutions to return to useful lives in the community (37). To fulfill its presidential mandate, the President's Committee must consider that currently there are approximately 186,700 mentally retarded citizens in large public institutions, and that the admissions figure to these institutions was 15,000 and the discharges figure 14,700 in 1970. In 1971, the discharges were greater than the admissions, the first time this trend has been reversed in many decades.

Although Chapter 11 is a more complete discussion of deinstitutionalization, it is important to mention here that the federal mandate for deinstitutionalization implies three necessary developments in our services to retarded persons: (1) we must continue to reduce admissions by offering to parents of the retarded alternate developmentally oriented services and residential placements; (2) we must increase self-help capabilities and job-ready skills of current institutional residents via highly skilled programs of service and training; and (3) we must increase community-based residential placement opportunities by spurring the establishment of community facilities.

The following schematic (see Figure 2.1) illustrates the past, current, and possible future national guidelines that flow from President Nixon's mandate to the President's Committee on Mental Retardation.

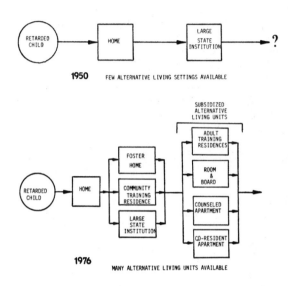

Figure 2.1   National Residential Services Trends
Alternatives Available to Parents of a Retarded Child

The major public advocacy organization working on behalf of the mentally retarded is the National Association for Retarded Citizens. Since the early 1950s, this organization has displayed an outstanding record of public service in the areas of public education, initiation of programs for the retarded, research into basic and applied areas that aim at prevention, and governmental affairs. One of their major priorities in the 1970s is the development of community-based residential services; their recent clarion call (see Figure 2.2) on this topic clearly calls for a renaissance in this

## Figure 2.2   NARC Residential Services and
### Facilities Committee

A RESOLUTION OF THE NATIONAL ASSOCIATION FOR RETARDED CHIL-
DREN IN ANNUAL CONVENTION ASSEMBLED, URGING THE GOVERN-
MENTS OF THE STATES TO ESTABLISH SMALL, COMMUNITY-BASED,
HOME-LIKE RESIDENTIAL FACILITIES FOR THE MENTALLY RETARDED.

WHEREAS, the subject of optimum residential services for the mentally retarded is currently receiving high-priority national attention, and

WHEREAS, it is now recognized as the normal and desirable right of handicapped persons, including the mentally retarded, to live their lives as normally as
possible, surrounded by the everyday community and integrated with that community life, and

WHEREAS, recently established accreditation standards, the expert opinions
of leading professionals in the field of mental retardation and the President's
Committee on Mental Retardation, and a landmark decision of the United States
District Court, Middle District of Alabama, reflect that existing residential facilities are frequently inadequate, inhumane, isolated, substandard and misdirected,
and

WHEREAS, it will be a function of the government of each state to reach decisions about replacement residential facilities, and to implement these decisions
within their state, and

WHEREAS, no such state government should undertake decision-making affecting the mentally retarded without giving full consideration to the recommendations of those persons who can best speak for the mentally retarded.

NOW, THEREFORE BE IT RESOLVED BY THE NATIONAL ASSOCIA-
TION FOR RETARDED CHILDREN:

That the National Association for Retarded Children recognizes that the public
interest requires that additional residential facilities for the mentally retarded must
be constructed, purchased, and leased.

BE IT FURTHER RESOLVED, that the National Association for Retarded
Children recommends that such residential facilities be community-based and be
integrated into the main-stream of community life.

BE IT FURTHER RESOLVED, that the National Association for Retarded
Children recommends that such residential facilities consist of small living units,
each replicating a normal home environment to the closest extent possible.

BE IT FURTHER RESOLVED, that the National Association for Retarded
Children recommends that such residential facilities take absolute precedence over
further capital investments in existing or new large scale "institutions."

vital area. Indeed, the initiation of community-based residential services for the retarded has become almost an obsession with NARC units across our country. Currently, this trend has the same momentum that the opportunity centers had in the sixties, and there is every reason to believe that this thrust will have the same national-state legislative repercussions, as in mandatory education laws.

In summary, each of these major national trends—the President's Committee mandate with its direct bearing on federal funding patterns and the repercussions of the NARC residential services policy statement as to the wishes of the consumers—acting in concert will, in my opinion, finally turn the corner away from the large public institution as a meaningful resource for serving our retarded citizens. During the transitional period between institution-based and community-based programs and services, it would appear judicious for local and state public officials to closely scrutinize and demand that the allocation of any public funds be consistent with the previously noted national trends, lest they continue to support ideologies or enlarged facilities that are clearly on their way to historical oblivion.

*Research*

Except for some scattered research activities at large institutions for the retarded, there was little research done in the field of mental retardation prior to the early 1950s. Indeed, the modern history of vigorous research efforts on behalf of the retarded directly involves the role of the NARC in its direct impact on this area since 1952. Commencing with its initial public information approach and collection of funds ("Pennies for Research") for this endeavor, it commissioned a study of the status of research in mental retardation in the early 1950s. The result of this study was a book entitled *Mental Subnormality* (38). This book emphasized that though some work had been done in the field of mental retardation, a number of key areas needed massive research attention and financial involvement, both in regard to professional commitments and support by public funds. NARC continued its research thrust through the late fifties, and by the early sixties it had provided a series of grants for promising young investigators in the field of mental retardation, "seed money" grants to help initiate or complete research efforts in this area.

Even more important, NARC evolved a very effective public information and governmental affairs thrust which had a direct impact on the posture and involvement of our federal government in the field of mental retardation. It resulted in the establishment of 12 mental retardation research centers and 22 university-affiliated facilities, all established and committed to discovering the causes of mental retardation and evolving professional training models for more effective treatment-management endeavors.

Currently we see research efforts in mental retardation focusing on the concepts of primary, secondary, and tertiary prevention. Although impetus in the area of primary prevention—the total prevention of a disorder—remains the key consideration, there has been increasing attention to effective treatment and reversal of the symptom of mental retardation (secondary prevention) and also towards ameliorating the effects of "fixed" mental retardation phenomena (tertiary prevention). Current thrusts are in the area of preventive biomedicine, in which studies are focused on topics such as slow viruses (infection mechanisms that have been recently implicated in neurological disorders such as multiple sclerosis and are now being strongly viewed as possible operative mechanisms in disorders such as the diffuse encephalopathies of early infancy), the inborn errors of metabolism, and early preventive approaches (amniocentesis, neonatology approaches, etc.). Similarly, concern for elucidating the basic mechanisms of secondary prevention challenges, such as the incidence of leukemia, diabetes, and premature aging in Down's syndrome, has also gathered much research interest.

In the area of preventive behavioral research, vital studies concerning the relationships between poverty and mental retardation (39), autism as a facade of mental retardation, the frequent relationship between psychiatric symptoms and the symptom of mental retardation (40), and the studies of motivational components of the mentally retarded (41) have all had direct impact on improving the social-adaptive levels of the mentally retarded. Finally, continuing studies of the purported memory and learning enhancers hold great promise for preventive behavioral considerations, not only for the retarded but for our aged citizens as well.

Home-training techniques also hold a great deal of promise in regard to secondary and tertiary preventive aspects. There is a strong move toward attempting to directly convert some past theoretical contributions such as deficit theory into direct programmatic packages. Specialized curricula, equipment tailored to the needs of the handicapped, and attempts to bring together cross-modality approaches all hold great promise for making home-training techniques more effective as direct impact on altering the developmental potential of mentally retarded young children.

Residential models have also become the focal point for a great deal of comparative study to determine the type of retarded individuals who can most benefit from varying models of residential care—at what age in their lives, what level of associated handicaps, etc. Of great interest here have been the programmatic aspects which are associated with specialized residential programs and the economic dimensions of the cost-service benefit ratio for evaluating such services.

In summary, we are noting an enhanced research approach to the primary, secondary, and tertiary preventive aspects of mental retardation. Increasingly, a mission-oriented type of research thrust is utilized, and there is every indication that this approach will be effective in bringing about new research possibilities and accompanying enlarged developmental horizons of hope and help for the mentally retarded of our country. (Chapter 3 is a more complete discussion of necessary research approaches.)

## Legal Rights

We must also be fully aware of what has occurred in regard to the recent legal movements on behalf of the mentally retarded. The changes which have come about in the last three to five years have been truly remarkable and allow us to make some predictions as to what the current-future trends will bring for the retarded by the end of this decade. The current decade should see legal action concerning the retarded accomplish three major goals:

1. *Recognition.* We are recognizing more and more that the Bill of Rights is a part of our Constitution that actually applies to our mentally retarded citizens as well as others. Indeed, we will see a time when there will no longer be right to education and right to treatment suits. In essence, current litigation in these areas will eventually rediscover the full recognition of mentally retarded citizens as to their personal civil rights.

2. *Implementation.* There will be a direct remedy to the recognition of the rights of the retarded. For example, the Nebraska right to treatment suit, with particular reference to least restrictive settings, has as its remedy the implementation of the community-based model of services as the affirmative answer to the needs of the mentally retarded. Accordingly, the implementation phase of the major legal

thrusts in this decade will provide the retarded direct implementation of the judiciary ordered changes, replete with state-national legislative changes and actions in each of our states. In this regard, it is heartening to note that the President's Committee on Mental Retardation, in its 1972 report entitled *Islands of Excellence,* strongly reinforced President Nixon's deinstitutionalization statement of 1971 with regard to the current movement in our country toward community-based programs. Implementation of the current state of recognition of the rights of the retarded will carry with it many affirmative remedies that will establish and indeed act upon the rights of the retarded to provide normalized programs in the mainstreams of our society, programs based on the principle of normalization and the developmental model. This implementation phase will embrace the view that has been very basic to our country in its commitment to provide an opportunity for all of its citizens.

3.   *Acceptance.* Although much has been accomplished in this area, especially in the last two decades, the recent litigation across our country—with its phases of recognition and implementation—will eventually bring about the full acceptance of the retarded and their integration into our social, educational, and vocational mainstreams. We will see some major problems in completing this goal of fully accepting the retarded in our communities, since this is the chronic problem which our society has always had in dealing with fellow citizens who are atypical and so easy to view as deviant.

The three trends of recognition, implementation, and acceptance of the retarded present major challenges to seeking the legal rights of the mentally retarded citizens in our country. There are approximately 24 law suits in progress now across our country concerning the recognition phase of the rights of the mentally retarded as full fellow citizens. The implementation phase is just beginning, and we are as a nation moving very rapidly toward community-based programs. Acceptance of our mentally retarded citizens as fellow human beings who have the right to enjoy fully the rights and opportunities of this nation will allow us to rediscover the very humanity that our forebears demonstrated in humanistic programs for the mentally retarded.

## SUMMARY

An operational overview of community programs for the mentally retarded has been presented within a perspective of past professional postures, current ideologies and practices, and a look into the future as to evolving trends. It has been stressed that attention to modern ideologies and programmatic trends, coupled with an enlightened view of what mentally retarded citizens can be helped to accomplish, can bring new vigor to the national wave of interest and active involvement in community-based programs for the retarded.

In building for the present and future we must embrace the new ideological underpinnings of the principles of normalization and the developmental model, with their basic focus on hope and help for the retarded. We must do this by building more meaningful systems of services and by continuing to expand the public informational vehicles for enlightening and instructing our fellow citizens as to the needs and rights of the mentally retarded. Similarly, we must also help establish and operate model programs showing what can be done today.

In the past, we have so often said that if we would only utilize what was already known concerning the research and the operational-programmatic advances in mental retardation, half of the retarded population would disappear. It is now time to bring reality to this statement by actively contributing to the repertoire of societal help for the mentally retarded as fellow citizens who have an equal right to seek fulfillment in this world.

*Chapter 3*

# A PRESSING NEED: APPLIED
# RESEARCH

Thirty years ago, research interests and activities in mental retardation were meager. Professional attitudes were negatively biased. This fact, coupled with minimal public awareness and governmental disinterest, was a major factor in producing the "hopeless-helpless" picture of the retarded person.

The advent of a strong consumer interest, such as the organized efforts of parents of the mentally retarded, cerebral palsied, deaf, etc., in the early 1950s was successful over the ensuing 20 years in spurring public, professional, and governmental efforts in research endeavors. For example, the National Association for Retarded Citizens, via its Governmental Affairs Committee, was instrumental in securing the passage of P.L. 88-164 which, starting in 1964, has provided $26 million in federal funds (the states and private sources supplied another $14 million) for the construction of 12 mental retardation centers across our country. A similar thrust by the NARC in the area of training has led to the establishment of 21 university-affiliated facilities for training future professionals in the mental retardation field.

Accordingly, at first glance one might well ask, "Since so much is already underway, why should research be viewed as a pressing need?" But it has become clear that these research and training efforts are very limited as to their scope, focus and quantity of activity. For example, the above-noted mental retardation centers continue to focus upon the prevention of retardation in the unborn and new biomedical treatments for the very young retarded child. In a nutshell, this research concentrates on primary prevention and some secondary prevention. The overwhelming majority of existing mental retardation research programs are not primarily mission-oriented. That is, the focus is often upon providing research personnel with freedom of inquiry rather than systematically studying research issues having direct relevance to critical problems. This contention is supported by Cramond's (42) discussion of research trends in mental retardation: "I cannot but agree with others who have expressed doubts about the value or relevance of much that passes for research in the field of mental retardation."

It appears that we currently need a more equitable balance between free inquiry and mission-oriented research efforts. Specifically, what is needed is a coordinated and mission-oriented research thrust aimed at answering questions pertinent to both the prevention and treatment of mental retardation. Stress must be placed upon the need to develop a series of well-defined research priorities in order to obtain maximum impact upon the lives of retarded citizens now and in the future.

It has been noted that existing mental retardation centers tend to become involved in various esoteric bits of research into causes and prevention of organic mental retardation, which represents relatively small numbers of the total retarded population. This research posture is in sharp contrast to the pressing issues, such as social-cultural determinants of mild mental retardation, which affect the vast majority of our citizens suffering from physically or environmentally induced retardation.

Similarly, the university-affiliated facilities (UAFs), with their focus on training future professionals at all levels, tend to provide a limited amount of actual service in order to provide training experience. Most of these UAFs are not funded to conduct research; the few groups that do engage in such activities tend to ignore the critical issues pertaining to optimum training models and developing excellence in the delivery of services.

Lastly, the consumer organization which initially spurred research efforts in mental retardation—the National Association for Retarded Citizens—has recently come to the same conclusions reviewed above, and it is now seeking a more balanced national research thrust. As the past chairman of the NARC committee studying this matter, I have been provided an excellent overview of these changing needs and directions.

## CURRENT RESEARCH ENDEAVORS

Despite the progress which is currently being made, research into the causes and treatment of developmental disabilities remains in an embryonic stage. Thus, while over 350 causes of mental retardation have been identified, the etiology is undetermined in approximately 75 percent of known cases.

One thing is certain; we simply do not know enough about retarded children or, for that matter, about the optimal education of so-called normal children. Our nation's educational system, at least in the public domain, assumes that when a child reaches the magic age of 6 years he is ready for formal education, and that the repetitiveness of the process will suffice to see him through. What does the usual teacher know about the individual differences among any 25 children who present themselves on the first of September with bright and shiny faces in her first-grade class? Or, for that matter, the next echelon of the educational hierarchy behind her, or the next, up to the highest echelons of the colleges of education?

And what about the school physician, the opthalmologist, the psychologist, or even the neurologist or psychiatrist who might on occasion be called in? How much do they know about learning and information processing and the best means to achieve such, generally, let alone the knowledge to cope with the process, even if an accurate assessment could be made of the child's potentiality to learn? They can test his visual acuity and correct that to 20/20; if his auditory acuity is down, they can put him in the front row; but is he able to perceive visual and auditory stimuli plus retain and recall these stimuli in a meaningful memory process?

What goes beyond the eye and ear? What goes on in that big brain in the cranium with 10 billion neurons—and billions more of synaptic junctions—with inhibition, choice, and decision-making at every step in life? What about attention? When and how does a child learn to attend? Without attending, he can look and not see; he can see and not perceive; he can perceive and not remember. The stage for learning to attend and learning to learn is set several years before that magic age of six—we must make an effort to find out when, how, and where. We should make an effort to assess the child's abilities and capacities before the age of 6, for he may have to unlearn or be rehabilitated before we begin the routine formal educational process.

In brief, we research. At times it is a matter of semantics whether we call it "basic" or "applied" research. If there is a problem to be solved, or if there is a method to be worked out to attain a goal, that is the important thing.

We should be able to learn a great deal about "normal" children by studying retarded children, and vice versa. In either case, we need to start long before the first grade. We cannot dissect the child's brain as we can an animal's; but, we don't need to if we can "dissect" his behavior. In fact, by studying children and animals developmentally, we will find that nature has "dissected" the brain for us through the process of maturation and development. There is much to be learned by this approach, both for the retarded and the normal child, the exceptional and the behavior-disordered child, the autistic, the poor reader, and so on. We need prospective as well as retrospective studies.

With regard to treatment, there is a pressing need for systematic research aimed at delineating more effective strategies for enabling mentally retarded persons to realize their full potentials. The current status of research in this entire area will now be briefly reviewed.

### Basic Biomedical Research

Although progress is being made in the prevention of mental retardation, it is proceeding, as might be expected, through a succession of small advances across a broad front, rather than by virtue of any single dramatic breakthrough. As stated above, the causes of approximately three out of four cases of mental retardation are still unknown. If the incidence of mental retardation in the United States is to be significantly reduced, increasing emphasis must be placed upon systematic research studies into the causes of this major handicapping condition. As new causal factors are identified, they must be carefully analyzed in order that specific preventive-treatment measures may be developed.

In addition to those research efforts designed to identify causes, a number of existing approaches to prevention
and treatment-management require additional study and
refinement. Although the rubella (German measles) vac-
cine represents a significant step toward the prevention of
mental retardation and other birth defects, the rubella im-
munity that can at present be given is incomplete and may
not be permanent.

Finally, steps must be taken to close the gap between
available technology and its application on a large scale. As
noted by Koch (43), "even today we are not applying and
reaping the benefits of knowledge discovered some years
ago" (p. 62). Through the recently developed amniocentesis, prenatal identification of a significant number of meta-
bolic disorders and chromosomal abnormalities leading to
mental retardation is now possible. However, the complexity of the procedure in its current form has generally
limited is availability to university and other large medical
centers.

## Preventive Behavioral Research

Available data strongly suggest that severe psychosocial
deprivation and understimulation in early childhood may
result in mental retardation. Further research is required in
order to more clearly define the apparent relationship between lack of environmental stimulation and intellectual
retardation. In addition, effective early intervention techniques of a behavioral nature must be developed to reduce
the incidence of mental retardation among high-risk
groups. The need for research in this area is underscored
by the fact that some 75 percent of our nation's mentally
retarded children are found in urban and rural poverty
areas where environmental deprivation is often a fact of
daily life (44).

## Alternative Models of Residential Care

About 150,000 retarded persons reside in 175 publicly operated residential facilities for the mentally retarded. These institutions are typically located in remote areas and are characterized by inappropriately designed, overcrowded, and antiquated buildings. The problem is compounded by the fact that most public institutions are badly understaffed, and most personnel underpaid and poorly trained.

The lack of meaningful habilitative programming and often shocking conditions which exist in many public institutions have been repeatedly and dramatically illustrated via national exposés, as in the case of Willowbrook. Accordingly, there is a burgeoning awareness of the need to replace dehumanizing institutional models with small, group-living situations located within the mainstream of our communities. Many state agencies and legislatures, however, are yet to be convinced that community-based alternatives are economically and programmatically superior to existing institutional models. A proliferation of relatively large, new institutions may thus be found in many areas of the country. Although carefully designed research —for example, a broad-based cost-benefit study—is needed to resolve arguments regarding community-based alternatives, no viable research studies have been mounted to date. Yet this very type of research is possible, as witnessed by the wave of community-based group homes that are rising in our country today, a prime area for applied research endeavors in the differing models of residential care.

## Home-Training Techniques

In the recent past, many parents of the mentally retarded grudgingly chose to institutionalize their offspring because of the marked absence of appropriate alternative services within their communities. Thus a recent survey (45) revealed that approximately 64 percent of our nation's mentally retarded children and young adults between the ages of 5 and 21 are being denied access to a public school education. Institutionalization could be precluded in a significant number of instances if parents were equipped to provide their children with needed education and training within the home setting. A number of techniques appropriate to this end have been developed, for example, behavior modification and programmed instruction, and are described in detail in the professional literature. However, there is a pressing need to actively translate these techniques into published formats that may be readily used by the parent within the retarded child's natural home.

## WHAT IS NEEDED IN RESEARCH ENDEAVORS?

The foregoing section suggests a number of alternative research pathways in the area of mental retardation which have national-international ramifications. A recent survey of 150,000 parents who have mentally retarded children revealed their following three top priority needs:

1. Research into techniques to enable parents to effectively train their handicapped children within the home setting
2. Studies of alternative approaches to traditional models of residential care
3. Basic behavioral research in the area of prevention.

Interestingly, all three of these priorities embody the concept of operational-programmatic research: what needed services, for which children, at what age, with what handicaps can be provided by current-future programs of treatment-management. These parental concerns are at the very heart of the term "applied research."

These above-noted three challenges encompass the following researchable issues:

1.    A focus on applied social-educational-behavioral and service systems research that is directly relevant to the lives of the developmentally disordered—such as family support systems providing needed services and different programs and designs for residential settings (for example, which programs and designs are best in differing geographical and social settings, for what age groups, with what type or level of developmental disorder?). Sociological analyses of the planning process in the community: What are the basic assumptions in community programs? What planning processes fail or succeed, where, and why?

2.    Ten years ago the community-based "hostel" for the retarded was considered a high-risk project. If the famous Boys Town in Nebraska had funded 5 to 10 hostels, at that time—in different geographic areas—for different age groups, levels or types of mental retardation, etc., we would have learned much and pushed others to follow. Similarly, today the concept of the crisis assistance unit is an example of a high-risk operational research challenge. We debate this residential component, though we really do not know how and if it will work. Will such units really relieve individual-family crises? What about program components, costs involved, and utilization rates? Can or should we mix children and adults of both sexes? Should such a unit be in town or in a vacation-type setting at the edge of town (ease of transportation versus more resources and fun, such as swimming pools for retarded citizens)? How should we architecturally design this crisis assistance unit?

3.    Similarly, operational research could harness what we already know about applicable techniques to help

the mental retardation. A case in point would be a review of current deficit theory research on the learning process and its translation into concrete guidelines for teaching the retarded. Some of the questions here are:

a. What is mental retardation?

b. Is it a global learning disability?

c. Are there specific deficits in attention arousal, motivation inhibition?

d. How are memory, retention and recall organized (long- versus short-term memory)?

The deficit theory has spawned thousands of research proposals and reports. In turn, they have yielded many practical recommendations for teaching the retarded (operant learning, transfer of learning principles, etc.). Yet if one asks the typical special education teacher how he could maximize his teaching techniques with the retarded, he rarely demonstrates a knowledge of these practical recommendations. Why? Because this body of information has not been properly compiled and translated into practical applications for teachers at the front lines. Instead, it is compiled in the yearly reviews, in prose apparently designed to frighten and confuse everyone but fellow scientists. Even our residents in psychiatry and pediatrics are just becoming acquainted with operant learning-management techniques in their teaching curriculum, although Ogden Lindsley illustrated the application of operant learning to disordered and retarded behaviors almost 15 years ago.

4. Studies into the causes of mental retardation, with a direct focus on the elucidation of factors which may permit primary prevention (eradication of causes), secondary prevention (early case findings and treatment), and tertiary prevention (amelioration of the extent of the residual handicaps). These research endeavors are crucial if we are to shut off the faucets of causative factors in retardation. Unless we attempt to make some real progress in this area,

our society will continue to fail to make significant progress in combatting the destructive toll taken by the symptom of mental retardation.

5.   A comprehensive cost-benefit analysis of the relative merits of community-based versus institutional programming. We could thus help put to rest the endless arguments as to the relative unit of service-cost relationships between institutional (large-to-small, etc.) and community systems of service. There is rapidly developing in our country a "Scandinavian backlash"—can affluent America afford the approaches of the "socialists" in Scandinavia? This is a researchable set of issues that have direct bearing on our local-state-national efforts and attitudes. Such a study should lean heavily upon the expertise available among many of our economist colleagues.

6.   A demonstration and investigation of a total prosthetic environment for developmentally disordered persons who have associated handicaps. Though much has been written about this applied research challenge, few examples exist in our country today. Not only would this type of programmatic research directly aid such citizens, it would be an example of what we can do for them, and it would spur societal changes and modify current attitudes of hopelessness in this area of endeavor.

7.   A study of representative systems for coordinating community services for the developmentally disordered is necessary; on this basis a model for an effectively coordinated service could be developed. This issue arises from reported experiences that in many instances agencies purportedly established for the purpose of service coordination (such as regional mental health and mental retardation centers) primarily provide overly elaborate diagnostic procedures and tend to shunt parents from one inappropriate service possibility to another. Such ineffective coordina-

tion has done much to unfairly contribute to the stereotype of the parent of the retarded as a diagnosis or service shopper.

    8.   Studying and developing a model system of education and vocational habilitation for the developmentally disordered. Allied challenges could include:

> a.   Further research into the merits of various degrees of integration of the mildly and moderately retarded into regular classroom programs.
>
> b.   Comprehensive investigation of the learning process and the environments in which it thrives, resulting in the development of recommended model curricula.
>
> c.   Evaluating the relative effectiveness of automated versus traditional teaching techniques.

    9.   We should focus on determining which operational-programmatic trends are now on the horizon. In other words, we would dedicate ourselves to selectively support, with seed money, "glimpses of the future" through the eyes of current research and help stimulate both pilot programs and then larger scale operational-programmatic research endeavors in these frontier areas of activity.

    The list of challenges is great. There is considerable need to try to define exactly what it is about poverty that leads to intellectual deficit. This requires biological, educational, behavioral, and social research. We need to study more intensively the best techniques for teaching slow learners, methods based not on so-called global intelligence quotients, but rather on components that lead to specific remediation procedures which are better than those we now have. We need to understand reading disability in children of normal intelligence. We need to better understand the mechanisms of intellectual malfunction in children with cerebral palsy in whose developmental disorder motor handicaps may play a primary or secondary role.

These general and specific types of operational-programmatic research efforts will have an immediate impact upon the current and future lives of the mentally retarded. They can produce the results needed to answer our currently unanswered questions for both today's and tomorrow's mentally retarded citizens.

## A COORDINATED RESEARCH APPROACH

When the above-noted research dimensions are directly coordinated, then the inclusion of mission-oriented basic applied research endeavors into areas such as the underlying processes of learning, the biochemical parameters of memory and learning, and psycho-social-cultural studies of the factors that produce family disorganization can produce a highly viable research thrust. Since this particular aspect of the research thrust is mission-oriented, it can be effectively coordinated with operation programmatic (applied) research issues as well as with the actual delivery of services to the retarded individual. The following diagram (Figure 3.1) illustrates the interdependence of those components, including training, for a research thrust that can meet the needs of today's and tomorrow's retarded.

Lastly, an active research information retrieval system will permit the continuing active utilization of data generated anywhere in the world as part of this unified thrust of a basic applied-service delivery program. This mechanism will permit us to quickly apply findings from around the world.

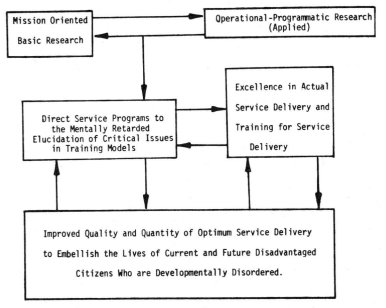

**Figure 3.1  Components for a Research Thrust**

## SUMMARY

The approach proposed here can meet the pressing need for meaningful research by avoiding the vicissitudes of most current research activities; unify what has been done, and embrace the challenges of the future with a posture that will permit us to move forward and attain new frontiers of knowledge (and hope!) for our retarded citizens.

SECTION II.

# UNIQUE SOCIAL-BEHAVIORAL CHALLENGES IN THE MENTALLY RETARDED

## Chapter 4

# OVERVIEW OF EMOTIONAL DISTURBANCES IN THE MENTALLY RETARDED

There are a number of major issues and problems relevant to the relationships between emotional disturbance and mental retardation. The definition of mental retardation underscores the presence of subaverage intellectual functioning and associated deficits in adaptive behavior. However, the majority of the disorders listed as capable of producing the symptom of mental retardation are more descriptive of symptoms rather than specific diagnostic entities. Add to this uncertainty of primary causes the problems of clinical description, and we have a major area of possible clinical confusion: symptomatic behavior which can be produced by a variety of causes. For example, the origins of a given child's hyperactivity may range from motor expressions of anxiety to manifestations of cerebral dysfunction. Similarly, a shortened attention span may be the end product of a range of determinants from an inadequate mother relationship in infancy—suggesting that the mother was unable to operate as a selective stimulation barrier for the child—to defective midbrain screening of incoming stimuli.

Thus the symptomatic nature of mental retardation, in association with the many possible causes for any given behavioral manifestation, increases not only the range of causation but also the possibilities for more specific treatment intervention in these complex disorders of childhood. Since emotional disorders in retarded individuals will be discussed at some length later in this chapter, it may be timely to review Chess's (46) definition of normal behavior as a baseline; the child gets along reasonably well with his parents, siblings, and friends, has few overt manifestations of behavioral disturbance, is using his apparent intellectual potential close to its estimate, and is contented for a reasonable proportion of the time.

There are a number of other definitions of emotional disorders that stress the individual's problems and malfunctioning in terms of a wide range of factors. Diagnostic systems of the emotional disorders embrace the symptomatic and developmental parameters that are such important considerations here. The spectrum of emotional disturbances range from the minor, such as adjustment reactions in childhood, to the major personality disturbances, such as psychoses of childhood. The considerations suggest that a description of emotional disturbance in the mentally retarded must include adjustment patterns which produce serious conflict within the retarded individuals, their families, and in the greater circle of their community transactions. Further, a disturbing personality influence such as pervasive anxiety may reduce retarded individuals' effectiveness and efficiency so that they have difficulty in dealing with emotional and stress situations, and thus it may further hamper their behavior.

A valuable concept in the emotional disturbances of mentally retarded children is that of developmental contingencies. This implies that the timing of and the reaction to intrinsic and/or extrinsic factors may be the major determining factor in symptom production at different neuroanatomical, physiological, and developmental stages of physical or personality development. The concept of developmental contingencies requires that a careful review of the personal and clinical histories be accomplished for any given child, with an overriding concern for capturing the dynamic flow of developmental events that produced the present set of behavioral symptoms. Figure 4.1 reviews some of the factors that can be assessed in such a developmental-interactional approach to seeking possible significant determinants of behavioral manifestations in the retarded.

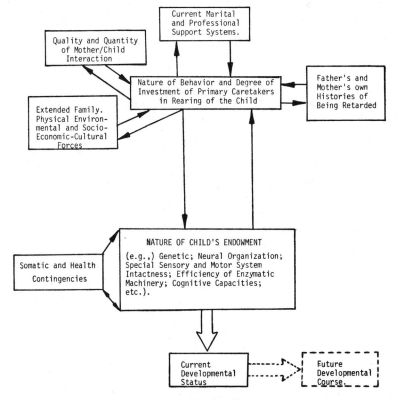

**Figure 4.1   Developmental Contingencies of Personality Functioning in Early Childhood**

These factors illustrate the complexity of evaluating the impact of different developmental contingencies in any given child (or adult). The figure also illustrates, by its relative complexity, the variety of dimensions that clinicians may elect to assess and attempt to therapeutically intervene. Indeed, each of the factors listed in Figure 4.1 have become points of theoretical-clinical departure for workers in this field. Yet the more difficult challenge may lie in considerations which emphasize the dynamic interplay between constitutional factors, validated cerebral trauma, the quality and quantity of mothering, and more recent possible determining factors such as family crisis.

## HISTORICAL PERSPECTIVE

As previously noted, professional interest in the personality dimensions of the mentally retarded has fluctuated for almost a century. Students of mental retardation are familiar with and respect the early contributions of such psychiatric pioneers as Itard, Seguin, and Howe. In the United States, the first successful efforts to organize professional services for the mentally retarded and to direct constructive public attention to their needs was largely the work of a small but devoted group of psychiatrists.

At the beginning of this century, the differentiation between the symptoms of mental illness and mental retardation in children was poorly understood. During the next 20 years, the following three professional viewpoints of mental retardation emerged: (1) it was described as a symptom of fixed neuropathology; (2) the genetic etiologies, with associated hopeless helpless prognoses, were overemphasized; and (3) the behavioral dimensions of the retarded were alternately viewed as being prosaic or as signals of potential danger to society (like the "eugenic alarm").

For the first half of the twentieth century, professional workers generally abandoned the field of mental retardation. Further, the most desirable recourse for both society and the individuals was thought to be the isolation of the retarded in large villages for the "simpleminded." Evaluation and treatment of emotional disturbance in the mentally retarded decreased as the object of professional attention. Retardates were viewed as the least ideal candidates for psychotherapy; it was presumed that little could be done for them.

In the 1920s and 1930s the rise of child psychiatry as a separate specialty at first further diminished interest in the emotional dimensions of mental retardation. However, it was the renewed interest in the psychoses of childhood and the emergence of potent parent advocate groups in the 1950s and 1960s which returned professional attention to the area in which psychiatrists had been pioneers.

The foregoing brief review of the relative lack of involvement of professionals in the behavioral dimensions of mental retardation may clarify the reason for the scarcity of available professional work and literature until the last 25 years.

This minimal professional interest continued until the following events occurred: (1) diagnostic clarifications of the cases which produce the symptom of mental retardation resulted in a sharp focus on the similarities and the differences between mental retardation and mental illness; (2) some consensus in definition of emotional disorder—as an abnormality of behavior, emotions or relationships which are sufficiently marked or prolonged as to both handicap the individual himself and distress his family or the community, and which continue up to the time of assessment; (3) research efforts in the biomedical, educational, and psychosocial determinants of mental retardation attracted increasing numbers of investigators to study behavioral characteristics of the retarded; and (4) citizen groups (NARC, etc.) joined forces with professionals to demand that more scientific attention as well as financial support be given to research dimensions of the behavioral adjustment potentials of the retarded.

Recent contributions to the interrelationships between mental retardation and emotional disorder have reflected this renaissance of professional interest. Since 1950 there has been a veritable explosion of interest in the behavioral dimensions of mental retardation, the differentiation between the symptoms of mental retardation and mental illness, and, more recently, the combined challenges of the presence of both symptoms in a given individual.

## FREQUENCY OF EMOTIONAL DISTURBANCES IN THE RETARDED

As previously noted, studies concerning the frequency and types of emotional disturbance in the mentally retarded are beset by some major methodological problems. The early studies (pre-1960) were accomplished primarily in institutional or hospital settings. The frequency rates reported ranged from 16 percent to 40 percent. These studies focused on institutionalized retardates in the mildly retarded range; since institutionalization has traditionally been used as a social mechanism for managing retardates with social-behavioral difficulties, they become a disproportionate percentage of the samples under study.

More recent studies, on institutionalized retardates report a similar frequency range of emotional disorders in the retarded, sharply question whether the (nonrepresentative) samples of institutionalized emotionally disturbed retardates reflect the increasing referral of "community program rejects" and the interrelationships of low-expectation of, and from, the individual, cultural-social deprivation, and the dissimilarity of personal expectations (maladjustment) to the social adaptive capacities of the mentally retarded.

For example, a previous study by the author on emotional disturbance in a sample of institutionalized children with Down's syndrome noted that though 37 percent of the total sample were emotionally disturbed at the time of the study, there were clear indications that 56 percent of the total sample had displayed clear indices of an emotional disturbance at the time of their admission to the institution. One must ask why they were sent to an institution for the retarded rather than to a mental health facility. Institutions for the retarded traditionally have employed a meager cadre of mental health professionals, and the admission of these emotionally disturbed retardates is quite inappropriate.

A series of reports of mentally retarded individuals who lived with their primary families or in their primary community at the time of study, have appeared during the last 15 to 20 years. These studies, especially those focusing on retarded children under the age of 12 years, rather consistently have reported a 20 to 35 percent frequency rate of emotional disturbances and have strongly suggested that the psychiatrist's focus must be placed on clear diagnostic study and subsequent treatment of the combined past and present findings of emotional disturbance and mental retardation. Interestingly, the presence of these combined findings may also reflect a professional bias by which the child's symptom of mental retardation is viewed as a signal not to treat the child's accompanying emotional disturbance. This bias was clearly articulated by Woodward, Jaffe and Brown when they noted:

> There are two prevalent attitudes on the part of many practicing child psychiatrists in the New York City area with which we differ strongly: 1) There is the attitude that a psychiatric diagnosis must be made in terms of either "organicity" (i.e., symptoms or signs of central nervous system

impairment) or "nonorganicity." Those holding this view seem unable to conceive of a mixed picture. Our experience would suggest that a mixed picture is common. To us it is irrational to say that a child with brain damage can have only one form of pathology, and that this explains everything. Why can't a child have mild brain damage and psychoneurosis? 2) There is the attitude that a child who has any evidence of brain damage at all, even a positive EEG without other evidence of CNS involvement, should not be offered psychotherapy. This attitude exists in spite of the known fact that children with brain damage may have normal intelligence. In our experience the results of therapy are always in proportion to the amount of psychopathology. There are some severely emotionally disturbed children who respond poorly to a psychotherapeutic program, and have no evidence of organic lesions. We believe that the decision whether a child should have psychotherapy depends on the estimate of his ability to profit by it regardless of the presence or absence of organic pathology. (47)

This pair of attitudinal biases may have unduly added to both the past and current reports of high frequency of emotional disturbance in the retarded and accomplished little or nothing to ameliorate the emotionally at risk status of these children. Indeed, these biases may well have facilitated the ultimate progress of similar retardates along the pathway to institutional patienthood as disturbed retardates.

Lastly, the frequency figures concerning the relationship between emotional disturbances and mental retardation reported in the literature should be placed in proper perspective as to the expected frequency rates of emotional disturbances in the nonretarded. The recent report of the Joint Commission on Mental Health in Children (48) suggests that emotional disturbances complicate the lives of 14 to 18 percent of the child population, whereas scientific population studies on mental illness in adults suggest that the incidence of emotional disturbance in the general population approaches 40 percent. Viewed in these perspectives, the reported ranges of frequency of emotional disturbances in the mentally retarded suggest a moderately increased susceptibility to emotional disturbances for them as a group.

## "AT RISK" BEHAVIORAL CHARACTERISTICS OF THE RETARDED

There are a number of considerations which tend to make the mentally retarded highly at risk for developing emotional disorders. It must be remembered that the heterogeneity of the more than 350 causes of the symptom of mental retardation embraces a wide spectrum of disorders, ranging from disorders in which mental illness is an expected symptom of the disorder (as in the untreated individual who has an inborn error of metabolism such as phenylketonuria), to instances in which the incidence of mental illness approximates the level of the general population (as in cultural familial retardation and the "invisible" mildly retarded young adult). Although it is hazardous to generalize across these many etiological determinants of the symptoms of retardation, we will review, by level of retardation, some of the major personality characteristics which place the retarded individual at risk in his vulnerability to emotional disorders.

### The Severely Retarded

Gross central nervous system impairment, multiple physical signs and symptoms, and a high frequency of multiple handicaps, especially special sensory and seizure disorders characterize the severely retarded. These at risk considerations directly impair these individuals' ability to assess and effectively partake in ongoing interpersonal-social transactions. Clinically, they manifest primitive behaviors and gross delays in their developmental repertoires. Primitive behaviors include very rudimentary utilization of special sensory modalities with particular reference to touch, position sense, oral explorative activity, and minimal externally directed verbalizations. In the diagnostic interview one notes much mouthing and licking of toys and excessive tactile stimulation, such as "autistic" hand movements which are executed near the eyes, as well as skin-picking and body rocking.

From a diagnostic viewpoint, the very primitiveness of the severely retarded individual's overall behavior, in conjunction with much stereotyping and negativism, may be misleading. For example, when minimally stressed in an interpersonal setting, these individuals frequently exhibit negativism and out-of-contact behavior, and this behavioral response may initially suggest a psychotic disorder of childhood. However, these children do make eye contact and will interact with the examiner quite readily, despite their very minimal behavioral repertoire. Similarly, one might form the initial impression that both the level of observed primitive behavior and its persistence is secondary to extrinsic deprivation factors, a functional disorder; however, these children display multiple indices of developmental-biological arrest which are of primary or congenital origins. It should be noted that these children never seem to possess a functional ego at the appropriate chronological age, and there is an amorphic or minimal personality structure. The previously noted at risk characteristics tend to appear against the backdrop of this amorphic personality.

Recent studies by Chess, Korn, and Fernandez (49) on severely retarded children with the rubella syndrome, and by Grunwald (50) on the multiple handicapped-severely retarded clearly document the high vulnerability of these children to psychiatric disorders. It has been noted that without active and persistent interpersonal, special sensory, and educational stimulation, including the active support of the parents, these youngsters fail to develop any meaningful contact with reality; they display "organic autism."

I have been impressed by the extent of personality development which the severely retarded can attain if early and energetic behavioral, educational, and family counseling interventions are initiated and maintained (51). True, they remain severely handicapped as to their cognitive and social-adaptive dimensions; however, there is a world of difference between the severely retarded child who graduates from a standing table to a wheelchair with a wide number of self-help skills, and the untrained severely retarded who responds with minimal affect toward any interpersonal contacts. Even in adequately managed severely retarded individuals, one notes that their paucity of language evolution remains as a high vulnerability factor in blocking growth toward more complex personality development. Interestingly, these youngsters tend to be accepted by their parental support systems and peer groups if adequate evaluations and anticipatory counseling are accomplished, perhaps reflecting empathy for the obvious handicaps which they display.

### The Moderately Retarded

The moderately retarded level encompasses some of the same etiological dimensions noted above, accompanied by a wide variety and high frequency of associated handicaps. The slow rate of development of these individuals and their specific problems with language elaboration and concrete approaches to problem-solving situations present both unique and marked vulnerabilities for adequate personality development.

In an outstanding study, Webster (52) viewed these personality vulnerabilities as stemming from the characteristic postures which moderately retarded individuals tend to use in their interpersonal transactions. More specifically, he reported the following clinical features: a non-psychotic autism (selective isolation), inflexibility and repetitiousness, passivity, and a simplicity of the emotional life. This simplicity of emotional life, a cardinal characteristic of the moderately retarded, reflects their undifferentiated ego structures and poses a clinical challenge in attempting to modulate their tendency toward direct expression of basic feelings and wants, as noted in their obstinancy, difficulties in parallel play situations, and so on.

Here again, the high frequency of special sensory and integrative disorders seriously hampers the moderately retardeds' approach to problem-solving, which makes them more likely to develop atypical or abnormal behaviors in a variety of educational or social settings. The limited repertoire of personality defenses coupled with their concrete approaches tend to form fertile ground for overreaction to minimal stresses in the external world. Proneness to hyperactivity and impulsivity, rapid mood swings, and temporary regression to primitive self-stimulatory activities are characteristic of their fragile personality structures. Limitations in language development further hamper their ability to fully communicate their inter/intrapersonal distress.

Unlike the severely retarded, this group of youngsters tends to be rejected by their parents and peers. Their significant attempts to approximate developmental expectations, along with the above-noted behavioral traits, appears to alienate them from those very interpersonal contacts which they so desperately need.

### The Mildly Retarded

I am hesitant to discuss the at risk personality contingencies of the mildly retarded level of the mentally retarded population because this group has been so harshly treated by professionals in the remote past (the eugenic alarm period) and in the recent past through indiscriminant labeling and the negative self-fulfilling prophesies of track system approaches in education. In addition, there is confusion over whether to view the mildly retarded as the statistical expression of the polygenic basis of the symptom of mental retardation or as the untutored have-nots of a society which tolerates only minor deviations from the norm (53).

In my experience, emotional disturbances in the mildly retarded reflect the well-known residuals of the individual who is labeled as deviant and then becomes caught in the dynamic interplay of disturbed family transactions. The typical delay in establishing that these youngsters have a distinct learning disability (usually not confirmed until six to nine years of age) presents the mildly retarded individual with a constant source of anxiety in his inability to integrate the major societal repercussions of being labeled a deviant at a crucial chronological-developmental time in his life.

Usually, during this quiescent period of psychosexual personality integration the non-retarded person is firming up his self-concept. Yet for the mildly retarded person, this period usually brings difficulty in understanding the symbolic abstractions of school work and the complexities of social-adaptive expectations from both his family and peer group. These stresses tend to establish excessive personality defenses against potential dangers to the self-concept, dangers which lurk anywhere and everywhere. The vulnerabilities of the mildly retarded are often not buffered or redirected by loved ones into new interpersonal coping styles to help correct earlier misconceptions about the self-in-the-world.

## TYPES OF EMOTIONAL DISTURBANCES IN THE MENTALLY RETARDED

Although both the frequency and types of emotional disturbance in the retarded historically have been colored by professional biases, they have always attracted much attention because of their possible import to understanding both normal and abnormal human behavior. Attention has focused upon the following types of emotional disturbance in the mentally retarded:

1.  *Psychotic disorders.* This usually refers to psychotic disorders of childhood, since the difficulties encountered in differential diagnosis and the resultant treatment formulations are usually more challenging and crucial in this age group. These disorders have encouraged further studies as to whether they represent functional psychoses masking as severe levels of retardation; or functional psychoses superimposed on primary mental retardation; or unique psychotic behavior in the retarded, which is defined by the extent of the emotional disturbance, with strong suggestions that it is a marked psychobiological over-reaction to stress in a retarded individual who has a limited central nervous system repertoire of response to stress, in contrast to the more clearly delineated functional psychoses.

2.  *Behavioral reactions.* These are comprised of symptom clusters, such as hyperactivity, which denote both intrinsic and extrinsic determinants of the same.

3.  *Transitory situational disturbances.* These crises are generally temporary acute reactions to overwhelming environmental or situational stress in a person without any apparent disorder. As the stress is reduced, the symptoms recede.

4.  *Psychoneurotic reactions.* In these cases, internalized symbolic responses to anxiety chronically are utilized to handle recurring patterns of interpersonal friction.

5.  *Personality disorders.* These disorders encompass extrinsically programmed personality postures towards interpersonal transactions in which frustrations and conflicts are avoided. Family expectations are crucial in the personality disorders, since the individual is protected from expe-

riencing the normalizing social values and the concepts of acceptable and non-acceptable behavior. In this particularly large category of emotional disturbances, the range varies from passive-dependent postures towards expected social roles, and acting out behavior which has legal implications (juvenile delinquency) to the sociopathic personality.

Each of these types of reported emotional disturbances in the mentally retarded will be discussed individually. For clarity, they will be discussed along the following guidelines of severity; the major disturbances, which encompass the psychoses, personality disorders, and the mentally retarded offender; and the minor disturbances, which include the psychoneuroses, transient situational disturbances, and special symptoms (such as hyperactivity).

## MAJOR EMOTIONAL DISTURBANCES

### Childhood Psychoses

Psychotic reactions of childhood have presented a major challenge to the clinician since their distinct recognition at the turn of this century. Delineation of types and etiologies have been delayed, in part by the fact that the psychotic child frequently functions at a mentally retarded level; in fact, early observers believed that all psychotic children deteriorated. Accordingly, initial studies in the first and second decades of this century tended to explain these illnesses as variations of central nervous system disorders and to focus on clinical descriptions. The third and fourth decades witnessed a sporadic number of reports concerning a childhood psychosis that resembled the schizophrenic psychosis of adults.

In 1943 a new syndrome, early infantile autism, was described and received much interest, including speculation as to whether it represented the earliest form of childhood schizophrenia. Following Kanner's (54) research, an increasing number of behavioral studies began to review the interrelations between childhood psychosis and mental retardation. Clinical and theoretical parameters of these interrelationships were referred to by Kanner as the "apparent" and "relative" forms of the syndrome of mental retardation. He summarized the renewed interest at that time as follows:

> This Journal issue [on mental retardation] is a logical outgrowth of a development which has tended to make the study of "feeblemindedness" and its ramifications an important, instructive and inseparable part of the field of Child Psychiatry. Nothing has contributed to this trend more potently than the work that has been done in the area covered by the term and concept of "pseudofeeblemindedness!" (55)

Experiences with the original and expanded diagnostic criteria for the syndrome of early infantile autism have not approximated the diagnostic clarity and prognostic overtones earlier stated by Dr. Kanner. Although the term autism is frequently employed in the differential diagnosis of the severe emotional disturbances in infancy and early childhood, to label a child "autistic" presents some formidable problems in regard to definition of the term, specific diagnostic implications, and treatment considerations for the child so designated. Too often the word is used as if it were a diagnosis, a synonym of childhood schizophrenia or an abbreviation for early infantile autism. Such usage obviously is imprecise and contributes further to the diagnostic confusion that abounds in the literature concerning childhood psychosis.

Prior to Kanner's studies, the concept of autism referred to disorders in the formal thinking processes; but many of the current concepts of autism include both thinking and particular types of behavioral relationships, especially withdrawal. The more recent, rather literal, definition of the term is crucial to an understanding of Kanner's concept of early infantile autism and some of the problems that continue to arise in its possible relationship to other disorders, such as behavior in the mentally retarded.

Currently, "autistic behavior" is characterized in the literature by reference to extreme preoccupation, a highly personalized and stereotyped approach to inanimate objects, and unrelatedness to people. In Kanner's initial descriptive study of early infantile autism he felt that his sample of 11 children presented two major primary symptoms: extreme interpersonal aloneness and a marked desire for the preservation of sameness. Utilizing these specific diagnostic guidelines, a wide number of clinical disorders that display autistic reactions in young children has been reported. The range of these reported clinical disorders is noted in Table 4.1.

**Table 4.1   Causative Factors Reported in Autistic Reactions of Childhood**

| | |
|---|---|
| Acute situational stress reactions | Deprivation: maternal, sensory, and affective |
| Central language disorders | Early infantile autism |
| Childhood schizophrenia | Idiot savant |
| Chronic brain syndromes of diverse etiologies | Mental retardation |
| Constitutional factors | Parental overprotection with infactilization |
| Convulsive disorders | Precipitate of severe parental psychopathology |
| Deafness | |

I had extended experience with these and similar diagnostic considerations during the study of a group of 1,025 young children who had been referred to the mental retardation clinic. This included the opportunity to treat and follow a group of 34 young children who represented autistic reactions of childhood. Seven distinct diagnostic categories were noted in this particular sample. A number of these children displayed prominent autistic behavior but were not psychotic, either by the definition previously given herein or by their future clinical courses. *This finding suggests that the symptomatic picture in these particular children was not predicted upon the degree of personality disturbance usually suggested by the rubric of "early infantile autism."*

An excellent example of the explicit application of Kanner's diagnostic criteria to a group of severely retarded children was reported by Schain and Yannet (56). Although the 50 children they studied exactly fulfilled Kanner's criteria for descriptive clinical diagnosis, the demonstrated causes of their disorders suggested a far different conceptualization of both treatment expectations and prognosis. These particular studies underscore some of the recurrent problems that one encounters in attempting to delineate a unique syndrome of early infantile autism and tend to confirm the previously noted emerging spectrum of reported causative variable in the autistic disorders of childhood.

The number of reports on early infantile autism and its possible relationships to the psychoses in childhood is really quite remarkable, especially in view of the relative infrequency of these disorders, the inconsistent diagnostic criterion commonly utilized, and the rather sobering follow-up reports that appear shortly after the initial enthusiasm of finding treatable disorders—childhood psychoses, in contrast to "untreatable" primary mental retardation. Reports on the interrelationships between the psychoses of childhood and mental retardation (57) are in essential agreement that the concept of pseudoretardation, a childhood psychosis masking as primary mental retardation, has limited utility since it usually reflects (1) errors in diagnosis; (2) attitudinal biases of the examiner; and (3) fixed views as to treatment-management expectations, with little delineation as to the degree of emotional and intellectual handicap.

Though one can become quite critical of this "rediscovery" of the old amentia/dementia paradox and the redefinition of developmentally primitive behavior into a loose diagnostic framework, it did bring about a wave of new professional interest in, and involvement with, the retarded. For example, the application of the psychiatric team approach to groups of the emotionally disturbed presented many opportunities for the direct study of psychotic children. Interpersonal pathology began to be established as a significant cause in children functioning at a retarded level, and a wealth of clinical reports of children thought to have a functional psychosis of the schizophrenic type ensued.

Current diagnostic terminology regarding psychotic reactions of childhood is inadequate and appears to be undergoing a slow evolutionary process. Some clinicians have felt that the designation "schizophrenia" was a label with questionable applicability to children; they chose instead "atypical child" or "children with ego defects." Interpretation of the clinical picture of psychosis in a child who is also suspected of being mentally retarded has explained it as (1) complementary parts of the same syndrome, (2) a primary emotional disturbance, (3) a multifactorial causal relation, or (4) the concept of the final common pathway from diverse causes.

As one reviews the case reports upon which such diagnostic formulations have been advanced, the need for detailed studies of these children becomes emphatic. There appears to be a tendency in child psychiatry over the last decade to classify rather diverse major emotional disturbances of early life as psychoses of similar historical and clinical parameters with differentiation based on the level of ego development noted rather than on an etiological basis. The term "autism" has been employed in various contexts; at times it appears to lose its original definition and is used as the description of a stage of personality development, a type of thinking disorder, a group of behavioral symptoms, or a specific diagnostic entity.

Another major point of confusion is the epistemology of the terms. *"Idiocy"* has the same derivation from the Greek that *"autism"* has from the Latin, meaning a person who lives in his own world, and when nomenclatural standards are applied to behavioral patterns in the moderate to severely retarded child, then the "idiot" is almost by definition an "autistic child." Those who have used Kanner's original diagnostic criterion for early infantile autism have apparently forgotten his cautions as to its possible spectrum of etiologies: "Possibly some of them are brain damaged, possibly some of them are schizophrenic. But in whatever category one wishes to place them, they do present a phenomenological constellation *sui generis*" (58). It would appear that similar phenomenological pictures—but from possibly diverse etiological factors—have led to the present dichotomy of viewpoints of Kanner's syndrome, ranging from purely functional to a secondary manifestation of major central nervous system pathology. The validity of considering early infantile autism as a separate and distinct category has been questioned by many clinicians (59, 60).

Despite the relative confusion which the labels "early infantile autism" and "autistic" have contributed to the general topic of the possible relationships of childhood psychoses and mental retardation, they still dominate the clinical-theoretical approaches to this general area. Accordingly, it may be fruitful to focus directly upon the continuing discussion concerning these disorders as possible sources of pseudo-retardation and/or the forerunner to childhood psychoses, and perhaps provide some signposts leading out of the current confusion.

THE RELATIONSHIP OF INFANTILE AUTISM AND CHILDHOOD PSYCHOSES TO MENTAL RETARDATION.    At this point a brief discussion of the concept of psychotic reactions in childhood is necessary, since this is probably at the core of the current discussions and conflicts concerning infantile autism and its possible relationship to mental retardation. The literature tends to refer to childhood psychoses, central nervous system disorders with associated emotional disturbance, childhood schizophrenia, atypical children, and early infantile autism almost interchangeably. It would appear that the theoretical inclination of the given investigator rather than the behavior of the child may determine to which factors primary etiological diagnosis is attributed.

Current viewpoints concerning the raw ingredients of the descriptive diagnosis of psychotic reactions in childhood embrace three major trends:

1.    Behavioral dimensions repeatedly stressed are bizarreness of manner, gesture, or posture; uncommunicative speech; no discrimination between animate and inanimate objects—this is felt to be one of the primary signs of such descriptive designations; excessive identification with inanimate objects; and deviant affective expressions.

2.    In the clinical encounter with the child, most commonly reported signs are sparse or totally absent reciprocal interpersonal relationships, the absence of which are manifested by lack of eye contact; minimal, if any response to structured play sequences; and markedly diminished spontaneous identification and interchange with the examiner. These descriptive signs and symptoms from the clinical encounter with the child strongly tend to suggest psychosis if they prevent any meaningful interaction with the child during the interview situation.

Additional descriptive features frequently noted in the clinical encounter include the language of such children; the voice tone, which is described as monotonous, with halting or stilted speech and echolalia without change of affective stress. Also in the area of language production there were noted pronoun reversals such as the "I-you problem" in a child with well-established speech development.

3. Stereotyped motor phenomena frequently are reported, such as repetitive and preoccupied manipulation of light switches, doors, and small electrical appliances; also persistent/unusual posturing, such as tiptoe walking and hand flapping.

In many ways, the general term "childhood psychosis" suggests a syndromic (from the Greek meaning different entities running together) approach to all psychotic disorders in early childhood, since it encompasses early infantile autism, childhood schizophrenia, atypical children, childhood psychosis, and mentally retarded children with psychotic reactions.

On the basis of their initial evaluation and follow-up observations, Rutter, Graham, and Yule (61) and Menolascino (62) consider childhood psychosis as a syndrome and view the clinical subgroups that are mentioned in the literature as depending on the age and stage of development of the child at the onset of psychosis, his underlying protoplasmic endowment, and the nature of the interpersonal environment in which he finds himself. In brief, this approach to syndrome diagnosis stresses the presence of a variety of etiological factors which converge into one final common pathway that becomes clinically apparent as a common syndrome of childhood psychosis and not the concept of unique etiology-unique syndrome.

Another syndromic diagnostic approach to childhood psychosis stresses the clinical gestalten that one obtains from the full evaluation of the child. This particular syndromic approach is well illustrated by the work of Creak (63) and her colleagues on the delineation of nine criteria for the "schizophrenic syndrome in childhood." Dr. Creak illustrated some of the basic problems encountered in applying the nine criteria to a schizophrenic syndrome of childhood by reviewing her experiences with a follow-up study of 100 cases of childhood psychosis. This is a significant paper, because she also underscores a major recurring problem: the differentiation of childhood psychosis from mental retardation. It may be prudent to note her cautions:

> Mental deficiency is the condition most readily confused with childhood psychosis, and indeed they have much in common. The psychotic child, while in the early withdrawn stage of his illness, is the most ineducable of any, and conversely, one meets among retarded patients odd skills, obsessional drives to no very obvious purpose, active withdrawal from social contact, and many instances of bizarre behavior. The distinction where these are psychotic children, or examples of psychotic behavior in severely retarded children, is almost an academic one. Such children function at a grossly retarded level, even if it often seems that it is the emotional isolation that closes the doors of learning to them. These cases show that even with reasonable care and long-term oversight, it is still possible to be in the dark as to the real diagnosis. Greater precision in diagnosis should be possible and the nine points were designated to help in this. We will always probably be faced with the problem, 1) Is he mad because he is limited, or limited because he is mad?—to put it crudely.

Such considerations become even more important when attention is focused on moderately and severely retarded children with multiple handicaps who have had a number of social-emotional episodes of deprivation. These particular children tend to be overly dependent on their parents and in the initial interview session may show a temporary regression, such as inaccessibility of feeling tone, which appears like psychosis unless one is aware of their past and present clinical and personal histories.

Therefore, to diagnose "psychosis" the examiner must spell out that it is based on observed reactions to different stimulus patterns. The quality of the interactions of the psychotic child is important. Such children appear to have a disturbed response to stimuli, which suggests a suprareflex pain-pleasure level and similar basic modalities of experience. At the same time, affective responses are derivatives of the raw visceral data received, and their appropriate elaborations depend on the intactness of the sensory organs and the central nervous system. Finley (64) has reviewed this particular area with a degree of objectivity and neurological-developmental elaboration that is rarely noted in the psychiatric literature concerning possible intrinsic determinants of behavior in infancy and early childhood. These considerations are highly relevant to Piaget's (65) findings that early personality development is highly dependent on the intactness of the primary sensory modalities. Parenthetically, lack of such intactness in the primary sensory integrative systems frequently is noted in the multihandicapped, especially in the moderately and severely mentally retarded children who experience associated major emotional disturbance.

One can summarize the previous comments concerning descriptive-diagnostic dimensions of a psychotic reaction in childhood by defining it as a disorder wherein there is a developmental failure or dissolution of the self-concept that is not consonant with the meaningful personal-social responses that ordinarily act to conserve both the identity and integration of the personality. Minimal diagnostic criteria are first, affective unavailability, which usually is present in the form of a refusal to interact with the examiner in the playroom. The psychotic child does not share his affect, nor does he react appropriately to the examiner's actions in the playroom situation. The clinical history strongly suggests a persistence of this type of relating as a reason for alienating the child from other personal-social relationships. A second criterion is a major interest in inanimate objects, the use of which is deviant from developmental expectations for the individual; there is no discrimination between these inanimate objects and animate objects, or there is a bizarreness of usage.

In regard to these rather perplexing areas, it is to be noted that moderately and severely retarded children are quite at risk as to ongoing personality functioning and tend to disorganize quickly, many times under minimal stress. At these particular periods, the mentally retarded child with an associated severe behavioral reaction usually presents acute features of primitive tactics to deal with primitive problems, usually in the area of motor control. In contrast, the mentally retarded child with a functional psychosis usually employs primitive tactics to handle rather complex problems, markedly diminished feeling tone, and the lack of interaction rather than problems of motor control. In similar fashion, one can differentiate the presence of a functional psychosis in moderately and severely mentally retarded children. Either of these entities, unless one uses a diagnostic caution, can mimic both the other and a primary functional psychosis in childhood.

In summary, classification attempts demand caution. For example, the heterogeneity of the descriptive-behavioral spectrum is the psychoses of infancy and early childhood, in contrast to the usually implied homogeneity. On the basis of the guidelines previously reviewed, a tentative classification of the psychotic reactions of infancy and childhood is proposed in Table 4.2.

*Pseudoretardation*

Having reviewed some of the specific diagnostic guidelines for psychotic reaction in childhood, we can now return to the previous considerations of the interrelationships between these specific behavioral syndromes which may mask as pseudoretardation or as a co-existing disorder with the symptom of mental retardation.

The concept of pseudoretardation has usually denoted an incomplete diagnosis, before treatment and follow-up

**Table 4.2 Tentative Classification of Psychotic Reactions of Infancy and Childhood**

| A | B | C |
|---|---|---|
| Developmental Arrest (primary or congenital). The child never had a functional ego. There is no concept of the self (there is an amorphic and formless personality—essentially no personality). Clinically, they reveal primarily self-generated activities with (1) little if any relationships with peers; (2) marked negativism (if pushed in an interpersonal setting one frequently notes negativism, withdrawal, out of contact psychosis); and (3) passive compliance to outside stimuli/demands. | Deviational-Developmental (e.g., "early infantile autism"). These patients never seem to develop a functionally complex ego early in life. This may be due to a primary integrative problem (e.g., minimal cerebral dysfunction, mental retardation, specific midbrain deficits Rimland, 1965); or possible secondary integrative problems (e.g., it can be secondary to a negative intake process such as psychotoxic mothering, deprivation syndromes, combined sensory-general environmental input difficulties, etc.). | Acquired psychotic (1) Regressive-dynamic: Primary (childhood schizophrenia). (2) Secondary (Propfschizophrenia). Organic Cerebral Insult/Dysfunction (e.g., infantile spasms syndrome and its residuals; traumatic etiologies, etc.). (3) Toxic psychoses (e.g., phenylketonuria). The toxic metabolic disorder literally disintegrates the personality relationship to reality—very similar to acute/chronic alcoholism in the adult. |

study have confirmed the diagnostic impression, and instances of misdiagnosis in which incomplete or inappropriate initial evaluation and/or professional bias can be found. Many case reports have strongly focused on pseudoretardation diagnostic formulations that have been difficult to substantiate by co-workers who have studied similar children. Conversely, when tentative diagnostic formulations —or better, an initial list of differential diagnostic considerations—sequentially are focused upon during the treatment phase, with follow-up study to assess differential outcome, then more distinct guidelines can be provided. The majority of recent studies strongly suggest:

1. The functional childhood psychoses are a separate set of phenomena as to causes, descriptive features, and clinical course, in contrast to primary retardation with superimposed behavioral symptoms.
2. The functional psychoses in childhood are infrequent phenomena—less than 0.1 percent of the childhood population—whereas the psychotic reactions that are superimposed upon a syndrome of retardation are more frequent—0.5 to 1 percent, are less intense, and less refractory to treatment than the primary psychoses of childhood.
3. The clinical courses, with or without treatment, are far different as to psychological adaptive abilities between the primary childhood psychoses and those which are superimposed upon a primary retardation syndrome.

Interestingly, today there is not the amount of fervor over diagnosis, treatment, and differential outcome concerning the functional psychoses of childhood and their interrelationships to mental retardation that there was 10 to 15 years ago. The previously noted follow-up studies, coupled with the rediscovery of the wide variety of primitive behavioral repertoires in the retarded—the same behavior that had been termed psychotic in the past!—and lack of relative differences in treatment modalities and corresponding responses to treatment all have tended to mute this earlier clinical fervor. Clinical research in mental retardation, especially over the last 10 years, has shown that the majority of the genetically and environmentally determined disorders tend to lead to mental retardation, especially in the moderate and severe levels, and not psychoses. The most common challenge in this relationship is not to determine whether the patient is retarded or psychotic, but to ascertain how much of his condition is attributable to retardation and how much to psychoses.

Earlier it was noted that the psychoses of childhood, especially following the work of Kanner, once again enkindled much fervor for the study of the interrelationships between mental retardation and the psychoses of childhood. Now, in the 1970s, the ferment has quieted and it is becoming quite clear that the number of functional etiologies of infantile autism and childhood schizophrenia is quite limited in scope. However, the reported findings of central nervous system pathology in the psychoses of childhood is the most frequent trend noted.

In summary, the clinical reports of the last ten years have rather clearly shown that (1) the psychoses of childhood, including infantile autism, are strongly associated with dysfunction of the central nervous system; and (2) the appearance of psychotic behavior, and/or autistic behavior, and mental retardation in young children most frequently denotes a common etiology of central nervous system dysfunction. If the reader views these two statements as based on too organic a viewpoint or too dogmatic for our current stage of knowledge, then a review of the previously noted diagnostic and follow-up studies will prove to be a rewarding experience.

## Personality Disorders

Personality disorders are characterized by chronically maladaptive patterns of behavior, such as antisocial personality or passive-aggressive personality, which are qualitatively different from psychotic or neurotic disorders. Since the diagnostic confirmation of a personality disorder hinges on clear documentation by review and validation of the past personal and clinical histories of maladaptive behavior of the individual being evaluated, the biases of the examiner become both a crucial variable and a source of diagnostic error. Studies reported in the earlier history of retardation tended to indiscriminately equate antisocial behavior with an expected behavioral accompaniment to mental retardation. Indeed, the much discussed earlier reports on the relationship between retardation and personality disorders, especially the antisocial personality, were couched as a moralistic-legal construct, rather than on definite descriptive criteria. The antisocial personality designation—formerly viewed as the sociopathic personality—continues to receive much attention and will be used to illustrate the current issues involved.

As one reviews the literature, it becomes clear that the individuals so designated (1) displayed rather spectacular behavior which centered much attention upon them; and (2) implied, through the chronic nature of their behavior and relative refractiveness to attempts at imposing external controls, an innate personality disorder. A perplexing number of formulations have sought to explain this disorder, giving rise to many misconceptions and bits of clinical folklore. For example, the clinical descriptive approach to the antisocial personality by Cleckley (66), while dramatically descriptive in citing case histories, contributed little to distinguish the phenomenology from that of mental retardation or to provide any therapeutic guidelines. But Humphreys (67) and Tarjan (68), while stressing the therapeutic refractivity of this disorder, reported that it was not frequently associated with the symptom of mental retardation. Indeed, Tarjan believed that the psychosocial family transactions were probably more important in relation to cause than the presence of mental retardation.

A corollary to these studies has been their focus on the antisocial personality disturbances as presenting basically unsocialized individuals whose behavioral characteristics— such as essentially no significant loyalties to individuals, groups, or social values; gross narcissism and inability to feel guilt—are predicated on the atypical/abnormal responses to interpersonal conflicts and culturally expected social adaptive responses to moral and social value systems-responses which literally have been negatively or inappropriately programmed by their families. Indeed, these characteristics tend to produce patterns of antisocial behavior, reinforced by family interactions, which became the hallmark of this disorder; immaturity or inability to postpone immediate gratification, impulsivity, irresponsibility, and failure in social learning from interpersonal transactions. This view of the etiology of the antisocial personality becomes the rational basis for the application of learning theory approaches to treatment intervention.

It would appear that one of the main reasons that the antisocial personality designation frequently has been inferred in mentally retarded individuals is the similarity of its symptoms to the developmental immaturity and associated delays in personality maturation that are noted in the diminished social adaptive abilities of the retarded. The symptom overlap would thus appear secondary to the bias of the examiner as to expected behaviors in both conditions, since a causal relationship cannot at present be confirmed.

Interestingly, other known personality disorders, such as schizoid personality, have been reported only rarely in the retarded. This fact is even more perplexing when one considers that some of these personality disorders are viewed as possible harbingers of psychotic disorders later in life. There appears to be a lacuna of professional interest between the study of overt psychotic disorders in the mentally retarded and the very conditions that are commonly considered as possible precursors to them. Indeed, the only other personality disorder in the retarded that has received much attention is the "inadequate personality," even though the application of exact diagnostic criteria would exclude this disorder as a primary diagnosis in mental retardation. For example, the current approach to this personality disorder as a primary diagnosis encompasses a behavioral pattern characterized by ineffectual responses to emotional, social, intellectual, and physical demands. While the patient seems neither physically nor mentally retarded, he does manifest inadaptability, ineptness, poor judgment, social instability, and lack of physical and emotional stamina (69). Unfortunately, this diagnostic statement leaves much room for examiner bias and value judgments unless it is correctly used.

In summary, personality disorders do occur in the mentally retarded, are primarily based on extrinsic factors, have no distinct etiological relationships to mental retardation, and, despite persistent folklore, are not increased in their frequency in the retarded population.

## The Mentally Retarded Offender

The mentally retarded individual who is viewed as a juvenile delinquent or a criminal has, like the sociopathic personality, elicited a variety of opinions as to the possible interrelationships between mental retardation and criminal behaviors as a sign of emotional disturbance, though there is a paucity of available factual information. Since this topic remains as a major challenge in modern approaches to the retarded, it is discussed at some length in the next chapter.

## THE MINOR EMOTIONAL DISTURBANCES

The appellation "minor" is utilized to review the following emotional disturbances in the retarded individual, because it implies (1) that they are separate from the mental retardation process itself, in contrast to the implied etiological relationships in the previous "major" disorders; (2) the extent of these disturbances do not appreciably interfere with social-vocational adjustment for any prolonged period of time; and (3) they are traditionally viewed as being more treatable than the major emotional disturbances. Under the rubric of minor emotional disturbances, the following disorders will be reviewed: psychoneurotic disorders, transient situational disturbances, and symptom clusters.

### Psychoneurotic Disorders

There is a paucity of older (pre-1950) literature on the frequency and types of psychoneurotic reactions in the mentally retarded. Previous reviews of this facet of emotional disturbances in the retarded suggest that the frequency of psychoneurosis in the retarded is quite low and the types of psychoneurosis reported are few in number. The low number of reports on psychoneurosis in the mentally retarded is not surprising if one recalls that the extent of these disorders—the disruption of ongoing psychosocial adaption—is relatively mild and that some of the long cherished notions about the role of anxiety, which is considered to be the core problem in psychoneurotics, in blocking intellectual function needs re-examination.

Yet there are a number of relatively recent studies (70, 71) that clearly delineate psychoneurotic disorders in young mentally retarded children. It appears that much of what was previously considered expected behavior in the retarded has, on closer study, been noted to be quite similar to emotional disturbance in the non-retarded. Each of these studies is quite explicit as to diagnostic criteria, and attributes the neurotic phenomena to factors associated with atypical developmental patterns in conjunction with disturbed family functioning. For example, the above-noted recent reports clearly delineate parameters such as the internal defensive tactics of retarded children (anxiety, fear of failure, insecurity, etc.) against externally derived phenomena such as chronic frustration, unrealistic family expectations, and deprivations. It is interesting that each of these reports suggest that psychoneurotic disorders are more common in children of the high-moderate and mild ranges of mental retardation. This trend has prompted speculation as to whether or not the relative complexity of psychoneurotic transactions is beyond the adaptive limits of the severely retarded individual.

As noted in other portions of this chapter, the recent renaissance of clinical interest in the emotional dimensions of mental retardation has produced a sharp division between the old literature and emerging reports of recent studies.

The paucity of past reports on the frequency and types of psychoneurotic disorders in mentally retarded individuals appears to this reviewer to hinge on a spectrum of professional bias concerning the preconditioning of the symptom of retardation to overall personality function. In the negative band of this spectrum is the rather fixed belief that mentally retarded individuals do not possess sufficient cortical material to view their interpersonal world in a fashion complex enough to warrant elaboration of the typical constellation of defense mechanisms comprising a psychoneurosis. In the middle band of this spectrum is the position that considers neuroticlike adjustments, or constructs such as displaced depression, manifested as general behavioral turmoil. Lastly, the direct observation of community-based samples of retardates has strengthened the growing impression that psychoneurotic reactions in the mentally retarded are similar as to both types and frequencies of these disorders in the nonretarded population.

## Transient Situational Disturbances

Although this rather large category of minor emotional disturbances is widely used in the assessment of the nonretarded, it is employed only rarely during clinical assessment of emotional disturbances in the retarded population. We feel that this lack is one of the major drawbacks of descriptive approaches to the retarded, and this topic will be dealt with at some length.

The *Diagnostic and Statistical Manual of Mental Disorders (DSM-II)* of the American Psychiatric Association (72) defines transient situational disturbances as follows:

> This major category is reserved for more or less transient disorders of any severity (including those of psychotic proportions) that occur in individuals without any apparent underlying mental disorders and that represent an acute reaction to overwhelming environmental stress. A diagnosis in this category should specify the cause and manifestations of the disturbance so far as possible. If the patient has good adaptive capacity his symptoms usually recede as the stress diminishes. If, however, the symptoms persist after the stress is removed, the diagnosis of another mental disorder is indicated. Disorders in this category are classified according to the patient's developmental stage as follows: 1) *Adjustment reaction of infancy*—Example: a grief reaction associated with separation from patient's mother, manifested by crying spells, loss of appetite and severe social withdrawal; 2) *Adjustment reaction of childhood*—Example: jealousy associated with birth of patient's younger brother and manifested by nocturnal enuresis, attention-getting behavior, and fear of being abandoned; 3) *Adjustment reaction of adolescent*—Example: irritability and depression associated with school failure and manifested by temper outbursts, brooding and discouragement; 4) *Adjustment reaction of adult life*—Example: resentment with depressive tone associated with an unwanted

pregnancy and manifested by hostile complaints and suicidal gestures; 5) *Adjustment reaction of late life*—Example: feelings of rejection associated with forced retirement and manifested by social withdrawal. (pp. 48–49)

The reader will note that the transient nature of these disorders is their paramount feature. The corollary, "if the patient has good adaptive capacity, his symptoms usually recede as the stress diminishes," poses the recurrent dilemma previously noted. If the clinician feels that retarded individuals have poor adaptive capacities, then little resolution is expected, treatment intervention is less than energetic, and other diagnostic categories are utilized. Similarly, if the mentally retarded are considered prone to emotional disturbances, then "transient" is viewed as the beginning of a chronic emotional disturbance that finally has emerged to accompany the retardation. Temporal factors are also operative, since one often evaluates the more obvious disturbance—the transient situational disturbance, especially if it is of severe proportions—and if the accompanying retardation is viewed as an instance of pseudoretardation, then the transient situational disturbance becomes the major focus of treatment and often is altered to reflect an emotional disorder that may produce retardation, such as an autistic reaction. The literature continues to be flooded with terms that imply misdiagnosis, treatment approaches that appear strangely out of place, especially on follow-up study, and professional biases fixed to the detriment of the child, his family, and society.

As noted, transient situational disturbances are, by definition, not a unitary syndrome as to types or levels of severity encompassed therein. This particular re-evaluation epitomizes one of the major conceptual problems that present a real dilemma to the behavioral scientist. More often than not, he must deal with descriptive diagnosis, since etiological determinants are frequently elusive. However, the nomenclatural systems currently available literally demand classification by etiology, whereas treatment-management techniques are based on behavioral and social constellation criteria. The problem here is a conflict between an etiological-prognostic classification approach versus a clinical descriptive-treatment indication approach and the associated and currently unresolved question as to whether or not there are meaningful interrelationships between them.

Although any system of classification is arbitrary, there are three ingredients of classification systems that recur continually: etiological description (diagnosis), treatment, and prognosis. The application of descriptive criteria in the field of mental retardation has clarified treatment and prognosis issues without having to be unduly concerned with etiology. For example, the descriptive term "trainable retarded" delineates specific intellectual and social adaptive levels of functioning and specific guidelines for treatment and prognosis. However, when a mentally retarded child of unknown etiology is noted to be emotionally disturbed also, the previously noted focus on a descriptive classification is often ignored in favor of delineating the current treatment needs and prognostic expectations. Undue focus is placed on the question of whether he is really emotionally disturbed or whether he is really mentally retarded. Too often, this obsession places too much emphasis on etiology and prejudices treatment and prognosis.

Examples of this recurring professional diagnostic posture in the interrelationships between emotional disturbances and mental retardation follow:

1.   A school-age mentally retarded child is referred from a special education class because of hyperactivity and temper tantrums; his mother is noted to have prominent psychoneurotic symptoms. The child and mother are en-

gaged in psychotherapy and their mutual emotional status improves. However, the child is still noted to be functioning at a retarded level. Accordingly, the case-closing diagnosis often is "mental retardation due to emotional disturbance."

In this instance, undue focus on presumed etiology precludes the descriptive assessment of multiple mental retardation and emotional disturbance and/or interacting disorders. The transient nature of the child's emotional disturbance is equated with the mother's psychopathology, and a complex disorder is erroneously reduced to a singular diagnosis.

2.  A four-year-old boy is referred because of obstinancy and frequent altercations with his classmates; his parents are noted to be perplexed by his behavior and only minimally interested in ongoing child-care goals. Examination reveals an adjustment reaction of childhood, a general level of intellectual functioning in the mildly retarded range, a borderline abnormal electroencephalogram, and scattered "soft" neurological signs. Psychotropic medications and/or anticonvulsant medications are prescribed; the case-closing diagnosis is "organic brain syndrome with behavioral reaction," and the parents are counseled on how to manage their "brain-damaged" son.

Etiological prejudgment has again reduced a complex disorder to a unitary disorder. A detailed descriptive assessment may have suggested multiple diagnosis and a specifically tailored treatment regime which focused on varying treatment-management approaches and prognoses for each of his disorders—mental retardation, adjustment reaction of childhood—and further family exploration-counseling to assess and help their mutual adaptive capacities.

3.  A quiet, withdrawn five-year-old boy who has stereotyped hand movements and no formal language is accompanied by his anxious mother for developmental as-

sessment. His general uncooperativeness precludes thorough assessment, and the diagnostic focus shifts to his overly anxious mother. His general clinical picture is termed infantile autism, and the presence of marked maternal psychopathology eventuates in an etiological diagnosis of early infantile autism or childhood psychosis. Intensive inpatient treatment is recommended for the child as well as individual psychotherapy for the mother.

Here, the etiological implications lead to an unwarranted conceptual jump to treatment/prognostic considerations without ample attention to the reported range of descriptive findings in the autistic reactions of childhood (73), attention which often results in the designation of less malignant diagnoses, more specific treatment-management approaches, and less dogmatic prognoses.

Briefly, the classification ingredients of etiology, description, and treatment/prognoses are not comparable or juxtaposable. This particular area of conceptual confusion is a major obstacle to further advances in the study of emotional disturbances. These considerations are of extreme importance to the apparent lack of major differences in the specific treatment program and results which are currently reported in heterogeneous samples of emotionally disturbed children, especially children with infantile autism and/or mental retardation.

In summary, just as it is difficult for the clinician to avoid prejudging whether or not a young child with atypical developmental indices is, or will become, mentally retarded, the more frequent use of the category of transient situational reactions presents similar challenges to the dogmatic or biased clinician who is asked to assess an emotionally complicated instance of mental retardation. Yet the utilization of this category of emotional disturbance in the mentally retarded individual will permit a direct and extended diagnostic study of both of these symptoms, clearly assess the extent and nature of adaptive problems noted therein, and then specify treatment-management approaches that do not prejudge, positively or negatively, long-range expectations for the individual's total intellectual and social adaptive abilities.

Lastly, when viewed as crisis situations in which there is equal opportunity for treatment and resultant personality growth or continuing stress and lack of personal fulfillment, these transient situational disorders present excellent opportunities for primary and secondary preventive approaches to emotional disturbances in the retarded (74).

## Hyperactivity: Syndrome and Symptom

Hyperactivity in the retarded is as often discussed as it is poorly understood. The older literature tended to view marked motor activity in the descriptive language of the psychoses ("maniacal excitement," "catatoniclike furor," etc.). It is from this body of reports that neurological studies have resulted in the delineation of marked and sustained motor overactivity—hyperactivity and hyperkinesis are used interchangeably to describe this symptom complex—as frequent accompaniments to known trauma to the brain (postnatal infections—especially encephalitis, toxic-metabolic disorders such as Huntington's Chorea, post-traumatic residuals as in the follow-up studies on head injuries, etc.).

When the etiology is not distinct, then the descriptive behavioral traits of overactivity, restlessness, distractability, and short attention span have been utilized to represent a nomenclatural syndrome, hyperkinetic-reaction of childhood. If no signs or symptoms of central nervous system dysfunction are noted, then this syndrome is viewed as resulting from family turmoil, behavioral disorder of child-hood. If signs of central nervous system dysfunction are noted in conjunction with the above noted behavioral traits, they are viewed as manifestations of an organic brain syndrome. Lastly, if signs of central nervous system dys-function, plus the above noted behavioral traits and dis-turbing interactions between the child and his parents are noted, then the organic brain syndrome is listed as the primary diagnosis and the family turmoil dimension as a secondary diagnosis. Needless to say, this is a rather con-fusing diagnostic challenge, and the cautions noted in the section on transient situational reactions and the overview of professional biases that were previously presented apply here.

These rather muddy diagnostic issues have lead to numerous reports that present no uniformity of diagnostic clarity and stress the relative importance of a wide variety of etiological determinants and treatment modalities. This diagnostic nonspecificity has also been documented by well-controlled studies which have been unable to objectify the motor overactivity that was clinically described or infer-red.

The major clusters of studies have focused on: (1) specific etiological entities (head injury, postnatal infec-tions, etc.) which can produce an abrupt behavioral change; (2) the developmental dimensions of expected hyperac-tivity ("the terrible twos") and factors that may prolong it; (3) family interactional patterns that precipitate hyperac-tivity as a primitive personality defense to marked and chronic stress; (4) neurophysiological immaturity which has been studied in an attempt to illuminate the frequently noted diminution of the syndrome/symptom after early adolescence; and (5) as a total personality response to an emotionally and physically barren setting (institutional life). Attempts at differential diagnosis (as to etiology) have focused on laboratory evaluations (EEG studies), family exploration as to timing and patterns of the hyperactivity (hyperactivity noted in the company of the parents, but not with babysitters or at summer camp), social class and expected behavior, and so on.

Similarly, treatment approaches have varied widely and usually follow one or the other of the above noted clusters of etiological determinants. Interestingly, one notes a trend in the recent literature to focus not on hyperactivity per se as a syndrome or isolated symptom but rather as a subcomponent of a more general problem in learning—a learning disability. To date, this recent trend has, unfortunately, only tended to muddy the waters further, and hyperactive behavior remains basically a symptom that must be evaluated thoroughly as to its import in the individual's total past and current levels of general social adaptive functioning.

This recent trend has focused away from the retarded as to expected hyperactive behavior, since most of the recent formulations exclude retardation as a basic diagnostic sign or symptom. This trend may also herald the effects of national successes in obtaining mandatory education for the retarded—and thus specialized-structured learning settings, which appear to benefit many hyperactive children—in contrast to the marked paucity of generic services for emotionally disturbed nonretarded children.

Recently I have noted that some clinics and practitioners, especially psychiatrists and pediatricians, complain, "Where have all the hyperactive kids gone? Is someone else treating them as something else?" These clinics and practitioners had, in the past, focused on a strong medical-evaluative approach rather than the social adaptive or family orientation to these children, and psychoactive drugs were a mainstay of their treatment approach. Such drugs, despite recent studies questioning as to their efficacy and moral dimensions, did provide a rationale for treatment and positive intervention for many practitioners who, without drugs, may have viewed this symptom as unmanageable.

## TREATMENT AND MANAGEMENT

Early reports on the treatment and management of emotional disturbances in the mentally retarded parallel the approaches and attitudes of early humanistic education approaches; the negative historical-societal postures towards those viewed as deviants and the accompanying tragic interlude during which the defect position and the eugenic alarm ushered in an era of custodialism to "protect society from the retarde"; and the resurgence of professional and public interest and involvement in the plight of the retarded in the midpoint of this century. Concurrent with these trends, fluctuation of reports on treatment and management of the emotionally disturbed retardate reflected societal approaches towards the "dementia" prototype, the educational approach toward "amentia," the suppressive approaches—isolation, restraint, sedatives—during the early part of this century, followed by the treatment approaches to the psychotic, the juvenile delinquent, the brain damaged, and, finally in the early fifties, some specificity of approaches towards this rather large group of individuals.

In retrospect, it is rather remarkable to note that from 1915 to 1951, clinical descriptive studies, low behavioral and social adaptive expectations, and the monotonous recommendation for institutionalization were the clinicians' standbys. This trend is even more remarkable when one considers that this same time period witnessed the rise of the movement to establish child guidance clinics, specific treatment-management approaches to the emotionally disturbed (usually non-retarded) adolescent, individual psychotherapy, and family therapy approaches. This professional lack of interest in treatment-management of the emotionally disturbed retarded gives full credence to the parents-founders of the National Association for Retarded Citizens, who viewed the establishment of their association as a backlash to the lack of interest of professionals in their children's adjustment difficulties.

Since 1950, an increasing stream of reports on this topic has been forthcoming. Treatment approaches have ranged from individual psychoanalytically oriented psychotherapy, therapeutic nursery schools with associated family therapy, psychoactive drugs, group therapy, play therapy, behavioral modification (75), and combined approaches. Each of these trends, over the last two decades, have grown, though the psychoanalytic approach has remained rather sharply focused on the severe and complex disorders of early childhood as its prime interest area in retardation.

The therapeutic nursery school approach has expanded to include a variety of levels and types of both retardation and emotional disturbance in the older chronological age groups. All of these approaches attempt to conceptualize a treatment formulation which encompasses an in-depth study of the child and his family in order to delineate the nature and extent of their adjustment difficulties, and to refine intervention techniques to resolve them. Reviews of psychotherapeutic techniques useful with the mentally retarded emphasized the prevalent fallacy that psychotherapy is not applicable to the mentally retarded. Similar results concerning the value of psychotherapeutic efforts in institutionalized samples have frequently been reported.

Rogers (76) stated that psychotherapy was not indicated for the mentally retarded because it requires insight, a high level of verbal communication, a capacity for self-reliance, and other factors inherent in normal intelligence. I strongly disagree with Rogers's assumptions by pointing out that relationships which stress warmth and acceptance are more important in assessing response to psychotherapy than the intellectual functions.

The rise of regional mental retardation resource centers and clinics in communities, such as university-affiliated mental retardation centers, has facilitated the availability of manpower to accomplish more treatment-management interventions, including psychotherapy, since a group of professionals and rapidly available community resources are necessary ingredients for the rather total family approach utilized by these centers. Although this movement has brought increased professional involvement in the emotionally complicated instances of retardation in community-based samples—rather than in institutionally based samples, with all of their confounding additions to the clinical picture and treatment potentials that were previously noted—this particular team approach also has many severe limitations.

First, it is in many ways a direct descendent of the child guidance clinic model and has carried along with it many of the professional rigidities—as in types of personnel needed—that have adversely plagued that model. Secondly, the rather cumbersome administrative guidelines and very high financial costs of such clinics tend to leave little promise that they will ever begin to serve the large number of emotionally disturbed mentally retarded individuals who are in need of such services. Wolfensberger, in a provocative article entitled "Diagnosis Diagnosed," suggested that the "diagnostic preoccupation" of such clinics not needed; is too costly; and is continued at the price of the actual delivery of services which can be accomplished elsewhere in the community (76a).

A treatment-management approach which has increasingly addressed itself to both the wide range of challenges present and the relative drawbacks of the previously described approaches is the modality of behavioral modification, based on the evolving perspectives in learning theory and personality and behavioral dimensions of the retarded. This approach has been used for over two decades in the objective descriptive, selective study and, more recently, in the general application of its techniques to individual, group, and systems approaches to the retarded. Since a number of excellent reviews of this treatment-management approach to the mentally retarded are available (77, 78) and a thorough discussion of its merits and demerits is beyond the scope of this chapter, only a brief review of the potential impact of this viewpoint and approach will be presented.

The behavioral modification approach to treatment of the emotionally disturbed mental retardate will, in my opinion, serve to both unite past viewpoints and illuminate new horizons of treatment response and prognosis. In contrast to past viewpoints, the behavioral modification approach:

1.    Strongly focuses on the minute descriptions of primitive, atypical, or abnormal behaviors.

2.    Objectively delineates—subjective phenomena that are not that difficult to describe, graph, or otherwise depict.

3.    Does not consider nomenclatural dimensions to be sacrosanct and hence does not permit them to limit full descriptive analyses of observed behavior—thus, nomenclature is relegated to its proper nonclinical role of administrative channels, rather than muddying the focus on descriptive dimensions.

4.    The observed descriptive parameters are used as the basis for a hierarchy of treatment interventions, not implied parameters or expected theoretical expectations as to "what the symptom really means." Again, this is a refreshing departure, in my opinion, from the professional fixation of hypothetical spooks in the box of the uncon-

scious, the family, or so on. Accompanying this approach is the studious avoidance of the historical social-professional bias towards the retarded that has been repeatedly emphasized in this chapter.

5.    Treatment-management contracts, based on the previously noted objectified hierarchy of treatment needs and accompanying tactics/techniques for their direct/indirect intervention and resolution can give direction to the treater(s), the individual, and the family. Since this arrangement can be subjected to cost-service benefit guidelines, it holds much promise for resolving the justified concern with the cost of human management service.

6.    The flexibility of the behavioral modification approach permits the focus on a symptom (for example, head-banging) or a syndrome/symptom complex (for example, psychoneurotic phobic reaction). Studies in this aspect of behavioral modification have posed serious challenges to cherished notions about the overdetermined nature of either singular symptoms or syndromes of behavior. To date such challenges have generated more heat than light as to whether the expected theoretical cautions do materialize. But the individuals and their parents have, in my experience, shown singular lack of interest of such professional debates, and have been more impressed by resultant alleviation of symptom and syndrome. This latter dimension —the viewpoints of the patient and their parents—also underscores another little-discussed aspect of the behavioral modification approach: the nature of the relationships of the treaters to the individuals and his family.

There is an evolving caricature of the professional in behavioral modification as a cool, detached behavioral engineer whose interest in his patient is akin to an animal investigator's study of his subject. Indeed, one suspects that this caricature is actively nurtured in some quarters as a prerequisite to involvement in this aspect of the treat-ment-management of the emotionally disturbed mental re-tardate! Yet the direct observation of a wide number of these professionals at work, not merely in their writings, has convinced me of their deep interests in the patient as a person.

Though behavioral modification approaches to the emotionally disturbed retardate are currently very popular and helpful, Baumeister's cautions are well taken:

> Operant conditioners have rediscovered a very fundamental principle: the empirical law of effect. Perhaps it is not too obvious to suggest that all effective teaching makes use of this principle, regardless of the label one attached to it and whether or not the teacher can actually verbalize the princi-ple. In this connection, it is instructive to look at some early methods employed in the treatment of mental deficiency. Over a century ago, Seguin, in his extensive writing on the physiological method, described procedures that are re-markably similar to those currently advocated in the name of behavior modification. There is another similarity worth noting. Seguin's methods were widely hailed during the nineteenth century, and indeed, provided the major theoret-ical and scientific rationale for the establishment of residen-tial schools in this country and in Europe. The early literature is replete with accounts of remarkable successes and cures using the physiological methods. In 1844 the Paris Academy of Science was moved to declare officially that Seguin had, at last, solved the problem of idiot education. That may have been a bit premature, for hardly more than half a century later a crippling pessimism had permeated professional opinion—a state from which we have not yet recovered. There were a number of factors responsible for this marked change in attitude, but certainly part of it can be traced to the ill-founded and exaggerated claims made for the physiological method. One can only hope that operant conditioning, both as a treatment method and as a way of conceptualizing retarded behavior, does not become an un-happy victim of its own publicity before its adequacy is dem-onstrated on purely scientific grounds. (19)

Baumeister's caution, in conjunction with the current renaissance of professional interest in treatment-management approaches to emotionally disturbed retardates, strongly suggests that future reviews of this topic area will reflect a continuing posture of innovative intervention techniques.

All of the above treatment-management approaches can encompass, on a primary or elective basis, the utilization of adjunctive techniques. These may range from enlarging the treatment from the one-to-one to the one-to-many arena, to two of the most commonly utilized adjunctive measures: parent counseling and psychopharmacology. Since these two adjunctive approaches are used frequently, they will briefly be reviewed.

## Psychopharmacological Adjuncts

Psychopharmacological agents have long been employed as treatment adjuncts in the emotional complication of the mentally retarded. However, most reported studies have been in institutional settings, and there is an apparent reluctance to combine such agents with outpatient therapeutic programs. Fish has concisely reviewed some of the concerns in this area as follows:

> Fears have been raised that drugs will dull perception, stifle learning, and disrupt the therapeutic relationship. Such fears have essentially proven to be groundless. Drugs tend to increase the effectiveness of the treatment program—in selected cases—and the supposed deleterious effects have failed to materialize. Recent years have witnessed a tremendous growth in the prescription of a variety of tranquilizer drugs in adult psychiatry. Actually, drug therapy was more popular and widespread in child psychiatry than in adult psychiatry even before the relatively recent interest in the tranquilizers. This is probably related to both the fact that there is a reluctance to resort to methods such as lobotomy and electric shock treatment utilized in the control of hyper-

active, aggressive adults. Thus, since 1937, benzedrine and, subsequently, dexedrine have been widely used in the treatment of disturbed emotional states in children. Specific therapeutic aspects of new drugs must be emphasized, because for many years a variety of sedative agents, most recently the barbiturates, have been utilized in mental disease to achieve control through heavy sedation. With more recently developed drugs, the aim is to ameliorate the symptoms and restore function and, in the child, to aid maturation and enable him to participate in educational programs. These goals cannot be achieved by heavy sedation. (80)

In attempting to provide a brief review of the use of pharmacological agents in this area, one is overwhelmed by the number of agents recommended and the conflicting claims as to their efficacy. Further complicating the picture is the placebo effect, since recent reports indicate that beneficial response is engendered not only by the patient's enthusiasm for the medication but also by the attitude of the physician. Similarly, attitudinal biases and resultant treatment approaches of behavioral scientists also directly effect the utilization and expectations of psychopharmacological agents in the emotionally disturbed retarded. Freeman (81) has succinctly reviewed this topic:

Those with a psychodynamic orientation may shun drugs as interfering with the therapeutic relationship; those with a behaviorist preference may do the same because they feel behavior modification procedures are more effective. Some physicians who are termed (somewhat disparagingly) "organic" may be little else than "directed drug therapy." Strong feelings are often expressed on these issues, as well as on drug preferences. The latter may be based on one's early favorable or unfavorable knowledge.

Freeman lists the following general guidelines for using psychoactive drugs in the emotionally disturbed mentally retarded: (1) agitated and/or hyperactive psychotic children; (2) withdrawn and/or hyperactive psychotic individuals; (3) depressed individuals; (4) hyperactive, impulsive and/or aggressive nonpsychotic children (for example, hyperkinetic syndrome); (5) highly anxious nonpsychotic individuals; (6) night sedation; and (7) tics (specific syndromes such as Gilles de la Tourette's Syndrome which tend to respond favorably to the haloperidol group of drugs). He reviewed all of the psychopharmacological agents that have been utilized for the emotionally disturbed mentally retarded. Though the number of agents currently available is quite large, he notes that there are evolving trends as to what classes of drugs (major or minor agents classified as to extent of action) are most beneficial for symptoms of emotional disturbances.

A number of relatively specific drugs as to adjunctive symptom management are available to the clinician; yet this topic has initiated bitter debate as to the relative efficacy of or need for their utilization. The recent controversy over the use of stimulants in school-age children (for a variety of developmental problems) has focused on these issues: (1) their value and role (psychopharmacologically), moral implications, personal perceptions of the drugs; (2) the role of the placebo effect and other major methodological problems in clinical psychopharmacology; (3) optimistic promotional materials from the drug companies versus toxicity precautions; (4) the indiscriminate utilization of these drugs to manage behavior at the cost of decreased ability for learning; and (5) the mixed expectations of the family for the drugs themselves. These and other dimensions of the personal-social-professional problems and issues involved in using psychopharmacological agents as treatment adjuncts for the retarded were succinctly reviewed by Colodny and Kurlander (82) as follows:

> In sum, the feelings, attitudes, and conflicts of all of those
> concerned with the use of (psychoactive) medications in the
> mentally retarded must be seriously explored before one

can tell whether it should be done at all, how it should be done and whether it can meet with success.

These psychopharmacological agents are primarily used as adjuncts to a total treatment-management approach; in the following three modes: (1) a major part of treatment in which the psychopharmacological agent and its possible benefits are focused upon by an authoritarian explanation and followup supportive visits, but with no major focus on personal or family counseling; (2) the above approach with a secondary focus on active individual and/or family counseling; and (3) active individual and/or family counseling with a secondary focus on the role of the psychopharmacological agent.

Though the literature on this topic is fairly extensive —it parallels the utilization of psychoactive drugs in treatment of mental illness—the modern era of psychopharmacology did not commence until the introduction of chlorpromazine in 1952. Previous parts of this section review some of the general advances since that time, yet the use of pharmacological agents to control the behavior of emotionally disturbed retardates (usually institutionalized) may not be past history. Lipman recently surveyed the use of psychoactive drugs at 109 public and private institutions for the retarded and found that 51 percent of the patients at these institutions received daily schedules of psychoactive drugs; the sedative drugs (such as phenothiazines) were the overwhelming drugs of choice and the dosage ranges were quite high; and 25 percent of the patients received these particular drugs for four or more years. He (83) used much restraint in summarizing this study as follows:

> Unless the writer's radar equipment has seriously failed, it would seem that, to an overwhelming degree, psychotropic drugs instead of paraldehyde and camisoles are being used for controlling the behavior of the aggressive, assaultive,

difficult-to-manage hyperactive patient. Given these survey results, it behooves us to ask: 1) What is the evidence to support the efficacy of chlorpromazine and thioridazine for controlling the difficult-to-manage? 2) What do we know of the effect of chronic phenothiazine treatment on the intellectual and physical development of the mentally retarded child? 3) What evidence is there to indicate that sedative phenothiazines should be the drugs of choice for this type of patient?

The utilization of psychoactive drugs for emotionally disturbed retarded individuals as true adjuncts to a total treatment-management approach, while beset with many basic methodological and clinical judgment quandaries can represent a judicious contemporary approach or subtly reduce the clinician to the suppressive-custodial approaches of a bygone era of mental retardation. Unless the adjunctive role of such drugs is clearly conceptualized and practiced, then a variety of medical pseudorelationships may be perpetuated—to the detriment of the retarded individual.

## Parental Counseling

Since parental counseling has been noted as a frequent ingredient of many treatment approaches to the emotionally disturbed mentally retarded, it is accorded a separate chapter (Chapter 9) for a more complete discussion.

## DISCUSSION

Emotional problems which often complicate the lives of mentally retarded individuals are being increasingly appreciated. Equally important in contemporary thinking is the knowledge that mentally retarded individuals no longer represent a homogenous group in any characteristics: intellectual, physical, social, or cultural. In brief, the mentally retarded individual is a thinking and feeling individual who, like any other person, is prone to similar emotional problems and social difficulties. Like the more normal child, the mentally retarded child may avoid facing his problems and may become anxious, aggressive, hostile, and antisocial. Similarly, he may be responsive, friendly, passive, and cooperative like other children.

It has become apparent that there is no natural line of separation between adequate intellectual functioning and abnormal intellectual functioning. The major differentiation between the retarded individual and his normal peer appears to be his overt and socially judged adaptive behavior. His limitation can seriously interfere with both his capacity to obtain satisfaction for his own efforts in regard to how he understands the world around him and in his capacity to meet environmental demands and expectations. The extent to which he is surrounded by supportive adults becomes the major difference in whether or not he makes a satisfactory emotional adjustment.

When adults are inconsistent in their attitudes or support and are demanding, undependable, and generally nonsupportive of the mentally retarded individual's efforts, his needs emerge with greater urgency. Such situations may develop in the home or in school and become chronic, even though parents and teachers are aware of the child's retardation. Parents may intellectually accept the problem the child has, but they may have strong emotional reasons which prevent their acceptance of the child for what he is. Some parents react with anger and withdrawal of love and consider their child stubborn, ill-tempered, or lazy; these attitudes increasingly push parents to view their child with nonacceptance or nonrecognition of his capabilities. The overall result is a retarded individual who has to cope with both his intellectual limitations and the psychosocial or emotional handicaps produced by the negative recurring interactions with his outside support systems, both in the family and in the general world outside.

In a disturbed family setting in which failure is answered with rejection, the child is continually subjected to increasing insecurity, and he may develop chronic anxiety with fixed pathologic dimensions, such as in a psychoneurosis. He may become diffusely anxious in many areas and may develop phobic phenomena or compulsiveness as defensive responses. Alternately, a child may remain passive and dependent, with particular focus on staying with the old and safe approaches to interpersonal relationships; this type of personality defense can drastically interfere with learning opportunities. Both types of disturbance are neurotic structuring of the child's inside world, and both are less likely to yield to environmental manipulation; in these instances, treatment of the child-parent interactional unit must use more formal psychotherapy approaches.

Psychiatric aspects of mental retardation become clinically more difficult to apply because of the many causes of mental retardation, the frequently associated multiple handicaps, the rapidly changing psychosocial needs of the developing child, and the complexity of family interactional patterns. The extrinsic factors may also mask, modify, or exaggerate the underlying pathophysiological processes.

## A Reflection

Parenthetically, the author has noted neurotic reactions in the mildly retarded, but rarely in any other levels of the mentally retarded. Although a quick answer may be gleaned through reference to the previously noted personality traits and vulnerabilities of the moderately and severely retarded—level of personality may preclude the complexities of neurotic symptom formation—there is another point of view: perhaps psychiatrists have attempted to fit the current nomenclature systems into their expectations of the behavioral repertoires of the moderately and severely retarded and have attributed mental illness to these stereotypes.

For example, in the past I studied a group of community-based Down's syndrome youngsters and noted a fairly high incidence of mental illness (84); during a later study of an institutionalized sample of Down's syndrome youngsters (85) I noted that many of them appeared happy, overly friendly, and would literally swarm around a visitor on the ward. On reflection, the bulk of stereotyped Prince Charming behavior in this particular subgroup of the mentally retarded appeared to be secondary to *affect hunger*, and a far different set of diagnostic considerations and treatment challenges emerged rather than the initial impression of their behaviors.

It is sobering to note how the past psychiatric stereotype of moderately and severely retarded as "happy and carefree" may have blinded psychiatrists from serving a lost generation of highly vulnerable retarded youngsters grouped together in institutions. Now their task is one of providing psychiatric services in conjunction with family/home/community opportunities for educational, vocational, and personal-social accomplishments within the mainstreams of society.

From this perspective, the goal in approaching the at risk personality contingencies of the mentally retarded must focus on helping them to develop more specific psychosocial skills for attaining interdependence in society. Previously there was overattention to the goal of personality independence, a task that is extremely complex for the non-retarded. Assisting retarded citizens to understand and manage their needs for dependent relationships while simultaneously fostering interdependent experiences with counselors, peers, citizen advocates, and employers will buffer and modify their personality vulnerabilities, thus permitting these individuals to more fully develop their social-adaptive potentials. This approach can bring about the projection that nine out of ten mentally retarded citizens can be trained to live effectively in the outside world (86).

## CONCLUSION

In this descriptive and treatment overview of the most common behavioral reactions noted in mentally retarded individuals, an attempt was made to delineate symptoms that are secondary to cerebral insults, the role of superimposed interpersonal conflicts and their residuals, and those instances in which all of these factors are operative. It was stressed that treatment approaches must first focus on the global nature of the child's interactional problems and only secondarily focus on specific handicaps such as a seizure disorder, motor dysfunction, or speech and language delay. Many behavioral disorders can be helped through widely differing treatment methods and approaches because of the multifactoral complex of forces that are usually present.

No treatment approach is successful unless a continuous working relationship with the family has been established. In comprehensive treatment planning, it is better to focus not on what the child presently is, but also on what he can become. Initial, tactful interviews can provide the foothold for the establishment of a good relationship with the family. Within the context of a mutual contract of help, between the therapist and the family, multidimensional treatment needs can be delineated, augmented, and followed through.

The mentally retarded are highly vulnerable in regard to both their intrinsic and extrinsic potentials for maximal developmental progress. The high frequency of allied handicapping conditions, delayed language acquisition, impairments in cognitive function, and the family-societal

attitudes towards these specific vulnerabilities all underscore the need for major inputs of early and continuing
professional help for these youngsters and their families.
Fortunately, the worldwide interest in the care and management of the mentally retarded remains at a high level
because of organized parent-advocate groups and a growing number of highly involved professionals. These individuals know what the retarded can accomplish as future
fellow citizens of this world; and thus they give of their
interest and compassion.

## SUMMARY

In summary, there has been much recent ferment in the use
of traditional, semitraditional, and mixed modalities of intervention to challenges in the treatment and management
of the emotionally disturbed mentally retarded individual.
Of particular importance are approaches that stress objective descriptive delineation of disturbing behaviors and a
noncommitant similar discipline to their management.
Such approaches not only promise more clarity as to treatment-management goals but also may clarify the diagnosis-
treatment-prognosis quandary noted in an earlier section
of this chapter. A corollary of the expanding viewpoints
and proposed treatment-management approaches reviewed here is the revitalization of professional interest in
an area once viewed as beyond hope or promise of change.

## FUTURE CHALLENGES

Throughout this chapter many of the diagnostic and treatment-management challenges confronting those interested
in the emotionally complicated instances of mental retardation have been emphasized. Future developments in this

area can be likened to the intitial approach to a formidable mountain. The trends reviewed here strongly suggest that we know where the mountain is. We know its height and physical characteristcs, and we have begun basic and applied programs of professional involvement, the meaningful first attempts of reconnaissance. In the area of the emotionally disturbed retarded, such reconnaissance can extend to:

1.   Descriptive studies that directly assess the behavioral myths of the past, such as the "Prince Charming" behavioral description of the individual with Down's syndrome.

2.   Ongoing attempts to replace nonspecific descriptive behavioral phrases ("infantile autism") with more specific behavioral delineations.

3.   More widespread appreciation of co-existing symptoms and disorders in order to avoid reducing complex disorders to unitary diagnostic/treatment formulations.

4.   Continuing detailed studies of the subgroups of the mentally retarded to illuminate their physical/emotional etiologies. For example, the excellent recent study by Chess, Korn, and Fernandez (1971) was directed to the question of whether the symptom of mental retardation renders an individual more prone to certain types of emotional distrubances or maladaptive defenses and clearly showed that the extent of handicaps in their sample was highly associated with the presence of an emotional disturbance, especially in the psychotic reactions noted. Does this relationship hold true for other etiological subgroups of the retarded?

5.   Studies of the types of emotional disturbances noted in the different levels of mental retardation are long overdue. For example, the writer is acutely aware that he has generalized unduly concerning emotional disturbances

in all of the retarded, even though there is a growing consensus that the behavioral dimensions and adjustment difficulties of the mildly retarded are qualitatively and quantitatively different from the moderately and severely retarded. What are these differences? Do the retarded have personality defenses that are akin to the non-retarded, or are there specific personality dimensions that are attributable to the concurrence of the symptom of mental retardation?

6.    Further evaluations of current treatment-management approaches, as to whether they are specific or nonspecific techniques for such intervention, are direly needed.

7.    Study of the interrelationships between the evolving scales for social adaptive behavioral assessment and traditional assessment techniques is necessary.

8.    Ongoing study of the confounding variables may alter what we see, what we treat, and why and how we do either. For example, the bulk of reports in the literature on this topic concern institutionalized retardates, and it may be a literature quite apart from that which is currently evolving from community-based services. Can we truly compare these reported studies and results?

9.    We need more information on the relative impact of early developmental experiences on both mental retardation and emotional disturbance, either singularly or as combined phenomena.

10.    There is a need for more direct observational data on the attitudes, feelings and experiences (phenomenological transactions) of mentally retarded individuals so as to delineate why some retarded individuals experience emotional disturbances while similar retarded individuals do not.

11.    There must be an extension of current and new theories on the relationship of personality dimensions—

frustration, expectancy, self-concepts, etc.—to the evolution of disturbed behavior in the mentally retarded.

12.  The current positive societal attitudes towards the retarded strongly suggest that professionals will be increasingly asked to develop new approaches to old challenges (such as the retarded offender) that will reflect direct results from this new optimism towards all retarded citizens.

*Chapter 5*

# THE MENTALLY RETARDED
# OFFENDER

Interest in the possible interrelationships between mental retardation and criminal behaviors, particularly as a sign of emotional disturbance, has far outstripped the available factual information. Approximately 500 separate studies on intellectual dimensions of the retarded offender have been published since Goddard's investigation in 1914. No other single characteristic of the mental retardate has been so thoroughly studied, yet these investigations have failed to provide conclusive evidence that intelligence level plays a role in delinquent and/or criminal behavior.

This chapter is an overview of past and current approaches to the mentally retarded offender. It also contains a description of a system of services to meet these individuals' needs.

## Historical Perspectives

The interpretation of the various studies concerning the relationship between criminal behavior and the symptom of mental retardation has produced a divergence of opinion, which in turn has led to the following one-dimensional viewpoints:

1.  The retarded are a type of "born criminal" (or "moral idiot").
2.  Intelligence is hereditary and directly related to the symptom of mental retardation via Mendel's laws, which accounts for the preponderance of male offenders.
3.  Characteristically, the retarded commit dangerous crimes of physical assault, particularly sexual assault.
4.  Because they lack the capacity to grasp the social values of their culture, including its social and legal definitions of right and wrong, the retarded are more prone to commit crimes.
5.  The retarded cannot foresee the consequences of their actions and hence cannot be effectively deterred by the usual punishments.
6.  The retarded respond indiscriminately to the criminal leadership of brighter persons because they are highly suggestible.
7.  Early and ongoing identification with delinquent models is common for retarded individuals due to the families and neighborhood in which they are reared.

Elaborations of these one-dimensional opinions range from the biological to the psychosocial. The biological concept of the mental retardate as a moral idiot or a Mendelian criminal type preceded historically the biosocial view of the mentally retarded offender as a product of social interaction. During the early decades of this century, there was still a predisposition to view mental retardation, delinquency, and societal dependency as inevitably associated biosocial phenomena. Sumner, in his brilliant source book *Folkways* (87) associated these three characteristics as representative of the submerged or maladjusted tenth of the population at the bottom of the social-class ladder.

Early estimates of the frequency of criminal behavior in the mentally retarded ranged from 0.5 percent to 55 percent, with the majority of the earlier studies reporting estimates in the higher ranges. Divergent points of view have persisted to the present time. The literature is interesting to review, as it illustrates one extreme or the other of the following range of expectations: either delinquency and criminality are frequent phenomena in the mentally retarded population and thus potentials for effective treatment are low, or delinquency and criminality, infrequent phenomena in the retarded, are dependent on environmental-family factors, and proper treatment will effectively quell these acting-out behaviors.

Many studies have indicated that the types of crimes most often committed by the retarded differ qualitatively from those committed by non-retarded offenders; a significantly higher incidence of crimes against the person (88) have been committed by the former group. These studies also point to the relatively higher incidence of mental retardation among the socially, economically, and culturally deprived segment of the population, which also produces a greater portion of prison inmates than does the general population. The studies further suggest that mental retardation and crime are more significantly related to these environmental factors than they are related to each other. Both points are well taken, and additional research is necessary before any judgments can be made concerning specific cause-and-effect relationships. Fortunately, we are now in a period of resurgent attention to the relationship between retardation and antisocial behavior; it appears that this professional interest will clarify the previously noted diagnostic quandaries while it will also facilitate more humanistic and specific treatment-management approaches.

## SOCIETAL VIEWPOINTS

Society historically has pursued the following three alternative courses with mentally retarded offenders: (1) ignoring their limitations and special needs; (2) seeking to tailor traditional criminal law processes to fit them; or (3) grouping them with the mentally ill, psychotics, and sex deviants. In *The Common Law,* Justice Holmes stressed the pitfalls of the early postures which ignored the limitations and special needs of the retarded offender as follows:

> Laws with external standards requires each at his own peril to come up to a certain height. They take no account of incapacities unless the weakness is so marked as to fall into well known exceptions, such as infancy or madness. They assume that every man is as able as every other to behave as they command. . . . An individual may be morally without strain because he has less than ordinary intelligence or presence, but he is required to have those qualities at his peril. . . . If punishment stood on moral grounds which are proposed for it, the first thing to be considered would be those limitations in the capacity for choosing wisely which arise from abnormal instincts, want of education, lack of intelligence and all other defects which are most marked in the criminal class. (89)

To concur that Justice Holmes accurately reflected the practical necessity of the law to impose a public policy that sacrifices the interests of the individual for the general welfare is to acknowledge with him that ignoring individual limitations falls most harshly on those with handicapping conditions such as mental retardation. Problems inherent in this legal-societal posture were illustrated by Kugel, Trembath, and Sagar in their study of the characteristics of court-committed patients to an institution for the mentally retarded, particularly in their conclusion:

> Society asks of the retarded a degree of conduct which does not appear to be one which is observed by society in general. Obviously, the retarded stand in a difficult position and the use of such categories as promiscuity, homosexuality, and behavior problems could allow for commitments with less than the safeguards to the more normal individuals. (90)

Our current legal and judicial processes exclude the mentally retarded individual by failing to acknowledge the fact that he has the right to receive special treatment because of his intellectual deficit. A retarded person, although not coerced in the usual sense, may be unable to make a genuine decision in relation to them. To a greater extent than the average person, he may be unaware of his constitutional right to legal counsel and of his right to refuse to answer incriminating questions. Additionally, when the interrogators advise him of these rights, he may be unable to appreciate their significance.

Serious consideration must be given to an arrest and its resultant anxiety when experienced by the mentally retarded person: How much does the retardate actually understand when the arresting officer conveys to him the scope of the Miranda warnings? This pitfall of the current legal approach to the retarded offender was clearly described in the President's Panel Task Force on Law report.

> The retarded are particularly vulnerable to an atmosphere of threats and coercion, as well as to one of friendliness designed to induce confidence and cooperation. The retarded person may be hard put to distinguish between the fact and the appearance of friendliness. ... Some of the retarded are characterized by a desire to please authority: if

> a confession will please, it may be gladly given. ... It is
> unlikely that a retarded person will see the implication of
> consequences of his statements in the way a person of nor-
> mal intelligence will. (91)

Often the retarded individual does not fully compre-
hend his situation, nor, because of his intellectual deficit,
can he handle his frustration.

There is a great variation in the statutes that purport
to define delinquent behavior in the retarded. For example,
the McNaghten* test of criminal responsibility is generally
held applicable to the mentally retarded, and the Durham*
ruling refers specifically both to "mental disease" and
"mental defect." Yet the rigidity of application of the
McNaghten standard—the prevailing one in the U.S.—
makes it highly unlikely that a mentally retarded person can
be brought under its protection. Failure to clearly define or
delineate the legal-behavior situation of the retarded
offender is pertinent both to the pre-sentence investigation procedure itself and to the conflicting data on the reported frequencies of criminal behavior of the mentally
retarded.

## CURRENT VIEWPOINTS

A current viewpoint regarding the association of mental
retardation with delinquency and criminality is that the
mentally retarded are as capable of delinquent criminal acts
as are their intellectually normal brethren. However, factors other than intellectual ones appear to be more important in the cause of such behavior, and these factors are
those commonly cited as important to the development of

*Judicial postures toward assessing whether a mental disorder or
mental dysfunctioning were instrumental in the commitment of a criminal act.

delinquent and criminal behavior in the general population. The lowered social-adaptive abilities of the retardate, when coupled with a lack of supervision, may make him more prone to criminal antisocial acts.

Prejudicial societal views toward specific behavioral maladjustments—particularly sexual acting-out in girls from broken homes or of lower socioeconomic status—result in legal charges and/or institutionalization being brought against a retarded person. Yet, the same behavior in a non-retarded individual does not result in similar consequences; delinquent behavior in a retarded girl from an intact, upper socioeconomic family typically results in a "illegal" referral to a child guidance clinic, while her counterpart from a lower socioeconomic class and/or broken home is referred to the juvenile court or is committed to an institution for the retarded.

Attention has focused on the interrelationships present in the descriptive term "the retarded offender." A recent study utilized an initial questionnaire survey of all correctional institutions in the United States; the study found that of the 80 percent who responded—representing correctional institutions that house 200,000 offenders—only 50 percent of their inmates had been tested, and 9.5 percent had intelligence quotients below 70. Nearly 1,500 inmates had IQ scores below 55. Noting the wide discrepancies in those tested and the variety of psychometric instruments used, the investigators elected to further study a random sample by: (1) a legal overview of the case; (2) an interview by a social worker; and (3) interview testing by a clinical psychologist.

Projecting the results of this sample to the total population in America in 1968, Allen reported, "There are in American prisons today nearly 20,000 adult offenders (10 percent of the total prison population) who are substantially intellectually impaired, some 3,300 of whom are classifiable as moderately to profoundly retarded" (92).

A new perspective has been brought to this old problem of the retarded offender by Allen and his co-workers. Their methodology and findings are commendable since they recommend, as a constructive alternative, an "exceptional offenders court" as a special component of a regional correctional system for the early identification and diversion into other community resources of those retarded offenders who need treatment and for whom traditional full criminal disposition does not appear required.

Similarly, if a retarded offender is actually sentenced to a correctional program, consideration should be given to special handling in the following areas: (1) classification and diagnosis; (2) treatment; and (3) pre-release planning and parole. With early identification of the degree of retardation and emotional problems (if any), a more realistic approach may be made to an individual's rehabilitation needs. The treatment of a retarded offender must include special education and vocational training so that he acquires the skills to get along in the outside world. Lastly, halfway houses (93) should be used for the transition from a correctional institution to the community, buttressed by a strengthened system of parole officers trained to manage retarded offenders with a more humanisitc approach that stresses acceptance and hope.

## Contemporary Services

The previously noted challenges in societal views, legal aspects, diagnosis, and personal rights of the retarded offender tend at times to cloud the allied issues that are involved in attempting to provide treatment, management, and services for these individuals. According to the International League of Societies for the Mentally Handicapped, the individual rights of the retarded are the same as those of any other citizen of the same country, age, family status, and so on. Included is the right to receive such special training, rehabilitation, guidance, and counseling as may strengthen his ability to exercise basic rights with a minimum of abridgement.

But examination of the legal processes and procedures of this country reveals the gross restrictions on the rights of the mentally retarded. Even when states have adopted legislation providing for separate treatment of the mentally retarded offender, the individual faces the possibility that "treatment" in this sense is only an acting upon the individual in some form. This was illustrated when reservations were expressed about the validity of the Maryland Defective Act if it resulted in incarceration without treatment. The court noted:

> But a statute though "fair on its face and impartial in appearance" may be fraught with the possibility of abuse in that if not administered in the spirit in which it is conceived, it can become a mere device for warehousing the obnoxious and anti-social elements of society. (94)

Accordingly, it is evident that a foundation has to be laid for the development of a constitutional right to treatment, the substantive right that is independent of a right to a procedurally fair hearing. Currently, the legal and institutional-based approaches to the management of mentally retarded offenders presents many dilemmas. For the retarded persons who have been convicted of offenses, the usual penal procedures of probation, fixed sentence, and parole do not successfully apply. Similarly, for those who have not been convicted—mostly younger offenders who have committed no serious overt acts but whose antisocial tendencies have been recognized and who have been committed on the basis of "prevention" to the state schools for the mentally retarded—most of the currently utilized treatment-management training methods also fall short. It appears that the current lack of activity in this area will continue, since only a few states are now planning to improve their treatment programs or facilities for the retarded offender.

A further problem in providing specialized services stems from the rejection of responsibility for retarded offenders on the part of most mental health and correctional professionals. For a variety of reasons, they tend to view the mentally retarded as being unsuitable for their respective treatment modalities, programs, and facilities. Brown and Courtless commented on this merry-go-round of treatment nihilism as follows:

> Mental hospitals claim such an offender is not mentally ill; the traditional institutions for the retarded complain that they do not have appropriate facilities for the offender . . . correctional institutions would like to remove such persons from their populations on the ground that programs available in the correctional setting are totally inadequate and in many cases inappropriate for application to retarded persons. (95)

The difficulties created by the presence of retarded offenders in institutions for the retarded have long been reported. In 1922, Fernald described the type of retarded offender seen in his institution as follows:

> Many of this class are defiant, abusive, profane, disobedient, destructive, and generally incorrigible. They honestly feel that they are unjustly convicted and frequently attack those who are responsible for their custody. They resent an effort to amuse them or entertain them. They cannot be discharged because they are not safe persons for community life. It is most unfortunate that this criminal type of defective should complicate the care and training of the ordinary defective—who constitutes the legitimate problem of a school for the feebleminded. (96)

This view persists to the present day; a superintendent friend of the author's viewed this challenge as "like letting gangsters into a kindergarten when those retarded offenders are committed to my institution!"

The doctrine of *parens patriae* made the disposing of unwanted juveniles, particularly the mentally retarded, convenient for the courts. Yet, over the years, very few specialized and effective programs have been forthcoming for the mentally retarded offender, despite the continuing complaints of their unsuitability for admission to institutions for the mentally retarded. If police were properly trained to recognize mental retardation there would be fewer arrests, and, where arrests were made, greater efforts would be made to obtain legal immediate treatment. Accordingly, recognition at the time of arrest is critical for subsequent court proceedings, for placement where sentencing is invoked, and for treatment.

## A Suggested Conceptualization of Services

There is an evolving treatment-management focus toward the retarded offender that stresses the need for the early and specific clarification of diagnostic issues, the legal right to treatment, and new systems of community-based approaches for their active treatment and management.

In establishing and improving programs for the retarded offender, the first hurdle is the issue of defining the individuals for whom the programs are intended. At present it is difficult to include retarded offenders in one all-encompassing definition. It would seem prudent to adopt the convention of defining the offender—the delinquent—by a common measure with stable dimensions, preferably some means other than official records. It is even more difficult to establish any causal relationship between an act and its antecedent causes if we delay defining retarded individuals until after they have commited an unlawful act. One method for measuring social conformity, irrespective of official records, is to mount research on the determining causes of these behaviors in both delinquent and nondelinquent subjects; that is, randomly selected individuals from the general population. This lack of a clear definition and the absence of empirical data on the relationship between antisocial behavior and intelligence are two of the reasons that research must be undertaken on the current status of the retarded offender.

A classification of the retarded offender which uses two age-specific categories, each subdivided into behavioral descriptions as a working formulation for more specifically defining and then implementing the treatment needs of these individuals, is suggested here. The two chronological and descriptive-behavioral categories are:

1. Mentally Retarded Adolescents and Young Adults
   a. *Behavioral problems.* Teenagers and young adults referred for the first time; usually adolescents with IQs of 40 to 80 who are management problems, those who practice promiscuous sex behavior, or who lack salable or social skills appropriate to community life.
   b. *Consistently antisocial, uncontrolled, or self-destructive behavior.* Usually individuals previously in residential services who failed to respond, or those coming directly from the community with a long history of social offenses.
2. Mentally Retarded Adults
   a. *Delinquent/criminal behavior with some community judgment of unsafe or unacceptable conduct.* Individuals exhibiting a generally low level of

successful socio-educational-vocational experiences prior to admission to an institution
or treatment setting. Actual or potential
threat for physical assault towards others is
documented.

b.  *Severe retardation with a history of habitual unacceptable social behavior.* Those individuals admitted to an institution because their families
or general society can no longer tolerate their
low adaptive abilities and maladaptive behaviors. Typically, their problem behaviors spill
over beyond the abilities of their family, generic agencies, and the community to control
or modify them.

The environment of the mentally retarded individual
tends to be reflected in his behavior, and the individual may
essentially reflect an index of the social conditions which
surround him. If a community has a large number of delinquent or socially inadequate retardates, it should take a
very hard, introspective look at the environments in which
all of its citizens live: their homes, schools, neighborhoods,
vocational opportunities, and recreational outlets. Considering these dimensions in the light of our knowledge that
most behavior is learned and that the interrelationships
between the individual and his environment produce a socially acceptable or inappropriate behavior, it is possible to
design a system of supportive services—preventive as well
as therapeutic—to aid the retarded offender. The evolving
treatment perspectives which currently appear to be ingredients of such a system are reviewed in Table 5.1.

An effective service program to correct and rehabili-
tate the retarded offender must include the elements of
prevention, advocacy, and treatment—the last offering the
most measurable and recognizable results. Ideally, a treatment program which interrelates these elements is pre-

## Table 5.1  Rehabilitation-Correctional Service
### Needs for Retarded Citizens

I. Prevention

    A. *Family and individual support of potential offender*

        1. Enhancement of home environment

        2. Counseling: educational or vocational

        3. School testing programs

        4. Specialized educational or vocational program

        5. Parent education and counseling

        6. Consultation to public school or vocational training personnel

    B. *Public and professional education*

        1. Teacher education

        2. Inservice training

        3. Professional consultation

        4. Law enforcement training

        5. Strengthen law enforcement and community relations

        6. Encourage public participation in prevention and control

II. Advocacy

    A. Personal

    B. Legal

    C. Legislative

    D. Therapeutic

    E. Public information and education

III. Treatment

    A. Early treatment intervention

    B. Thorough evaluation and prescriptive treatment

    C. Individual and group therapy

    D. Parent and/or spouse counseling

    E. Spectrum of specialized residential services (e.g., structured-correctional hostels)

    F. Follow-up supportive services to the family

    G. Continuing educational, vocational, and socialization experiences

ferred, since it recognizes that the treatment scheme must be flexible in order to permit highly individualized preventive-treatment challenges. For example, the mentally retarded offender recognized late in adolescence could be referred to a structured correctional service. He would most likely be a physically mature person whose behavior is self-destructive, consistently antisocial, and at times uncontrolled or difficult to manage. The structured correctional service, which must be supervised by a corrections or mental health professional, must be established in a halfway house physical setting. The number of offenders should be limited to six to eight people and subdivided by sex. Specialized personnel should be used for individual and group work. Other staff members should be available as suitable identification models. The facility should be located near community rehabilitation programs such as special education classes or vocational training centers.

The purpose of the structured correctional service must be intensive teaching of adaptive social behavior within a highly structured setting with a high staff-client ratio and a full daily program of activities in an only partly restrictive atmosphere with minimal physical-architectural restraints. The highly specialized nature of this service would permit length of stays from short-term to intermediate.

In brief, the purpose of a structured correctional service would be the teaching of adaptive social behavior. Positive reinforcement of changing behaviors must be programmed to the consistent and immediate and must continue over a period of time. The goal is to effect behavioral change that would be maintained after the program. To enable the courts to make referrals and commitments, it would be necessary to place limits on the degree of freedom facility residents enjoy. A high staff-client ratio and a physical setting that provides for intensive supervision can be used to (1) provide specialized treatment-management inputs for this program and (2) structurally impose controls from outside until the individual can be helped to further develop his own internal controls.

## SUMMARY

The relationship between intelligence and delinquent/criminal behavior is still unresolved, but the issues of controversy differ from those prevailing prior to and shortly after the first scientific investigations into this subject. During the first three decades of this century, it was widely believed that virtually every mentally retarded individual was a potential juvenile delinquent and that most criminals had subtle covert or overt manifestations of mental retardation. The negative fallout of this old, persistent belief and its current implications have been noted by Krause: "When retarded children and youth become enmeshed in our juvenile justice system, its deficiencies are multiplied many times over. . . . To be poor, retarded, and caught in the toils of the law is too often an invitation to tragedy" (97).

The recent trends which have led to the gradual acceptance of a more humanistic and scientific view of the retarded offender and how these developments are inextricably bound to our improved understanding of mental retardation, the legal offender, and methodological advances in behavioral science research, have been reviewed. A conceptualization of needed services for the mentally retarded offender, based on current ideologies and program components, has been suggested in an effort to spur these trends toward an early fruition.

*Chapter 6*

# SEXUAL PROBLEMS IN THE MENTALLY RETARDED

Basic human hunger for friendship, affection, and love is not the exclusive property of the non-retarded, though society frequently chooses to ignore this. It is far easier to disregard the similarities between the retarded and the non-retarded and assume that "subhuman" beings should not have sexual feelings or engage in sexual activity.

Due to fear, ignorance, and prejudice, society barely endures the presence of the mentally retarded in the community; sexual misbehavior in the retarded is frequently considered such an implicit threat to societal welfare that it is quickly counteracted by restriction. Erroneous assumptions have been invoked to justify such "treatment" as suppression of sexual stimuli, severe punishment for "inappropriate" sexual behavior, and legislated involuntary sterilization (98).

The relative inability of the retarded individual to interpret, communicate, and constructively channel his basic feelings hinders him in coping with and solving sex-related problems without outside help. The retardate living in the community can and must be educated to recognize and to handle his sexual impulses in a manner that is both socially acceptable and legally permissible. Special areas of concern include masturbation, homosexuality, the heterosexual relationship within and without the institution of marriage, the concept of responsibility—that is, marriage and/or parenthood—and finally, the extremely important techniques of contraception.

The following case histories will serve to illustrate how the mentally retarded have suffered from the lack of social training and how they can respond to such training once they get it.

The first case concerns a retardate living in the primary community, who needed behavior modification to fit within societal norms of sex-linked social conduct. The second is an example of the social retardation typical of nearly all individuals who reside in institutions for the mentally retarded. The problems of these two types often result from diametrically opposed causes. The retardate living in the community behaves inappropriately because of an almost excessive social stimulation, a superabundance of exposure to socialization patterns which he is not able to interpret adequately nor make competent value judgments of; the retardate living in an institution behaves inappropriately often because of minimal social stimulation, a literal lack of social contact which forces him to aimless or random activity, usually of a pleasure-production/ pain-abating nature, as in self-stimulatory and other auto-erotic behaviors such as masturbation, rocking, and head-banging.

## CASE HISTORY 1

A 25-year-old woman was referred for evaluation by her vocational rehabilitation counselor because, "We trained her as a housecleaner for one of the local motels. Though she does her job very efficiently, she has the habit of wanting to jump into bed with almost any guest that looks at her twice!"

This young lady is the youngest of six children and was raised in a rather chaotic family setting. In addition, the family social and economic status was below normal. Because of the lack of special education facilities to meet her mild degree of mental retardation within the school system, she quit school during the fifth grade. Thereafter she remained at home, helping her mother do the housework. According to the referring counselor, "she may have had too much contact with some of the unsavory characters who bounced in and out of her mother's life between three divorces."

The girl apparently began to have frequent sexual relations at age 13, including among her partners some of her mother's suitors. A social worker who maintained contact with the family became concerned about the possibility of her being pregnant when she was 15½ years old. The girl was referred to the juvenile court and subsequently admitted to an institution for the mentally retarded. At the institution she was regarded as "a behavioral problem with special interest in and to the opposite sex." With the advent of a local vocational rehabilitation program, she was sterilized and discharged approximately one year before the author saw her.

During our interview the woman was rather sullen and distant. She didn't quite understand why she had been referred: "Is it because I like men and they like me?" She stated that she was planning to marry and was very definite concerning her prospective mate. In reviewing her previous sexual encounters, she commented, "Everybody did it anyhow, and I don't have to worry about getting pregnant anymore."

*Comments*

The fact that this mildly retarded young lady did her job very efficiently indicates that her vocational training had been successful. However, her training had focused almost entirely on job skills and hardly at all on the repertoire of necessary interpersonal skills that would permit her autonomous adjustment.

As she had been living in a group home situation in the community, arrangements were made to move her into a behavior-shaping halfway house that served the purpose of keeping her from returning to the institutional setting while at the same time seriously curtailing her mobility within the community until she mastered the fundamentals of more suitable social-sexual behavior. At the present time these changes have been accomplished, her anticipated marriage has been used as a future goal in remotivating her and redirecting her sexual impulses, and an extensive program of social and vocational re-education is in progress.

## CASE HISTORY 2

A 10-year-old Down's syndrome boy was evaluated at an institution for the mentally retarded. The ward nurse complained, "He just sits in his chair all day and we really wouldn't mind that, if he would only stop masturbating. He looks up at us, smiles, and keeps masturbating. You would think it would ruin his health, but he is happy about it and does it all the time. We want to slow it down—somehow." It should be noted that although this young man had been referred for psychiatric consulation, there were 9 other youngsters (of a total of 40) on his ward who actively engaged in a wide spectrum of self-stimulatory activity.

In the interview this youngster readily engaged in play transactions, showing good eye contact and eager participation in active games such as ball-throwing and play telephone conversations. It soon became clear that much of the boy's masturbatory activity was in response to the lack of external physical stimulation.

His daily schedule was rather drab. He rose at 7 o'clock in the morning, had breakfast at 7:30, watched television on the ward until 10 o'clock, and went to school for one hour until 11 o'clock, when he ate lunch. The afternoon schedule was identical, with the exception of no further schoolwork. When I inquired about the boy's parents, the social worker stated that they lived 250 miles away from the institution and "they don't have much money, and barely can get here more than once a year to visit him."

*Comments*

This case illustrates how the "abnormal sexual activity" frequently associated with the symptom of mental retardation can be a result of the individual's hunger for meaningful personal relationships, which in turn may be a result of institutional staff orientation that programs the retardate's behavioral repertoire in a negative manner. With the initiation of group recreational activity, a full day's school program, and contact with a foster grandparent who visited the boy on the average of three times a week, the boy's self-stimulatory behavior disappeared completely within two weeks!

These two case histories have reviewed the most frequent types of sexual problems in the mentally retarded which generally are referred for psychiatric consultation. What is the solution to this situation? How can we alleviate many of the underlying sexual frustrations in the individual retardate? Let us examine a guiding principle in this area of human endeavor: the principle of normalization and how it is applied by those countries which are in the forefront of mental retardation services.

## SOCIETAL ATTITUDES IN SCANDINAVIA

The Scandinavian attitude toward sex and the mentally retarded is an outgrowth of the Scandinavian attitude toward sex in general. Couples who are fond of each other readily engage in sexual relationships and generally make no secret of the fact that they do so. Society takes their relationships for granted, and no one is surprised when they result in marriage. What is surprising (to the American observer especially) is the fact that the Scandinavian divorce rate is about one-half of that of the United States.

The major difference in Scandinavian management of sexuality may lie in the fact that people are more open; they freely acknowledge premarital and extramarital living arrangements, rather than refusing to admit that such cohabitation does exist. In Scandinavia, such cohabitation exists for the mildly retarded also, on the assumption that the mildly retarded can be expected to follow the social and legal patterns of their society generally.

A multiplicity of Scandinavian firms both produce and distribute so-called girlie books and magazines. Just as such publications are sold freely in Scandinavian countries, they are also found on canteen bookshelves in their institutions for the mentally retarded. The rationale for all this is that it is emotionally healthier for the retarded to become aware of such material in the controlled environment of their own residences and homes than to risk emotional upset later when casually encountering such items on bookshelves in the community.

Another surprising departure from tradition has been the Swedish attitude toward literary comprehension of the mentally retarded. Since most of the world's inspirational love literature has been written on a level far above the the scholastic attainment of the mentally retarded individual, many such stories, among which are *Pygmalion* and *Romeo and Juliet,* have been rewritten within lowered vocabulary and comprehension levels. Also of interest is the fact that these books are regularly used as part of the sex education curriculum in classes held for the retarded in Sweden.

In reference to alcohol, the Scandinavian laws regarding personal responsibility for acts committed while "under the influence" (i.e., drunk driving), are much more strict than those of the United States. However, there is a firm belief that the best way to avoid alcohol abuse is education concerning its appropriate usage. Such alcohol education is available to the mentally retarded as a matter of course; by point-of-law in Sweden, the retardate's need for education constitutes his right to such education!

## MARRIAGE

In their *Declaration of the General and Special Rights of the Mentally Retarded,* The International League of Societies for the Mentally Handicapped states, "The mentally retarded person has the same basic rights as other citizens of the same Country and the same age" (99). The 1969 President's Committee on Mental Retardation report states, "The retarded are due the same inalienable rights to life, protection of the laws, dignity of person, and opportunity as all other Americans" (100).

In a broad sense these position statements may refer to the retardate's individual right to sexual fulfillment; they may also lay the foundation for the subject of the retardate's right to contract and enter into the responsibilities of marriage. It well may be that the concept of marriage and the moral and theological teachings on this subject constitute the most confusing, myth-ridden, fear- and guilt-producing thoughts on the sexuality of the mentally retarded.

Many sweeping indictments of the mentally retarded overly stress that it is difficult for the retardate to make a meaningful choice of a love partner and to be faithful. However, even the absence of these qualities does not impede the retardate's legal right to marriage. How many members of the non-retarded population have encountered these same problems in the course of their own experiences?

Another common statement is, "The more the severly retarded the individual is, the less able he is to conceptualize the responsibilities and emotional interactions of the marital relationship." One goal of sex education for the mentally retarded should be thoughtful interpretation of the institution of marriage. As in all marriages, if a marriage between retardates is meaningful to the two individuals involved, it fulfills the morality of our societal norm. The retarded couple may need more support than the normal couple, but the same is true for any handicapped member of society—the blind, the physically handicapped, the incipient or borderline mentally ill, or the second-generation economically disadvantaged.

A continuing myth is that "the retarded are likely to reproduce the retarded, and at a far higher rate than that of the 'normal' non-retarded population." The facts are different. The incidence of mental retardation directly attributed to genetic factors runs to 15 percent or less of the total causes. A large portion of the moderately, severely or profoundly retarded are either physically unable to complete the act of sexual intercourse or are infertile and therefore unable to reproduce under any conditions, let alone to constitute a serious threat to the welfare of society. It is curious that society is not nearly so concerned about what antisocial acts actually are perpetrated upon retardates—witness the tragedies and overt dehumanization in our residential warehouses for the retarded!—as it is about the possibility that at some future point in time one single retardate might force his will sexually upon a non-retarded member of the community.

Moreover, with the advent of relatively inexpensive and easy to use contraceptive agents, the answer to a threatened "overpopulation by the retarded" is the same as for the nonretarded population: adequate sex education, including a survey of and instruction in the use of available contraceptive techniques.

That the mentally retarded, in many instances, do need a specialized living situation is a valid consideration in discussing the subject of marriage. It is difficult for some to visualize the ideal physical setting for married retardates. However, as has been demonstrated in the Scandinavian countries, once we begin to actively study and implement viable alternatives, the most desirable setting will quickly prove itself by the recognized criteria of human management: increased human fulfillment associated with decreased adjustment problems (101).

One final cause for widespread public alarm is the child actually brought into this world by retarded parents. The myth is that the retarded are totally unable to function adequately as parents. Studies have yielded information that the retarded will be less successful as parents than the non-retarded, but they will be much more successful than was originally predicted. With proper support in matters of social policy, education, and so on, the retarded can function in the parental role. This aspect of their sexual adjustment hinges upon two basic factors: emotional control and adequate child-rearing instruction. Just as they themselves need instruction regarding culturally acceptable dating and sexual/interpersonal modes of expression, one day they will face the same adjustment problems vicariously during the adolescence of their children. This is a point of similarity between all parents, whether retarded or not.

Today we are witnessing major changes in societal attitudes toward sexuality in general. These changes will also tend to produce an altered view of sexuality for the mentally retarded and help us to achieve full sexual normalization for our mentally retarded fellow citizens (102). Acceptance of the sexuality of the mentally retarded will, I believe, sharply reduce the urgency of the issues discussed in this chapter, the sexual problems of the mentally retarded. Close and lasting interpersonal peer relationships between retarded adults who have learned to cope judiciously with their sexual needs will permit them to avoid, when their parents die, one of the most devastating experiences of the human condition: loneliness.

Section III

# PRACTICAL ISSUES IN
# MANAGEMENT

## Chapter 7

# PROVIDING CHILD DEVELOPMENT SERVICES FOR THE RETARDED

This section will focus on specific practices in child development services which are consistent with modern ideologies and principles. There are recurring issues and challenges which are vital to the key ideas in child development.

## GOALS

A major ideological issue related to child development is the matter of goals. Goals in child development services come into focus when we view the child who is either too young for acceptance in public schools or who is too low-functioning.

We could classify goals into a number of levels, from very general and very high-level goals to very specific and small ones. Typically, when this subject is raised in child development centers, the questioner is likely to receive a variety of answers—and it is often difficult to find fault with these answers, for their validity depends on individual levels of meaning. Are we talking about very general or very specific goals? "Level of meaning" is important here, because what we state as a goal may be rapidly internalized in a very superficial manner and thus cause us to lose our perspectives on the subject.

For example, one goal that is frequently voiced in child development centers is "preparation of a child for acceptance into a public school." This is actually a sort of medium-level goal—not a high-level or narrow goal. It is a somewhat broad, but not a very general goal. The normalization principle does suggest that we should try to get a child into public school (or other generic service) as soon as possible. The reason however, may be administrative, and thus does not tell us a great deal about goals. We might work with a child for two or three years and succeed in getting him into the public schools, but we may have taught the child very little besides a few superficial skills during this time span. But at a high goal level, we should be trying, in our child development services, to shape the child, to normalize him in his psychosocial skills and intellect. In other words, we should try to prepare the child for life, not just for entering public schools. This should be a key step in seeking high-level goals. We should view public school entry as an intermediate, specific, and concretized step by which our high-level goals are implemented and achieved.

Similarly, our approach must be consistent with a management-by-objectives approach, so that not only can we speak about very specific goals, but we can share them with others in terms of realistic timetables. We must strive, then, to assess a child's development at a given time and then stake out a goal for him; if we find that he now runs 100 yards in a given time, we can state that we want him to improve his running speed by 20 percent over the course of three months. Here the goal is specific, a timetable of improvement may be set, and so on.

When we work on specific goal levels, it is very important that progress be charted in a form that is intelligible to the child. One of the more effective techniques is to have a person compete against himself. This can be accomplished with retarded children and adults through charts and various visual devices where things are pictured, through stars or bar graphs, for example, to show what the individual is doing now. Then we can attempt to motivate him to improve his level of functioning. Thus the child is removed from competition with a group, competition that may well have been very painful to him in the past. Instead, he competes with himself. The child will invariably grow and show improvement, and, by seeing this improvement, will be encouraged. This is an extremely useful tactic for teachers who currently have such information on record and do not have to repeat their efforts.

This technique highlights a recurrent criticism of past child development services such as the old opportunity centers. There one observed the youngest group learning a task, then watched the second older group doing the same thing, and a third older group following the second —grown men and women doing the same thing as young children who had just entered the center! I vividly recall one such opportunity center where teachers were focusing on color discrimination. This "goal" was being taught from the lowest through the highest levels. The older men and women who had experienced this course for over ten years were learning it again—a sight that prompts the question, If they haven't taught them colors by now, isn't it a little late to start? Certainly, colors might still be learned at this age if other techniques are used. If the old techniques weren't effective at age 3 or 5, they are not going to be effective at 23 or 25!

We must be both realistic and precise in our teaching methods. It is more difficult to *re*learn than to learn right in the first place.

One of the major goals inherent in the general statement of normalization is developmental shaping of the intellect. In this respect, it is interesting to note that curriculum guides and programs for the severely retarded child in public school systems and developmental services indicate that teaching establishments have yet to catch up with scientific developments, or incorporate into their curricular goals the actual shaping or upgrading of intelligence. Teachers are still thinking in terms of the beliefs of 10 or 20 years ago; that intelligence is constant, that a child is born with a given level of functioning and will only grow at that same rate, that he will grow physically but his developmental quotient will remain the same. Today, we know this is not true. We can shape a child to accelerate development as we push him towards his potential.

Nevertheless, we seldom accomplish this goal anywhere with any children, retarded or otherwise. We fail with non-retarded children in public schools, children who are nowhere near their developmental potential, and we succeed even less with retarded children who need it more. But it is apparent that proper use of the first techniques, methods, and materials currently available can often enable us to improve the retarded child's developmental quotient by 10, 20, or perhaps even 30 IQ points. This should be the teachers' commitment, a commitment evident throughout their curricula, attitude toward admission, and exclusion policies.

Today, typically, so many child development centers continue to function solely as babysitting centers. True, babysitting serves an important purpose; it relieves stress for the family and mother even if nothing else is accomplished. Yet, it is obviously not sufficient to settle for babysitting when, with almost the same amount of money—or a little more—we can do infinitely better. When one visits a typical child-developmental center, a great deal of baby-sitting is evident. With the gentle techniques of baby-sitting, teachers will often produce a child who is himself a gentle and well-behaved child. In the past, many opportunity centers have produced young adults who were, after five or ten years of babysitting, fairly socialized in some of their behaviors. They were gentle and obedient, and they went along with a lot of things, whether they made sense or not. But this just isn't enough. Inherent in this approach are the low expectations teachers come to have for the child. "Bring him along at his level. Don't expect more than growth equivalent to his IQ."

## DEVELOPMENTAL EXPECTATIONS

An important goal in modern child development services is that of developmental expectations. Teachers must commit themselves to seek high developmental expectations and stick with these expectations. A child will respond positively to such attitudes and, conversely, will respond negatively to low expectations. Consider various studies where one group of teachers was told nothing while another was told that tests had shown their pupils were late bloomers. The latter children did bloom. Their IQs rose by a very large degree compared to the other children. The first group, where teachers had not been oriented and expectations had not been changed, did not respond as they might have.

Child-development theory of 20 to 30 years ago stated that a child is born with a certain endowment—he merely develops, almost grows like a plant. One cannot accelerate him. The only way one can slow him down is by brain injury or some similar misfortune. Essentially, this theory was based on the idea that heredity was the major determinant of the development of the child. For example, the Gesell approach defined what a child would normally do at a certain age; he would not do it much earlier or much later. Somehow, when the time came, it would happen. Today we know that it will not happen unless there is a strong interaction between the child's endowment and a continuing set of experiences in his environment. The entire developmental course can be greatly accelerated by the quality and intensity of the child's interaction with his environment.

However, while this is supposedly general professional knowledge, it is not evident that professionals have applied such knowledge to their work in child development centers (103).

One clear expression of the teacher's developmental commitment is evidenced by the length of the learning day. When a teacher expects only two-and-one-half hours of learning from her young retarded student—or any child—then there is a lack of commitment to the shaping of intellect, because it has been repeatedly shown that a child's intellect is shaped throughout his waking period. The question then becomes: who will do the shaping while the child is awake, the teacher, his peer, his sibling, or his mother?

Much of the interaction of the child in the home is somewhat developmental, but it is not skilled or systematized. Indeed, it is often only partially helpful and sometimes achieves the opposite of developmentally oriented goals. This is particularly true in families with chaotic home conditions and a lack of stimulation coupled with very confused inputs. Accordingly, the teacher must make a commitment to lengthening the child's learning day. It may be necessary to start with a shorter day and, as rapidly as possible, increase the day to at least six hours or more. We can use that time better for developmental purposes than it would be used in the home.

Teachers, then, must take a close look at their schedules: Are they offering long enough days? Are they bringing a child up to longer hours fast enough? Or are they just simply expecting that it will happen?

Other evidence of commitment is the teacher's attitude towards admission policies. Do they include young children as early as possible? Or are they excluded because they are not yet three or four or five years old? Do they exclude them because they are not toilet trained?

A past example of the stupidity of exclusion and non-commitment to a developmental attitude is one from the author's own state. Regulations there excluded the severely retarded from public schools until they were eight years old —and then they had to be toilet trained, and have an intellectual quotient of 40! Thus some of the best developmental time was already past for the child. This posture illustrates a rather total lack of commitment to the concept of the malleability of intellect. The establishment of such regulations tended to confirm the self-fulfilling prophecy of low developmental attainments by the retarded. We are, fortunately, gradually overcoming this attitude.

Exclusion of a child because he is too handicapped is also a negative attitude. The more handicapped the child, the more he needs developmental shaping. An ongoing close review of the inclusion and exclusion criteria of child development centers will assure that we are not omitting children who need these services the most when they need it the most or can profit from them the most.

## CURRICULUM

What should and should not be stressed in the curriculum? The same questions can be asked about the nature of daily schedules. Curriculum and schedules go hand in hand and effect each other intimately. A frequent error is the excessive use of rest periods which are essentially do-nothing periods. Another problem can be permitting children excessive free play unrelated to their developmental needs. This should be distinguished from a set of techniques as in the Montessori approach, which may be confused with excessive emphasis on free play or arts and crafts periods. This is one of the curses of our past: the old theory that when a child is retarded, forget the mind and train the hand. Thus children are programmed to spend many hours a day in arts and crafts that are not developmental but merely time-filling. Another error is the tactic of excessive unstructured outdoor activities. Children need outdoor activities, but not in excessive amounts or of an unstructured nature.

We should ask these questions: Are motor activities developmental and sequential? Do they contain an internalization of developmental stages of children's growth? Are they providing children with those perceptual motor activities appropriate to the individual's particular level of development? It must be remembered that if the teacher introduces an inappropriate activity—which may be appropriate for a different child or for the same child earlier or later—time is wasted for both the teacher and child. The teacher must strive for a profound understanding of the subtle developmental changes in the child, and then provide the types of activities which are exactly matched to the individual's current stage and readiness. Accordingly, we need tough but reasonable expectations in our curricula— we must define tough goals, but ones which are reasonable —and we must pursue them single-mindedly.

As previously noted, one of our major goals is to shape the intellect. There are two aspects which underlie what we define as intelligence, and they are virtually the basic components of intelligence: perception and language. Of the two, perception appears to be more important than language. Nevertheless, when one considers current educational material and professional literature, there appears to be a great deal of confusion regarding these two aspects.

For example, some studies have provided disadvantaged children with an intensive language program—then have imposed such a program upon a developmental foundation that is totally inadequate. The child then learns superficial speech or language responses without having developed the perceptual foundations—the input/output functions—which underlie everything else. Accordingly, one of the most important functions in attempting to shape intelligence is the development of the perceptual foundation. Upon perception we can build language, and upon these two lies the road to advances in general intelligence. Focusing on perception and language, the teacher can shape and teach, and the child can grow by leaps and bounds; by 20 and 30 IQ points if the program is pursued with a specified curriculum and professional commitment to it.

Curriculum emphasis, then, should be perceptual. This emphasis will be reflected in the materials used, for perception is particularly stimulated through developmental materials.

## NORMALIZATION

Normalization is a high-level goal, one with a number of important implications. For example, in a developmental center where there are children from both a residential facility and their primary homes, one must take great precautions to mix the children equally in an effort to avoid creating what may be perceived as a "little institution." A mixture of at least half of the children from the residential facility and half from their primary homes will facilitate integration, and aid in the realization of other normalization elements.

Other major implications of normalization in child development services are the issues of separation and specialization. Retarded adults and retarded children should not be grouped in any manner that would allow society to perceive these adults as being childlike. Specifically, the presence of young adults in the same facility with five-year-old children creates a societal perception much more damaging to the young adult than to the child, the concept of the retarded person as the eternal child who will never grow.

There is another element here. Sometimes older retarded adults who have not received early help may not exhibit the types of habits and behaviors that we want children to learn. If we do not separate them, children will look up to adults, as big brother or older peers, and will tend to pick up very primitive behaviors. For the sake of both adults and children, then, normalization demands that we provide separate, specialized adult and child programs, not in conjunction with each other.

Another aspect of this issue is the separation of the place of residence from the place of program. A child developmental center should not be in the child's home. It is normal in our society for a school-aged child to leave the place where he sleeps and go elsewhere for school, treatment, organized recreation, peer relationships, or worship. Accordingly, we should ensure that the child leaves home for his child development activity—and not just next door, but a little distance which can be developmentally explored, so to speak—a distance of at least several blocks, which eventually he may learn to walk on his own. Or, if there is a bus, a distance where he takes the bus, at first with help and supervision—maybe he walks a block or two to the bus, and then a block or two from the bus to the child development center. There are some excellent five-day group homes in the author's own state. These facilities were considered breakthroughs when they were initiated. Yet they are right next door to a Child Developmental Center, and it probably would have been more developmental and more normalizing if the children had had to learn to walk a few more blocks to the center. We must, then, actively consider the optimal physical and perceptual distance of the developmental activity from the sleeping activity.

Specialization also means further separation of the parent role from the teacher role. For normal children, the parent and teacher are not the same people. The retarded person must experience the same normalized set of relationships. There may be exceptions or transition periods that demand compromises along these lines. This is acceptable as long as they are truly compromises and there is a commitment to eventually separate these roles. There should be houseparents and teachers, and though there is a continuity between the two, they are not identical. The goal is continuity of programming without perpetuation of role identity.

## INTEGRATION

There is also the matter of integration to be considered. Normalization stresses that the retarded child and the development programs be eventually integrated with the non-retarded. This does not mean integration with other handicapped children, since the retarded have little to gain from integration with the cerebral palsied or the blind, for example. Of course, the retarded child may have any number of other handicaps, but he primarily needs integration with his non-retarded peers. There are many good reasons to believe that the retarded child will learn more in an integrated setting than in a segregated setting. Teacher expectations are higher, and peers who are faster learners provide models from whom the retarded child learns by imitation.

Integration directly confronts the issue of expectation, an issue which has a very sad history in the education of the mentally retarded. For 70 years professionals have deceived themselves, the public, and parents by stating that if a child is handicapped or retarded he should be taken from the crowded general classroom and put into a small group where he can express more individuality. "Here, we can offer him better methods and better materials." "We can spend more money on him." "We can do so much more than we could in the regular classroom." Yet all the child typically does in these special settings is sit around and fall further behind.

Though these have been the rationale for segregated special education all these years, what have the retarded really received? For 70 years there have been classes available for the mildly retarded. These were small classes (15 to 25) with specially trained teachers and special materials. At that time, there were classes for the more severely retarded—even smaller, and even more expensive. Today, there is a wealth of research evidence that overwhelmingly demonstrates that with all our special teachers and small groups, our retarded children learn less in a special classroom than they do in the regular classroom, even if they are a few grades behind! This is an established research finding. We have to confront the fact that special education need not and should not mean segregated education, since we can have special education that is integrated.

Why, with special teachers and special materials and special small groups did our retarded children learn less in special segregated classes? There is probably one answer that encompasses all others: low teacher expectations. *Once you label and segregate a child, the teacher gives up.* The teacher "knows" the child is slow because of his retardation or learning disability. The teachers then tend to progress at a leisurely pace. Teachers do not consciously assume this attitude; they simply do not ordinarily confront this negative posture since it is, after all, an unpleasant confrontation.

There are teachers who say that retarded children who have attended normal public schools until the third or fourth grades become upset and frustrated that the experience has not been worthwhile or fair to them. True, a number of studies show that a retarded child has greater adjustment problems—both social and emotional—in the regular classroom than in the special classroom. Indeed, it is typically noted that retarded children in special classes learn less academically and intellectually but are better adjusted than retarded children in the regular classroom. We can thus combine the best of both worlds by providing for the learning-developmental process as well as for social and emotional growth. Special education has to come to grips with this challenge. We can do it, if we commit ourselves to the problem. We need not abolish all special education classes. We can accomplish our goal gradually and systematically over a period of time, but we must view these concepts and commitments as necessary goals.

Some critics ask, if it is appropriate to place retarded children into integrated regular classrooms, how does this satisfy the previously noted emphasis on specialization? Although it may appear to be contradictory, it actually is not, because specialization implies a consistent manpower model, utilization of physical facilities in the mainstreams of our society, and a human management model consistent with the retarded person's needs. We can have integration into what is essentially a specialized program. There is no inconsistency in a public school program of education for all young children. It has a human management-development model consistent with its materials and methods. The manpower model structure goes along with it, so there is really no conflict.

Integration does not merely mean that we place deviant children in classes with other children. We can have integration on many levels, and in many ways. Even the establishment of special classrooms among other classrooms is a measure of integration, as in the remote county school where a whole wing is devoted to special education. Here, there is integration to the degree that there are regular classrooms in the same school. Some towns, however, have built special schools for the retarded at the edge of town. Even though these may be good schools in design and equipment, they are essentially entirely segregated areas for the retarded. Other examples are the blocks of classes in one wing or one floor of a school, dispersal within a particular school or within an entire school system, and so on. There are, then, various degrees of integration. Hopefully, we can break down one barrier at a time.

The mildly retarded can be integrated much more readily than the severely retarded. The younger child adapts more easily than the older child. When we study a Montessori-type program, for example, we find that they are so accustomed to having children of different sizes and different ages together that no thought is given to integration. The children themselves think nothing of working closely together on the same developmental level, despite apparent differences as to physical sizes, ages, and level of abilities. This is the whole social structure in that particular developmental system, where there really is no problem of integration. It becomes more problematic, however, when we move into more typical educational systems with their rigid grade classifications.

Another advantage (or rationale) for integration is that not only does a retarded individual learn more in such a setting, but what he learns tends to be more normative, and more culturally typical. Also, other children will probably tend to develop more positive attitudes toward the retarded. By definition, this would change what retardation is, what it is perceived to be.

When we started integrating handicapped children into a particular local public school program, there were many negative attitudes on the part of the teachers and parents of the retarded and the non-retarded. After a while, such attitudes disappeared, as the people slowly changed their minds. They would not have changed unless both the parents and teachers concerned had had these experiences. Undoubtedly, the non-retarded children involved will also grow up with more tolerant attitudes. When we accept deviancy, the deviancy in many instances disappears, because it is of our own perception. We make a person deviant by repeatedly labeling him as deviant. A classic example is the current quandary, "Is a hearing aid more damaging to a person socially than actually being hard of hearing?"

Almost by nature and definition, segregation creates inequality; it is almost impossible not to have inequality along with segregation. Integration certainly tends to lend more dignity and acceptance to the person perceived and defined as deviant.

Methods for achieving integration were previously noted in the discussion regarding placement of the retarded into generic services. In general, we should strive to abolish special programs and continue efforts to obtain generic services. An area may begin its efforts with one child development center, but should, however, continue to try to establish services in the public school system. We must, then, try to get children in child development centers into the public schools. Exceptions are children who have severe problems or those who must be taught some special skills before they can move into integrated programs. Highly specialized and segregated services should not be enlarged into service empires merely for the sake of enlargement. Instead, they must be self-limiting in their striving for power, influence, and money. Our idealism should lead us to a mobility of program expectations by which generic services abolish the need for highly specialized services.

Non-retarded children can be brought into special services, such as day-care centers where retarded children are admitted. Eventually, through such action, a 50-50 mix can be achieved. This is, in effect, very similar to putting retarded children into generic day-care centers.

## SAFEGUARDS FOR MONITORING PROGRAM QUALITY

A major technique for bringing about integration in child development services is to utilize contracts-for-service with other agencies. When the retarded child is identified, follow-through services with agencies are established, and a group of concerned individuals is engaged to monitor the program. Essentially this approach calls for contracting generic agencies to render services to retarded persons. However, the contract-for-services mechanism should also be explored with families. Contracting with families is very close to family subsidy. We may reach an agreement by which a family receives a certain amount of money, services, materials or support if they agree to maintain or board a child in their home. For example: a child may be placed in a home Monday through Friday, and, for a certain amount of money, the individuals concerned provide parentlike functioning for the child five days a week. This contract-for-services can be managed with a generic day-care center, and the contract may specify the services to be rendered.

There must be safeguards if such contracts are to be effective, since we must be assured that when the retarded children or adults are moved into generic services they are not disadvantaged or forgotten, pushed aside, or handled badly. A good safeguard is to demand that the major responsibility and concern for the retarded be vested in an agency that is concerned primarily with the retarded, that is, a regional mental retardation specialty agency, local public agency, or local parent association. Even if this agency does not render any direct services, it should be the agency which maintains responsibility and accountability. It should also exercise very strong regulatory power over the agency to which it provides funding and, in some cases, perhaps, to which it does not provide funding.

Another major safeguard is a written agreement in which the contracting agency spells out the conditions under which a goal such as integration is to be achieved. Similarly, the financial terms and other guidelines governing the relationships between the special mental retardation agency and the generic agency should be clarified as to their management of the retarded child.

A fourth mechanism for any agency contracting for services to retarded persons is strong consumer representation, for example, a board of directors which includes consumers or parents of retarded children. In addition, watchdog committees or special committees can work together with a particular agency or an entire group of agencies, as in a watchdog committee for one generic day center or a watchdog committee for all day-care centers in an area. The services would include periodic visits to assure that retarded persons actually receive appropriate attention and management. Similarly, a citizen advocacy program can engage local citizens in one-to-one relationships with retarded persons.

Another safeguard is the placement of retardation specialists into generic agencies. The specialist makes himself available to help teach others how to work with the retarded. For example, an agency may say, "Yes, we're ready to take a retarded person and serve them, but we don't know too much about it. Can you help us?" and a special resource person in a school system can help integrate retarded children into regular grades or provide consulting services to the agency or contracting agency. This is a role that author has assumed with many local public agencies during their initial efforts to admit retarded children. They could be assured that if a crisis occurred, help would be available. Initially, there were a number of crises, and under the ordinary course of events these problems might have resulted in the exclusion of retarded children. Backup consultation is important. When agencies are assured that help is near—initially on a free-of-charge basis—they will eventually put this service into their budget. Such an arrangement can go a long way to help make integration a success.

Finally, there is the question of backup specialty services. Here is an example of how such a service can work effectively: At once time ENCOR (see Chapter 10) was considering the establishment of four or five sheltered workshops in Omaha, and up to seven Child Development Centers. ENCOR has since been quite successful in integrating children into generic programs. Also, the schools have so broadened their entry requirements that they are taking many of the children it was initially thought necessary to serve in child development centers. Thus, ENCOR now serves a great deal fewer children than it had originally considered. It has also been discovered that there are a number of retarded persons who do not necessarily have to be served by a special mental retardation service. It is possible that in the near future ENCOR may be able to omit one or two child development centers. Perhaps it will take only the most severely impaired children, or children just entering the service who need to be somewhat shaped and socialized before they can be contracted into more generic services. Therefore, ENCOR may eventually need only one or two child development centers and will act primarily as a regional system of backup services.

In summary, the foregoing safeguards for monitoring contract-for-services for retarded individuals in generic services represents an excellent approach to providing normalized services for the retarded in a cost-beneficial approach.

## ACCULTURATION

Let us focus, for a moment, on a vital process in the growth of an organization, the process of acculturation: *becoming part of a culture.* As Wolfensberger (104) has noted, there are three major levels in normalization: the person and intermediate social systems, the interactive dimension and the interpretation dimension. Initially, we teach the child some skills; then we focus on teaching the normative exercise of these skills. This last dimension is particularly concerned with teaching a child cultural ways and practices which have intrinsic social meaning. This is vitally important, for if he lacks familiarity with these functions, he risks the stigma of being labeled or degraded.

We can teach a child to walk, for instance, but we may not pay attention to how he walks. Yet we must be sure he walks in a way that does not draw attention. Or we can teach a person to brush his teeth, but when he knows how to brush his teeth, does he actually practice toothbrushing as a habit? It isn't merely the skill itself that is important, but the habitual exercise of that skill until it literally becomes a social habit.

We must, then, consider how our retarded children look, how they act, how they are perceived—because what we do may well determine whether or not they are perceived as deviant, whether or not they are degraded, how they are labeled, and—most importantly—how they are treated by others around them.

## CONTROVERSIAL ISSUES

There are a number of controversial developmental issues, and some are particularly relevant to the provision of developmental services for the retarded. One has to do with the developmental structure of programs: should they be highly or minimally structured? Generally, opinion ranges from one extreme to the other. Some individuals favor a totally unstructured developmental environment; others favor a structured one. There are many good examples of each extreme in operation. What is the answer? Sometimes, in truth, it's better for a child to be in one type of structure than another. The issue of individualized program structure often depends on the child's past history of parenting. A child who is extremely structured at home, for example, might do better in a less structured developmental environment, and vice versa.

We should remember, however, that research evidence shows retarded children appear to function better in a structured rather than an unstructured environment. Apparently, more learning goes on under relatively structured conditions. Yet structure does not necessarily imply an excessive focus on direction. For example, a child development environment which is strongly Montessori-oriented will often have a child engaged in free-choice activities for the entire day. Viewed in terms of materials, the use of materials, the way the children learn to move about the environment, the way they learn not to be loud, not to interfere with other children—all of these are aspects of a structured environment. Yet, the child can engage in whatever activity he wants to. We must make the distinction, then, between direction and structure, and remember that for retarded children structure appears, in general, to be more developmentally optimal.

Another controversial topic in child development services is the cost-service benefit ratio. Many people in child development services are apparently unable to foresee that society cannot increase its financial support infinitely in one particular area of social services. Economic support for mental retardation has improved in recent years. Yet one day it is going to level off, and we may find that we are getting extra dollars only because our national productivity continues to grow. In other words, the dollars increase but not the percent of the national-state-local budgets. This is one of the weaknesses in Scandinavian programs for the retarded. In Scandinavia, they have been receiving a larger percentage of state, national, or local budgets every year since the mid-1950s, and they have not yet made provisions for the day when the cash flow levels off. Teachers and program administrators must prepare for similar problems and commit themselves to the hard fact that one day we are going to be asked (mandated?) to serve all retarded children and provide all their needs within a limited budget and find economical ways of doing it!

We cannot afford to forget that society has many priorities, some of which are lower and some higher than mental retardation. Societal survival, for instance, is number one; it may come to the point where environmental conservation is our highest priority. Today we lack orientation and experience to do the job as economically as possible and do not like to admit that sometimes we are given more money than we know how to use wisely. We must learn to follow the example of one state where the local association for retarded children completed mental retardation plans, then returned to their county commissioner money it had not spent! Such actions tend to create trust in public officials, and they are then much more inclined to give you what you truly need. We will fail in our provision of child development services if we continue to go along with traditional educators' ways of avoiding the hard talk about the cost-service benefit ratio as to the actual costs for actual services delivered.

Our commitment is to serve the largest number of children in need of service at any given time, at the greatest benefit and least cost. It is very uncomfortable to see a service that spends $2,500 per year per child for 20 children while 80 children go totally unserved. We should take the $2,500, provide less service for these 20 children, and provide at least some service for the other 80 who are getting nothing.

On the practical level, many developmental day-care centers are too small to be economical. There is a level at which these centers become more economical and where the cost per child goes down as the number of children served rises. We do not want institutions which serve 100 or 200 children at one place. But when we have 10 or 15 children in a center we are not at our best cost-serving benefit ratio levels, and we will have better economy at about 40 to 50 children. This is a sort of optimal compromise between size and cost. The same principle, of course, applies to the one-to-one staffing myth. Commitment to serving children well with the least possible manpower ratio to provide the services needed—is one of the overriding challenges in the provisions of child development services for the retarded in the present decade.

## SUMMARY

The reviewed practical issues in the provision of child development services for the retarded are attainable goals at the present time. We must be clear-headed and critical of our purposes and the means by which we hope to attain them. We must be aware of the need for public involvement and education as well as the importance of that public's concern for financial rectitude. Then we must turn this awareness into action on behalf of all retarded persons.

*Chapter 8*

# RECURRENT PROBLEMS AND ERRORS IN BEHAVIORAL MANAGEMENT

Over the years, as a psychiatric consultant in mental retardation, I have noted some frequently recurring problems and errors in the behavioral management of the mentally retarded. These recurring challenges will be reviewed with a focus on possible methods for obtaining more successful treatment-management outcomes.

## THE MYSTIQUE OF OBSERVATION

One major problem relates to the function of observation. For some reason, people attach a great deal of magic to the concept of observation. When a retarded person is placed into a special observation setting, he is observed—usually for weeks—and then a decision is made about his assignment, behavioral management, or whatever; all this in the belief that such an approach is appropriate and will somehow prove helpful.

Such an approach appears sound in theory, but when we set out to observe, we often fail to really see! For example, we rarely chart behaviors, such as in the precision teaching approach (105), and we rarely use any specific types of observation techniques. Accordingly, these exercises are often a waste of time. We go through stereotyped, unproductive routines which fail to solve any problems whatever, and final patient assignment is often made on information that had been available initially, information that could have been collected from those who had previous contact with the retarded person (teachers, parents, other professionals, or physicians).

An allied recurring error in the creation of observation environments is the lack of any clearly structured role expectancy upon the person observed. When we put a child into a residential facility educational setting, expectations are fairly clear. These are continuing programs, and when a new child or adult is added the programs exert powerful role expectancies. The retarded will tend to behave in accordance with these expectations. Yet, in many observation environments, we let a child or adult sit idly about; we expect little and he does little, and seldom demonstrates what he is really capable of doing. We neither learn his range of behaviors nor observe his reactions to challenges.

Another major error in establishing observation units is frequent shifting of observed persons. After the person is observed for a number of days or weeks, he is often plunked down in some other environment for further observation or assignment. These changes or transfers are generally very undesirable, because each shift causes a drastic change in environment and often makes the habilitation process much more difficult. For example, a child is often admitted to an institution for the retarded and placed in an observation unit for six weeks. He is then assigned to a living unit with another change in personnel, discontinuity in relationships, an entirely new environment, new structure, and new demands. Yet even these changes and the child's responses to them are usually not studied.

Why not focus on the background personal-social history? Why not let the observer have the freedom to say, "Let's see whether it works out or not." If such an approach is successful, the new child doesn't have to be reassigned, and the observation task has been resolved. If we do have to reassign, then it is no more than would have occurred if the child had been in a separate observation unit. A decision-theory approach would also indicate that we should make our initial assignment directly into the habilitational environment which we think is appropriate and take our chances.

## INDISCRIMINATE ENVIRONMENT SHIFTING

A second frequent challenge in behavioral management of the retarded is the matter of indiscriminately shifting emotionally troubled retarded persons around at the time of crisis. This is one of the most knotty problems in many management settings, because it is the least conceptualized and is often done unconsciously. In brief, it is the professional posture that, when a problem arises in a management setting—the classroom, a living unit, or a sheltered workshop—we are apt to "solve" it by removing the person from the trouble spot and reassigning him elsewhere. If we have a work team of six retarded workers and one member of the team doesn't get along with the rest, we are apt to transfer the one member into another work team. If a trainee doesn't get along well with his supervisor, we are apt to assign him to another supervisor or assign the supervisor to another part of the workshop. The same occurs with children in special education classrooms and child development centers; we are apt to abruptly remove them from the environment in which they are having adjustment problems. In institutions this takes the form of frequent transfers from one living unit to another: the retarded person's record reflects a series of generally meaningless moves. If he acts out, he is transferred immediately, and the cycle begins. This pattern tends to be repeated again and again, because it appears to be the easy or logical way to accomplish a need.

Actually, this is a negative approach, because we are reinforcing maladaptive behavior; positive reinforcement of the avoidance behavior is often implied. "If I don't like my work assignment, all I have to do is misbehave and I can get out of it"—that is what the retarded person often learns under this misdirected behavioral approach. He learns a pattern of misbehavior that gets him out of trouble spots. This practice also creates discontinuity in relationships between the behavior manager (teacher, supervisor, trainer, etc.) and the person involved. Continuity of relationships is very important in behavior management, because quite often it is this relationship itself which carries and supports the training and habilitation function. Since it is through these relationships that normalized behavior is frequently mediated, when we disrupt them a superficiality of relationships develops. Accordingly, we tend to inadvertently teach manipulative behavior to the retarded person. He learns that he can manipulate others, can get other persons or himself transferred, or can get others into trouble.

A major lesson in life management is that most problems have to be solved within the very context in which they occur. If a person has problems with his job supervisor, he is going to have to cope with them in some way. Only rarely do we have the opportunity to escape such situations; we do not change jobs very often or leave home-area locations; the retarded person, like the rest of us, has to learn to handle these social behavioral skills. If we fail to confront this behavior in the context in which it occurs, we are taking the easy way out professionally. We must pinpoint or analyze the behavior, then plan a course of management uniquely suited for the person concerned. This is a demanding and challenging course, but if we can work things out in their current setting, we can accomplish more growth in the person involved than by any number of transfers.

In brief, every transfer or discontinuity created in the life of a retarded person reduces his rehabilitation potential by a large magnitude. We must be certain that the advantages of moving a person from one environment to another far outweigh the disadvantages experienced.

## DISCIPLINE

Another major behavioral management issue focuses on discipline. In defining rewards and punishments and the in-betweens where we ignore behavior, we must be certain we understand what types of behaviors are rewarding, which ones are neutral, and which are unpleasant. A major recurring error in considering discipline is failure to clearly define the types of activities which are obligatory to a person in his role and station in life and which are privileges. Confusion often permeates this crucial area. For example, when we operate a vocational services center, work should be conceptualized as an obligation, since the prime goal is to train the person to become a worker and learning to work is as much an obligation to him as for the staff. Conversely, going to dances and a ballgame are privileges, not obligations. There may be learning or normalizing values in recreational activities, but they still have the overtones of privileges.

The major principle of management here is that privileges should be revoked but not obligations. Accordingly, if a person misbehaves in the workshop, he should be removed from this setting only as a last measure. If he is sent home from the workshop, he learns that if he does not like his work, all he has to do is misbehave. We are actually teaching misbehavior by systematically rewarding such misbehavior. Instead, we should tell the person that no matter what he does, he does not get out of his work. Then, perhaps, he will learn that there is no point in misbehaving on the job. Removing someone from an obligatory assignment should be done only under conditions which would resemble those in ordinary life; such action only follows a serious offense. We should use comparable criteria when we deal with our retarded citizens.

We must then analyze carefully the privileges and obligations provided for our retarded citizens, and, if we can help it, never revoke obligations, but only privileges.

Actions can be particularly risky when managing the behavior of a person who lives at a hostel and also works at a vocational services center. A question frequently raised by personnel in vocational service centers is, "To what degree should we revoke a privilege that is really a part of the expected behavior of living in a residential setting?" From a behavioral management point of view, it is much more meaningful to revoke a privilege that is somehow tied in with work—a raise or dock in pay—than a privilege associated with a different sphere of living. Similarly, one could revoke the privilege of eating with other individuals. The person punished then eats by himself but isn't removed from the situation in which the problem occurred. If misbehavior occurred on the work floor, extra work might be assigned. The object is to tie the reward, as well as the punishment, as closely as possible to the specific behavior that is to be shaped. One should not separate the misbehavior from the privileges in time, space, or function, if at all possible. Saturday ballgame privileges might be revoked because of a misbehavior that occurred in the work setting, if we have fully used more relevant measures. We must not risk smothering a retarded person whose life we rather totally control, as we may well do when we have a child in a hostel or in a day care center or provide his recreation.

We must also be aware of the multiplicity of relationship contacts the retarded person has—with housekeepers, teachers, advocates, and so on. If one of these relationships does not work out for the best, the individual should have others to whom he can turn. There must be a firm balance here between the continuity of principles of behavior management and of ongoing relationships with key management people. Yet relationship options should be available so that if a child misbehaves in a classroom he will not be hounded for 24 hours a day and thus made miserable in all spheres of his living.

## INTERPRETATION OF BEHAVIOR

The next issue is the role of interpretation in the shaping of behaviors in the mentally retarded. A common error is overemphasis on shaping the verbal behavior of a person who is not very verbal and to whom verbalization has little relevance. I recall a work activity program which was operated by an elderly gentleman on a part-time basis. This individual would go around the work group of adult retarded individuals and show them how to do things while talking incessantly to them. He would go on and on, without stopping, on his own level, and in his own particular manner, and as a result, the workers listened less and less and soon completely tuned him out. They had learned, usually after one or two days' exposure, that they simply could not keep up and could not understand. The trainer was good at showing, but not at explaining.

We must, then, be sure we function not in our own style or in the mode to which we are accustomed, but in a way that communicates meaningfully to the retarded person on his level. We must relate to him on a level he can understand—just a shade above, and no more. Our goal must be to challenge, not confuse.

We do not need to focus strictly on verbal communications. There are many other communications route available. We can teach severely retarded children to chart their own behavior, a technique that helps them learn to interpret their behavior to themselves. We can chart their behavior for them and develop many visual aids that show them what their behavior is and how it is changing. On the work floor, for example, we can plot the retarded worker's productivity. Even the severely retarded can tell whether their work curve ("output") is going up or down. Counting devices can be utilized by which the retarded individual aims for goals through which he attempts to improve upon prior accomplishments by competing with himself.

Using this method of interpretation and communication involves the precision behavioral management approach. Behavior can change in a very phenomenal fashion. A study in a sheltered workshop in England reported a group of retarded workers who improved their rate of performance and then leveled off and remained at a static level for many weeks. It looked as if they had reached the peak of their performance, that they were going as fast as they could and accomplishing as much as they could. At this point, an entirely new system of rewards was instituted. The workers immediately became more productive and continued to improve, showing they had been capable of higher performance all along. They had learned, but hadn't performed. The new system of rewards used charting, plotting, interpretation, and similar tactics for the quantification of behavior.

One should not verbalize endlessly with a retarded individual about his performance. Verbalizing is of limited value. Instead, show him, if possible; demonstration deals directly with his comprehension level. Do interpret directly, especially in areas concerning discipline. This is particularly important if negative discipline is involved. Interpret repeatedly and clearly while the discipline is in effect, not merely beforehand.

## PREVENTION OF COMMUNITY INSTITUTIONS

It is important to avoid establishing small institutions, through the development of community-based group homes. Group residences in a middle-class neighborhood can be fairly well integrated and are generally viewed as a step forward. However, residents returned from an institution and placed in such a residence can bring along with them the culture of the institution. There is such a thing as institutional culture, and it can be transferred directly to community group homes. This must be prevented. Once such a culture is established in an adult residence it may remain there for decades, since it tends to become self-perpetuating. One way to break the cycle of institutional culture is to prevent physical isolation of the group home. Another is to prevent social isolation; a physically integrated home can be socially isolated from the community and the mainstream of culture.

In the rush to diminish the number of residents at large institutions for the retarded, there has been a strong tendency to transfer entire groups into new group homes, thus re-establishing the institutional culture in new locations. In one Eastern group residence, neighborhood citizens objected to residents sitting on the porch and rocking. Visitors driving through this middle-class neighborhood would suddenly notice 20 men rocking on a porch; this did little to promote acceptance in the community. Even if there had been only 12 men on the porch, passersby would say, "There's an institution."

To break the cycle of possible community institutions, we must seek interim solutions. If possible, we must initially establish group residences with a small number of community residents—perhaps adults from the waiting list of a local institution. We can begin with three or four, then add one person from the institution—not two or three, but one. Two or three constitute a group, with group processes and reinforcements. One person can be isolated from his institutional underpinnings and integrated into an established social system because group expectancies will pressure the newcomer into conforming. When this individual has been integrated socially, a second person is added, then a third—one from the institution, and perhaps another from the community.

A plan such as this must be developed for adult homes, or we are going to witness many institutional culture disasters and behavioral problems in this area. A major scandal in one group residence can severely damage the whole community-based movement. Events that are commonplace and unnoticed in institutions can wipe out a community residence. These considerations are of utmost concern during the early, critical stages of the evolution of community-based group living systems in a state or region. Planned integration of the community institution population slows the process of establishing places of group living, yet it must be done so that the system itself isn't jeopardized by unpleasant incidents. We must approach group residence development by first establishing a community social system, then adding residents at a regular rate.

## GENERAL ISSUES

Three general issues concerning inappropriate behavior are: (1) body contact; (2) respect for the individual who is retarded; and (3) inappropriate joking, and the frequent errors they represent in relating to the retarded.

It is important to stress appropriate body contact for the retarded. In the institution it is commonplace for residents to literally swarm over visitors or staff—touching, kissing, and so on. Yet this behavior is seldom handled appropriately in child development centers and community-based residential settings for the retarded. Such demonstrations must be replaced by more appropriate relationship behaviors. When retarded persons are provided with adequate human relationships—relationships with parents or parent surrogates—they do not have to seek physical intimacy with strangers. If relationships are strengthened with houseparents, teachers, workshop personnel, and particularly with citizen advocates, we can discourage inappropriate body contact, especially since excessive or indiscriminate body contact is one of the obvious signs of deviancy.

Secondly, we must consider the matter of respect. There is nothing wrong with talking about a retarded person within his hearing range, as long as that person is involved in the discussion. In this manner, personal respect has been shown the retarded person. If you are going to talk about a retarded person and you do not want him to hear, talk about him where he cannot hear. In other words, show the same respect to retarded persons as we generally show the nonretarded.

Similarly, sexual behavior in the retarded is an area in which we have not completely considered our appropriate roles. Our thinking on this topic generally tends to be chaotic and unreasonable. In one state institution residents who engaged in any kind of sexual behavior were immediately punished by attendants. Yet, these same attendants would tease the boys and put pin-up pictures in their units. This kind of behavior promotes a great and unhealthy confusion in the mind of the retarded person.

The last topic concerns inappropriate joking. This is a common error; people continually joke about, and with, retarded persons. They joke about their competency and their sex life then tell make-believe stories and tease them about things which are "unreal" for them. Professionals who are otherwise quite competent are guilty of this type of behavior. For example, the author recalls a vocational counselor who teased a male worker, "Are you in love with this girl? Are you going to marry her?" Indeed, he did have a crush on her; he became confused, and took the comments literally, for he was unable to distinguish between reality and teasing. Eventually, he made a fool of himself through no fault of his own. It takes a rather abstract skill to understand what is and is not a joke.

In summary, the recurrent practical problems in the behavioral management of mentally retarded citizens demand a re-examination of both societal and professional viewpoints on expected behaviors. The guidelines reviewed will hopefully provide cause for reflection by those who are privileged to serve the retarded.

*Chapter 9*

# A CRISIS MODEL FOR HELPING PARENTS TO COPE MORE EFFECTIVELY

In this chapter, some differential patterns of family interaction and management in the area of mental retardation will be reviewed. Included are frequently encountered issues ranging from initial consideration of the family's attitudes toward their child to treatment approaches that enlist parental cooperation in initiating an emphatic and energetic program aimed at fulfilling the child's developmental potentials. The stages of parental acceptance relevant to current management approaches will be reviewed initially. From there, we will take a close look at an operational framework that extends this approach into a crisis-oriented approach embracing both diagnostic and specific treatment guidelines.

We shall stress the fact that the rewards of successful management far outweigh the additional efforts that are frequently necessary in respect to professional involvement and time. Indeed, successful initial assessment and management of these family attitudes and problems may avoid institutionalization by default, especially in parents of severely or profoundly retarded children.

## STAGES OF PARENTAL ACCEPTANCE

It has become clear to clinicians in the field of mental retardation that the initial interpretation interview is a cornerstone for future action. If we fail at this point to help parents understand their child's problems, we may well be sending them further along the path of carousel medicine, or what has been termed shopping patterns for further diagnostic services, rather than effective treatment intervention.

The initial interpretation interview is thus crucial to all further treatment and habilitation attempts. However, the practice of diagnostic interpretation and parental counseling in the area of mental retardation is a most demanding one, and the clinician who embarks on such a course needs certain skills in order to be effective (106). Among these skills are:

1.    Knowledge of the disease states or syndromes which can produce mental retardation as one of the symptoms. Such knowledge allows the clinician to share his diagnostic conclusions with the parents without feeling uneasy with terms, findings, or parental questions as to prognostic implications.

2.    The ability to explain and discuss diagnostic findings in a manner in keeping with the parental level of understanding, both intellectually and emotionally. Here we must avoid the tactic of many parents to attribute their child's clinical picture to some "organic" entity in an effort to relieve any self-guilt and/or perplexity concerning the course of the child's retardation. The initial diagnostic interpretation to parents who do not even suspect mental

retardation—for example, the initial shock of Down's syndrome—will be totally ineffective unless the emotional reactions of the parents are anticipated and handled before firm diagnostic statements are made.

3. An intimate understanding of the family dynamics, obtained from a previous review which includes marital interactional patterns, the nature of the support systems as to the extended family, and so on, is necessary in order to know when and how much to interpret. For example, in 22 percent of the children seen in our initial sample of 616 cases (107), the parents had already either known or strongly suspected that their child was mentally retarded. Thus, proper management of the initial interview with this particular group led to emotional acceptance of their child's disabilities and rapid movement toward realistic treatment programming. It was in the other 78 percent of our parent group that we noted mechanisms that have been well delineated in the clinical literature as stages of parental reaction and acceptance or rejection of the diagnosis of mental retardation.

The stages of parental acceptance can be briefly reviewed as follows:

The parents may not have fully accepted the diagnosis of mental retardation in their child. Here one frequently notes:

a. *Shock.* "It can't be true," or "How can they tell?" or "What did we do to deserve this?" Strong religious overtones are common.

b. *Denial.* "He is just a little slow" (with appropriate and seemingly endless catching-up fantasies).

Unsuccessful intervention and management of either of these two parental responses can lead to further medical shopping for the diagnosis.

2.  The parents may have varying degrees of guilt feelings about their own possible roles in the causation of the child's condition. This usually presents itself clinically as the mother worrying unduly about "the bad fall I had," inference statements such as "My wife has some rather strange people in her family tree," or more direct attempts to displace perceived guilt by sidestepping and/or resenting reality, followed by energetic efforts to find some external family source onto which they can project the problem. Favorite targets of and for projection here are the family doctor (delivery, instruments, vague febrile episodes that were "inadequately treated," etc.).

The lack of intervention at this point can lead to increasingly more pathological coping devices manifested by an obsessive search for magical solutions (108).

In the older child, derogatory comments concerning local special educational facilities are frequent. Accordingly, failure of successful therapeutic intervention at this point leads rapidly toward more primitive defense mechanisms, both individually on the part of each parent, and collectively in regard to the family's approach to their child's problems and needs. Overly agressive, almost paranoid, coping devices come to the foreground, and a very strong undercurrent of depression is frequently apparent in each or both of the parents. One notes a shift from direct focus on the child's needs to unsuccessful attempts on the part of both parents to quell their internal turmoil.

3.  A similar parental response is one in which a reaction formation is employed as a thin veneer to solve unconscious wishes to be rid of the burden their child has come to represent. The reaction formation type of defense is usually manifested clinically by overreaction and/or overcompensations in the form of excessive protection and concern about the child, or by aggressive demands for spe-

cial and additional attention for their child. At this point, previously noted diagnostic shopping tends to change slowly to therapeutic shopping ("Maybe he's not mentally retarded; perhaps he's an autistic or schizophrenic child?"). Here we frequently see a shift from the denial of the child's developmental problems towards a vague position on causation ("damage to his brain") on which parents can project "reasons" for the child's developmental problems. The request for inappropriate treatment at this time literally spells out the irrational (unconscious) nature of the parents' reaction to the child's problems—distortion of the external reality referents of their child's developmental problems into a paradigm which so structures the situation that they themselves can also obtain professional services.

In summary, the initial multidisciplinary diagnostic evaluation of the child and his family must include an assessment of the family's current state regarding knowledge of the nature of their child's problems, acceptance of those problems, and a willingness to cooperate in a mutual treatment approach. Utilizing this type of overall orientation, the interpretation interview can quickly determine how parents are working out their own emotional responses to their child. One can then move toward differential management considerations that focus on family counseling and/or guidance.

It is important to realize that parental guilt is common in these areas. Since the parents conceived the child, they feel responsible for his difficulties. Parents of emotionally disturbed children handle the guilt problem in a different manner; but parents of a mentally retarded child can't project their guilt—onto school authorities, or so on—since the ultimate projection must be onto themselves. This has particular relevance to the crisis of personal values, a subject that will be covered shortly.

## Evolution of a Crisis Orientation to Diagnosis and Parent-Management

In scanning the early literature on mental retardation, one is struck by the fact that very little mention was made of parents, or their feelings. In the mid-1940s through the early 1950s, a trickle of armchair papers began to discuss relevant parent dynamics. Then, in more recent years, a virtual flood of such papers appeared.

It is also curious to note that the parents discussed in the literature of the time are rarely representative of parents of the retarded in general. Instead, they often tend to be (1) mothers; (2) of middle and upper class status; (3) white; and (4) consumers of outpatient diagnostic clinic services. Generalizations are only too readily drawn about parents of the retarded. Failure to include fathers in research, over-reliance on maternal information, and an assumption that such information, particularly regarding the father, is valid, are very common. Regarding the latter, Ross (109) has noted, "Reading the scientific literature in this field, a student unfamiliar with our culture might easily get the impression that fathers play no part in the rearing of our children."

Many writers who comment upon parents' initial reactions to learning that their child is retarded are actually referring to only a minority among parents. In only a very small number of children can the diagnosis be made at birth. In the vast majority of cases, diagnosis is made at school age, and if mild retardation is already suspected by the parents, awareness is usually gradual and does not have the sudden impact so often implied in the literature. Even in severe and profoundly retarded children, the diagnosis usually arises from observation of retarded development. More often than not, formal diagnosis only confirms the parents' apprehensions. The act of confirmation may be abrupt, while suspicion or even knowledge of retardation may have been present for months or years.

## A Review of Parental Management Approaches

Early conceptualizations of parental response to retarded children were heavily influenced by psychoanalytic thought. Major emphasis was placed on the role of guilt, which was seen as a near-universal phenomenon in parents of all types of handicapped children. These parents were commonly viewed as conflicted and almost certain to engage in defense mechanisms such as denial and projection. It was expected that such defenses would be of neurotic proportions. Virtually everything the parent did was interpreted as constituting rejection or nonacceptance of the child, and parental behavior containing positive elements was, at worst, labeled as reaction formation or, at best, as ambivalence.

The psychoanalytic interpretation reached its apex with two elaborations. One of these was by Beddie and Osmond (110) who equated parental response to a retarded child as equivalent to a "child loss" (death of a normal child) resulting in grief that required "grief work" in order to be overcome. Institutionalization was seen as a "death without the proper rites." The other elaboration, by Solnit and Stark (111) coined the term "chronic mourning" for the "object loss" to which the advent of the retarded child was equated. This grief motif became widely accepted, and management approaches flowing from these psychoanalytic concepts tended to incorporate several elements:

1. The parent was placed in the role of psychiatric patient, which he was expected to accept if he was to be helped.

2. Help consisted primarily of therapeutically oriented individual or group counseling which explored the parent's feelings about his own parents, as well as those about the child and his condition and problems.

3. The parent was encouraged to express his deep-seated feelings of responsibility for the child's condition and was provided interpretation, reassurance, and support in an effort to dissipate guilt. Management seldom went much beyond this point. On the one hand, it was now assumed that parents were able to make the best adjustment possible under the circumstances and, on the other, there prevailed a very pessimistic, almost nihilistic, view about treatment horizons for the retarded child. Thus, there seemed little to do except recommend institutional placement and make the necessary arrangements for it.

More recently, stress has been placed on the realistic demands and burdens that parents of retarded children often bear. Parents were seen as being under a great deal of situational and external stress, and symptoms of such stress were perceived as essentially normal or at least expected under the circumstances. The neurotic interpretation of parental reactions was specifically attacked and rejected by Olshansky (112). He pointed to certain social factors of our culture which induce parents to feel devalued for having a damaged child, and to other co-existing factors which inhibit his ability to externalize his sorrow so as to dissipate it. Such a conflict was seen as apt to result in long-term internalization of a depressive mood which Olshansky termed "chronic sorrow" as an understandable, non-neurotic response to a tragic fact. The management suggested by Olshansky emphasized ventilation of parental feelings, readiness on the part of the professional to act as scapegoat, and provision of concrete services such as nursery schools, special classes, sheltered workshops, and guidance with the practical problems of child-rearing.

Farber (113) advanced a sociological and relatively sophisticated theory of parental response to a retarded child. Briefly, parental conflicts were seen to spring from two types of "crisis" situations: one, a "tragic crisis" occurs when parents are unable to cope with a retarded child over a long period of time. This theory has given rise to a number of studies by Farber, his students, and others, but since the main interest in this work has been theoretical, there has been little elaboration in regard to management implications.

## A New Management Framework

Each of the conceptualizations briefly reviewed here has made some contribution toward a better understanding of families of the retarded. However, the approaches have emphasized only limited aspects of either the problem or the possible management options. We will attempt to unify some of these various concepts and to propose a framework designed to handle a wide variety of problems and situations.

It is proposed that parental management needs arising from the advent or presence of a retarded child tend to have three major sources: (1) novelty shock, which results when parental expectancies are suddenly shattered; (2) value conflicts due to culturally mediated attitudes toward defect or deviance; and (3) reality stress resulting from the situational demands of raising or caring for a retarded person. Each of these sources will be discussed in detail.

## The Novelty Shock Crisis

Novelty shock is a very natural response that occurs when parents learn that expectations regarding their child deviate substantially from reality. Novelty shock may occur when a parent of an older child learns relatively suddenly that the child is or may be retarded. However, most commonly, novelty shock occurs upon the birth on an obviously atypical child, such as a child with Down's syndrome.

Parents usually have great anticipations about new babies. Most immediately, there are certain basic normative expectations as to size and weight. Parents hope the baby will have racial characteristics similar to their own. Aside from these basic normative characteristics, parents—especially if they have not had children before—are apt to idealize the expected baby. As Solnit and Stark (114) have stated so well, parents often do not merely expect a typical infant but a perfect one. Aside from expectations as to the qualities of their baby, parents have strong hopes for the future. In our culture, most parents expect their children to pursue an education, to marry, and to practice an occupation. Some parents not only establish college education funds for unborn children, but pick the college their child is to attend and the occupation he is to assume.

The time of birth itself is, under the best of circumstances, a time of severe physical and emotional stress for both mother and father. It is a period accompanied by uncertainty and emotionality. Any additional stressful events superimposed on such a state of vulnerability and depletion are apt to cause bewilderment, confusion, disorganization, regression to increased dependency upon others, and maybe even temporary psychosis. Obviously, an unexpected and stressful event associated with the occasion itself, such as the birth of a grossly atypical child, is particularly apt to induce such a state, conceptualized here as novelty shock.

Actually, the fact that the child is damaged and likely to be retarded may not be the critical issue. The general disruption of expectancies may be more traumatic than the specific nature of the reality. For illustration's sake, we might say that novelty shock might be equally severe whether the baby is diagnosed as Down's syndrome, or whether it is three feet long, very premature, has purple horns, is of unexpected racial characteristics, dies unexpectedly, or turns out to be more than one baby. Often it is not even the unexpected event that induces shock as much as the way the event is interpreted by all involved, including medical personnel. Imagine an authoritatian medical figure towering over an exhausted, lonely, perhaps half-conscious mother, booming dramatically: "Madam, you have just given birth to a mongolian idiot who should be institutionalized immediately!" Incidents of this nature are by no means rare and have been documented in many instances.

The literature also shows the parents can go into novelty shock merely by becoming aware that some terrible event has happened—even when they lack all understanding of the terminology thrown at them, or of the nature or meaning of the event. McDonald (115) documented a case where a father walked the streets in confused agitation for two nights and a day after being told that his baby had a cleft palate; he came back asking what a cleft palate was. Kramm (116) told of a mother who, informed that her child was a monogoloid, set out with the help of neighbors and dictionaries to find out what a mongoloid was. Eventually she concluded that it was something kindred to a mongrel dog. Other parents have been kept from seeing their child or have been induced into not wanting to see it. One such family finally came in fear and apprehension to see their institutionalized baby; on the basis of the guidance they had received, they had pictured this child as an unspeakable monster. Instead, they found a sweet, beautiful baby with Downs Syndrome whom they would probably have taken home, loved, and raised it if there had been better interpretation earlier.

It is apparent that management for novelty shock must often entail undoing damage wrought by others. First and foremost, parents in novelty shock need gentle, undramatic interpretation of the facts, delivered in an atmosphere of maximum emotional support. Reading matter and audiovisual devices might be highly useful. Also, interpretation should stress those elements which are realistically positive, such as the positive aspects of likely child development and the availability or expected availability of services and resources. To cope with their grief, parents should be helped to get to know fellow-parents, such as "pilot parents" from local Associations for Retarded Citizens, who have experienced similar traumas and who have made model adjustments. Where a newborn baby is involved, management should not terminate when the mother leaves the hospital but should continue as needed.

In order to be able to provide facts and information to the parents, it is necessary to assess the condition of the child. However, a comprehensive assessment may be neither possible nor desirable at the time. On the other hand, since parental novelty shock occurs almost invariably either at the child's birth or during the first years, one must postpone many judgments until there has been opportunity to see the child respond to environmental conditions and services. Thus it is important to incorporate a reasonable balance of caution, uncertainty, and positive elements within the fact-oriented management aproach. Managers should not attempt to attain a certainty that is not attainable at the time; instead, assessment must be viewed and interpreted as a time-bound process. Such emphasis upon the uncertainty of the future should not be mistaken as merely a device for softening the emotional impact upon the parents; uncertainty is valid even in some very clear-cut and relatively homogeneous syndromes such as Down's and others, where occasionally remarkable deviations from typical syndromic expressions may occur. The benefits of an early, sudden, and somewhat dramatic diagnosis appear to have been greatly exaggerated. Such a diagnosis-compulsion on the part of the manager may often be detrimental rather than beneficial (117).

It appears that parents in novelty shock tend to become very inward-directed, usually in a selfish and self-pitying manner. Successful adaptation often requires that the parent broaden his concerns to the spouse and the child. Thus, management that emphasizes future assessment of the child's progress can help the parent to move from a helpless, disordered dependency toward a more adaptive concern about maximizing the child's development. One might say that it is better for the parent to move toward a reality stress situation than to remain in novelty shock.

The novelty shock reaction is likely to be well circumscribed and definable, and management implications tend to be rather clear. However, such reactions, though perhaps memorable because of the extremity of parental response, are relatively rare. In a few instances, an unexpectedly atypical child is born and recognized at birth. In a few other cases, a child is suddenly recognized as significantly atypical sometime after birth. But in the vast majority of cases, recognition comes mercifully slow, or some events prior to or associated with pregnancy have sensitized the parent to the possibility that the infant may be atypical.

## The Reality Stress Crisis

Even to rear a child that is gifted, healthy, and beautiful is a tremendously demanding task. Relatively normal adults fail in the task of rearing children who, at least initially, were rather typical infants. Therefore, it must be recognized that the task of rearing an atypical child is very likely to constitute such a demand that typical parents cannot be expected to manage adequately without being provided with extraordinary resources and services.

It is to be expected that parents of retarded children will increasingly present themselves to psychiatrists and agencies such as psychiatric clinics in search of help. While the parents may display signs of stress and occasionally even psychopathology, we must recognize that such symptoms may be no more than normative reactions to situational stress.

It is important to realize that crises or conflicts due to excessive reality demands are essentially normal and are only to a limited degree under the control of the parents. Psychiatric management of families of the retarded has sometimes ignored the realistic burdens associated with rearing an atypical child and instead has tended to become preoccupied with parental psychopathology. Indeed, in the literature one can find endless examples where parents are stereotyped as guilty, rejecting, unaccepting; where they are viewed as "the patient," and where excessive faith is placed on therapeutically oriented counseling rather than on education or provision of concrete relief measures. The physical demands made by a hyperactive child can rarely be handled by counseling alone, and the demands of caring for three children still in diapers are not lightened by probing the mother's anal fixations and deepseated feelings about feces. If any kind of counseling for such a mother is appropriate, it is of the type that introduces her to operant behavior shaping and supplements that didactic approach with home visits.

All professionals who participate in the management of families of the retarded should avoid the temptation to provide management that might be better provided by others. Instead of maintaining management dominance while doing something that they have been trained to do but that is irrelevant in the specific case, a professional would do better to act as an effective advocate or aggressive referral and follow-up agent in seeing to it that somebody will provide the management that is appropriate and needed in a given case.

Measures of major and most poignant relevance to the relief of reality stress are the following: concrete and direct services, such as obtaining acceptance of a child in a day-care or special education program or inclusion of an adult in a vocational training or sheltered-work program; seeing to it that homemaker, visiting nurse, or home economist services are initiated; getting the family enrolled in appropriate clinics and health services; initiating casework to obtain public assistance for which the family may be eligible; exercising advocacy functions to safeguard rights and prevent exploitation, especially of the poor and disadvantaged; providing the family with education in regard to problems of child care, especially feeding, dressing, and toileting the handicapped child; providing the family with equipment, perhaps on a loan basis, that facilitates child care or accelerates child development—for example, walkers, standing tables, toilet chairs, feeding aids; helping find competent babysitters; or assisting in arrangements for residential placement.

## Value Conflicts

Clinicians tend to be more adept at tracing individual psychopathology to pathogenic events and patterns in persons' backgrounds than in dealing with the powerful effects of social and subcultural values and attitudes which are transmitted in relatively "normal" fashion and which may rule a person's behavior. In our society, there are many perceptions and interpretations of mental retardation that have been transmitted to us from the past. We must recall that, by definition, retardation is a deviancy. In other words, retarded persons are significantly different from others, and in our society the difference is generally negatively valued. Thus, common historical role perceptions of the retardate have included the retardate as a menace, as subhuman (animal-like or even vegetable), as an objective of ridicule, and as an object of pity (118). Some role perceptions have been more common in some of our subcultures than others. For instance, Catholics appear to be more accepting of retardation than Protestants or Jews, and Hutterites are so accepting that they will not institutionalize any retarded member of their community (119, 120, 121).

Many well-known books and articles written by parents of retarded children (122, 123, 124) strongly reflect value conflicts and both adaptive and maladaptive ways of responding. There have been numerous reports of parents who were well equipped with intelligence and resources who found themselves blocked by inner value conflicts from raising or relating to their retarded children; other families have struggled hard against poverty and situational burdens and managed to succeed in raising retarded children to productive citizenship.

It follows from the above that many parents have conflicts about a retarded child not because the child is an extraordinary burden of care, but because they intensely disvalue the meaning which the child represents (125). Thus, a value conflict is a very subjective thing but no less real or necessarily less stressful to one family than the burdens of care are to another. A parental value conflict may result in various degrees of emotional and physical rejection of the child. When mild, it may be manifested by ambivalence and overprotection; when severe it is inclined to result in the child being discarded—usually by means of institutionalization—and perhaps even in the denial of his existence. Unless a parent is exposed to, or spontaneously undergoes, existential management experiences or experiences existential growth, the value conflict is likely to last a lifetime.

Appropriate existential management may include psychotherapy, but other measures may be more effective as well as efficient. One of these is counseling that is not oriented toward psychodynamics and unresolved childhood fixations but toward the meaning of life and its ultimate values. Various schools of existential thought specialize in this type of counseling; for example, the school of logotherapy. Another and very underutilized measure is religious counseling. Much, of course, depends on the selection of an appropriate pastoral or religious counselor, but most religions permit multiple positive interpretations of a retarded child (126). Some persons, though actively involved in a religion or church, are not aware of these interpretations. However, a person is likely to accept them in the proper context, for these interpretations, although perhaps inconsistent with other values he may hold, are consistent with the large and deeply meaningful values and beliefs that are mediated by his religion.

The rationale for a third measure of assisting parents of retarded children was apparently first fully elaborated by Weingold and Hormuth (127). They pointed out that since value conflicts are mediated by a process of socialization involving various groupings of society, a very promising management should be group-derived resocialization. While group techniques had been used earlier, Weingold and Hormuth were the first to present a truly systematic rationale for the use of group counseling with parents experiencing conflicts in attitudes. If this rationale is valid—and it has much surface validity—congregational support should be one of the most powerful management options because it can combine group-mediated resocialization with adaptive religious interpretation. Congregational support implies that a parish, church or church group show its acceptance, or continued acceptance, of a family with a retarded child in a number of ways, both large and small. This would include friendly and frequent socializing with the family, offers of babysitting and other assistance, and active expression of interest by the pastor. A major manifestation of congregational support would be the operation of Sunday School classes or day-care services for retarded children with active voluntary participation on the part of church members.

There are, of course, other alternatives. The important point is for the parent's helper to truly understand the principles and processes involved in a value conflict and then to invoke management alternatives flexibly, creatively, and in ways which take account of local and specific circumstances.

In Table 9.1, a theoretical framework is summarized concerning the sources of management needs. Some normative behaviors of parents in novelty shock, in value conflict, or under reality stresses are listed; some major management needs are given; and positive and negative parental adjustments are indicated.

## PROGRAMMING THE MANAGEMENT PROCESS

It is proposed that those who seek to effectively aid parents of the retarded should explore a general strategy of management which appears to have high parsimony and to be consistent with decision theory by exploring and meeting family-management needs in a rank order of immediacy of the problems, by minimizing superfluous or irrelevant assessments, and by testing management options selectively so as to maximize the probability of their effectiveness. This strategy involves three stages, which will be discussed, and each is summarized in Figure 9.1.

## Stage 1

Immediately upon referral, the family helper should assess the parents' response to the diagnosis and work toward generating, obtaining, and using services that have immediate relevance. By intimately tying a theory of parental stress dynamics to a strategy of assessment and management, we can more confidently answer the old question, Assessment for what?

During any stage of the management cycle, great care should be exercised in the use of referrals to other agencies. Often such referrals constitute unconscious defensive maneuvers on the part of professionals or entire agencies and may start a family on the runabout circuit. If referrals appear to be indicated, they should be accompanied by aggressive follow through on the part of the referring professional or agency until it is ascertained that appropriate services are being provided from another source, or until a conscious and deliberate decision has been reached to terminate or suspend management. Too often, management is not terminated by a conscious decision but is permitted to fizzle out and casually drop out of awareness.

## Stage 2

For parents in any state other than novelty shock, the realistic situational demands upon the family should be assessed. Generally, steps should then be taken to relieve these situational burdens. This may imply a number of measures such as those discussed in the section on reality stress. Until concrete relief measures have been instituted in order to alleviate the immediacy of a stressful reality, it is senseless to be concerned with problems of real or suspected psychopathology. Here, it is useful to think in decision-theory terms: alleviation of reality demands might alleviate psy-

**Table 9.1  A Theoretical Framework for the Management of Parents of the Retarded**

*Three Major Sources of Parental Management Needs*

| Nature of responses | Novelty shock | | Value conflict | Reality stress |
|---|---|---|---|---|
| Formative initial parental responses | Confusion Disorganization Helplessness | Dependency Anguish Anger | Profound existential pain and insult to ego<br>Ambivalence about acceptance of facts | Stress symptoms Deterioration of health Family tension |
| Management needs | Immediate supportive counseling to realign expectancies<br>Medical-diagnostic interpretations that are realistic yet focus on positive developmental expectancies<br>Preparation of parents for planning and utilization of services<br>Provision of societal and peer support, as by referral to parent groups | | Existential type of therapy or counseling (for example, pastoral counseling)<br>Resocialization, as with group counseling, congregational support<br>Finding a niche for the child in the parental value system<br>Exposure of parents to models of positive conflict resolution, as in the parent movement | Correct assessment of reality-based family needs<br>Knowledge of and rapid provision of concrete services that relieve situational demands |

**Table 9.1 (Continued)**

*Three Major Sources of Parental Management Needs*

| Nature of responses | Novelty shock | Value conflict | Reality stress |
|---|---|---|---|
| Adaptive parental adjustments | Acceptance of reality factors<br>Seeking or acceptance of guidance<br>Realignment of expectations and plans | Resolution of existential parental quandary<br>Value change<br>Investment of value in the child<br>Empathy for the child | Search for resources<br>Utilization of resources<br>Participation in the creation of needed resources and services<br>Placement of child outside the home where appropriate |
| Maladaptive parental adjustments | Rejection of the child<br>Inappropriate discarding of child<br>Precipitous institutionalization<br>Denial of reality<br>Surrender to irrational guilt<br>Conflicted management of child<br>Withdrawal<br>Irrational affixing of blame | Rejection of child<br>Inappropriate institutionalization<br>Denial of child or his condition<br>Severe and continued ambivalence<br>Shopping for invalid diagnoses and cures<br>Reaction formation<br>Conflicted management of child<br>Sense of unfulfillment<br>Chronic sorrow<br>Prolonged emotional disorder | Rejection of child<br>Premature separation from child<br>Unnecessary institutionalization<br>Family dissolution<br>Passive surrender to situational demands |

263

chopathology, no matter whence its source, but alleviation of psychopathology might be either impossible or of little benefit if reality demands are still excessive. Thus, concrete and direct measures that provide relatively fast relief from situational stresses not only may accomplish the greatest benefits at least cost, but may also open up the way for a more valid assessment of possible psychopathology.

Once concrete measures have been instituted, enough time should be permitted to lapse so that those stresses that can be relieved by these measures may have a chance to dissipate or at least lessen significantly. During this time, it can be expected that those signs and symptoms of family stress that can be reasonably assumed to have resulted from the situational demands will dissipate enough to permit the assessment of more deep-seated conflicts. At this point, it is time to move to the third stage of management.

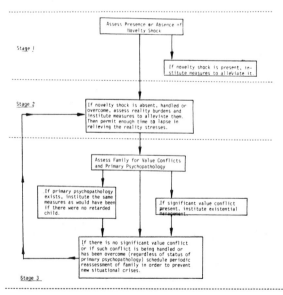

Figure 9.1    An Approach to Exploring/Meeting the Family—
Management Needs of Parents of the Retarded

## Stage 3

Once it is reasonably certain that the parents are no longer in novelty shock and that the family has found some relief from the burdens of a demanding reality, it is time to assess "primary psychopathology"—that is, problems of personal adjustment which may be aggravated by the presence of a retarded family member but which basically have their origin elsewhere; and personal and social values and attitudes relative to retardation which interfere with adaptive behavior.

Primary psychopathology can be managed much as it would be if the retarded family member were not retarded. Value conflicts would be managed as indicated in the earlier section on them.

## CONCLUSION

The provision of services to the families of the retarded can be justified by pointing to three potential beneficiaries of such services. First, there is the retarded person himself, whose life course can be profoundly affected by the services he receives. Often the only way to help him and to insure that services rendered to him are not wasted is by working with and through the family. Second, services may provide significant or even crucial assistance to members of the family so that they (singly or as a unit) can function in a relatively normal or at least adequate fashion. Third, society itself benefits by preventing individual and family disorganization or the need for even more costly services later.

In this section, a broad concept of management has been presented—a highly selective literature review, and a theory proposing the management needs of families of retarded parents who appear to be experiencing novelty shock. For families experiencing this condition, emotional support as well as information, education, facts, and reading matter should be provided, and the child's condition should be interpreted in a way that places a realistic emphasis on positive developmental expectations and resources likely to be available in the future. Also, affiliation with a parent movement should be encouraged, and the necessary names, addresses, phone numbers, brochures, etc. should be provided. Such help should be delivered as speedily as possible; a matter of days or even hours might make a difference in the future life course of the family. If the parents do not appear to be in novelty shock, stage 2 is invoked; this should also be done once parents pass from novelty shock into a period of stress caused by awareness of the realistic burdens of caring for a handicapped child.

## GENERAL REMARKS

No matter what problems exist, what management is conducted, or what results are obtained, families should be scheduled for periodical reassessments. Novelty shock crisis tends to be a nonrecurring event of short duration. Value crises tend to be long-term, but once resolved they are not likely to move from cycle to cycle and from crisis to crisis as the retarded child and his family pass through various developmental life stages. Thus, reassessment should be oriented primarily toward situational stresses. Reassessment may take place at regular intervals or during those developmental phases most likely to be fraught with stress. At any rate, management of families will increasingly be perceived not as a one-shot effort but as a lifelong process. We will probably see the development of services and service delivery systems more appropriate to such a conceptualization than those that exist at present. The following case histories illustrate both the complexity of family management and the need for a rational approach to it.

## Case History 1

Robert is a 9-month-old boy with Down's syndrome. He is the youngest of five children. He has a 17-year-old sister, a 14-year-old brother, a 10-year-old brother, and a 2-year-old adopted brother. His father is a professional person, 44 years of age; and his mother is a 43-year-old housewife.

When his mother became pregnant at age 42, she requested amniocentesis in order to test if this child might have Down's syndrome. She was counseled against the testing and assured that the chances were very high that she would have a normal child. When, in fact, the child did turn out to have Down's syndrome, it was a very difficult situation for the mother to accept. In addition to the normal crisis situation with the birth of a Down's syndrome baby, Robert's parents have felt very guilty for not pursuing and insisting upon the amniocentesis. Now they feel responsible for having brought a defective child into the world, a child whose birth, they feel, could and should have been prevented.

Robert has always been very healthy and has had no other problems except Down's syndrome. However, the relationship between this child and his parents is not healthy. The mother was told on the day of the child's birth that he had Down's syndrome. She left the hospital within three days of his birth, leaving the baby there. When the boy was a week old his father went to the hospital to bring Robert home and at that time asked the pediatrician for help. The pediatrician referred him to the local community-based service for the retarded, which he called when the baby was three weeks of age.

Generally a mother accepts a retarded baby much more readily than a father, and many times fathers have a great deal of difficulty in the first few months. In this case, however, the father accepted the child's birth while the mother was upset and having much more difficulty adjusting to him. This is not because she feels she is too old to have a child; after all, their adopted child is only 15 months older than Robert. It is, rather, her inability to accept the child's Down's syndrome.

As previously mentioned, the mother and father had great difficulty in developing the early parent-child relationship with the baby. They made comments to the effect that "it is too bad that he has an empty head." They seemed to feel that there was nothing there, that he wouldn't develop; and they held back in making an emotional tie to this child. It made us rethink our idea about telling parents immediately that the child is retarded and allowing them to begin the process of adjusting to the fact. Perhaps it is not so wise to tell parents that the child is retarded before the normal parent-child bond is made in the first two or three weeks of life.

Eight weeks after Robert was born, the parents went on a vacation to Utah, and at that time we felt that they might leave this little boy with the mother's brother; we were surprised when the family returned with him. They had taken the other children on a side trip to California and left the baby with a sister.

The family is taking good care of this nine-month-old child, and the older children are less upset than they were at the beginning. Yet the child is not fully accepted in the family, and there is not the normal parent-bond that is commonly seen with other children.

Since the child was three weeks old, the family has been served by a counselor from the regional retardation service and has had an infant teacher going into the home. Since this is the youngest of five children and training a young Down's syndrome children is basically early infant development, the counselor and the teacher have been of great support and developmental assistance to these parents. There is a pilot parent involvement with them, but in this case it is felt that an infant development center at which the parents and baby could come together with other parents and babies on a regular basis and be involved more on parent-to-parent relationship rather than on a mother-to-teacher relationship would probably be more supportive and might help this mother develop a better feeling for this baby, for herself, and for the family.

Earlier the older children were picking up the anxiety and guilt of the parents, and they, too, were having great difficulty in dealing with this baby. They were really grieving for him, more than we see in the siblings of other children. Now they are beginning to reflect the increasing security of both parents as they themselves resolve this family crisis situation.

COMMENT.    The shock crisis features in this family were of major proportions—from fear before birth, to disengagement of the mother from the child in the first few days of life, to a rather stormy early settling-in period for the mother-child relationship. The aftermath of demolition of this family's expectancy for a normal child almost led to their disowning the child as their product and as a rightful member of the family. The need for very early counseling and development services is clearly noted in this instance.

## Case History 2

Tom is a pleasant but somewhat different looking 4-year-old boy who functions in the mildly retarded category, about one to one-and-a-half years delayed. This child is the only child of a 54-year-old father and a 34-year-old mother; both are in their second marriage. The father has grown children, but Tom is his mother's only child. He weighed 10 pounds at birth, with a one-minute Apgar score of 7 and a 5-minute Apgar score of 8.

He is mildly hyperactive and not toilet trained, but he does speak two- or three-word sentences and seems to have good receptive language. He has been fitful and restless since early life and at different times has been placed on Ritalin, Vistaril, and Thorazine; at present, he is on Mellaril.

Tom's father seems a rather stable man. He works as a custodian for a large firm, and he has good insurance coverage. His wife is rather unstable and has great difficulty in coping with Tom. Any type of noisy behavior is interpreted by her as "hyperactive," and she seems very anxious.

About a year ago Tom's mother made contact with the local community-based service for the retarded. She requested help for him, stating that "He is driving me crazy." Yet any attempt at that time to identify her or make contact with her resulted in her hanging up the phone. For a two- or three-week period, she called on one particular staff member several times a day. Finally she identified herself and the child's doctor, information which was sufficient to enable the staff to contact the doctor and obtain advice on how to best handle the situation. The doctor suggested visiting the home and talking with her about putting Tom in a child-development center—a move he had been suggesting to the mother over a six-month period with very little success.

When the community-based staff person went to the house, the mother became very upset. She kept saying, "Go away." At that point, a change in tactics was in order and the staff member wrote a note to the parents telling them that she too was the parent of a handicapped child, and suggesting they call her at home. She also offered to have a staff caseworker come out to the house to help the family with the child. A few days later she received a letter from the mother stating, "I know all about caseworkers and how they come out for a chat and then ask all kinds of personal questions." Apparently the family at some time had had contact with a welfare caseworker, and this negative experience was another barrier to serving the child. For six to eight months the service heard nothing, then another children's service called with a referral of this child. We contacted the family, working through the father. Tom was placed in a child-development program within two weeks of the referral.

The mother appears not to remember the contacts with the local service agency a year ago and is very happy having the child in the development center. In addition to school for the child, the caseworker has arranged for public housing and food stamps for the family. Application for county health aid to cover medication is being explored, and application has been made to Social Security for disability benefits for the child.

The mother has benefited from Tom being gone six hours a day. But when Tom returns home from the center he is tired and cranky and his mother didn't feel able to cope with him for the evening hours. A respite care program from 5 to 9 P.M. on Wednesdays was arranged. In the future, carryover training in behavioral management in the home will be offered to these parents.

The family is under financial strain, has very few relations or friendship-support systems, and is further handicapped by the serious emotional instability of the mother and her lack of parenting skills. It is likely that we can strengthen this family unit temporarily, but it is not unrealistic to expect that Tom may need a foster or group home placement before he reaches early adolescence.

COMMENT     This family illustrates a multiplicity of crisis features ranging from the mother's being unable to fit the boy's behavior into her expectancy of childrearing to her psychopathology and the family's loneliness and lack of interpersonal support systems. The last factor nearly overshadows the value crisis elements that are present. Take the family's relative isolation from interpersonal contacts: this feeling of aloneness in the community and the poor parenting readiness are hallmarks of child abuse cases. This factor alone—far beyond the child's handicaps—signaled the need for active and persistent attempts by the mental retardation system to make an effective entry into this family. Without such relatively early interventions, this child would have been greatly at risk for personal injury, a rapidly escalating major emotional disturbance, and low developmental horizons.

## Case History 3

Frank, age nine, is a sturdy, youngster of great vitality, who is interested in physical activities. He has been labeled as suffering from infantile autism but now is classified as a childhood schizophrenic. Tests of his intellectual ability are difficult because of his behavioral problems, but test results place him in the moderately retarded range. Professionals have not really agreed as to the exact nature of his problem or how to effectively deal with him. He is the oldest of two children of highly educated parents. His father is a college professor and his mother has graduate degrees. His younger sister (age seven years) seems normal intellectually and behaviorally.

Because of his parents' concern and their knowledge about obtaining services, this child has been seen and served by most agencies in the area. Frank attended a preschool for retarded children and a private school for educable children. His behavior made it impossible for him to stay in these settings, and he then spent six months in the Children's Program of a local psychiatric hospital. When he left there he returned to a child-development center and did fairly well for about one year.

During the past year, Frank has grown larger and more aggressive and has begun to bully his mother, attacking her with a knife on two occasions. Because of his size and strength compared to the mother's small stature, and because of the absence of the father from the home on monthly trips for the university, the situation has progressively worsened. The mother sees Frank as dangerous to her and possibly to his little sister. As a result, she is afraid of him, a fact of which he is aware; thus he is able to take advantage of her physical fear. If he doesn't have his way, Frank attacks her or throws tantrums. Generally, she is unable to cope with him.

About 18 months ago Frank spoke well, but now he usually mutters incoherently, although he does say a few meaningful words. He is, however, more outgoing. He used to be "inside himself," but now he relates to adults in a social way. He also now acknowledges the existence of his seven-year-old sister. When he was younger he literally walked into her and behaved as if he could not see her, or as if she didn't exist.

This is not a case of a family with inadequate parenting skills. They have become very knowledgeable in behavioral management, studied behavior modification from books, taken courses, and enrolled in child guidance sessions, both individually and with a group of other parents with difficult children. With most children they would be considered as very adequate parents.

This past summer, Frank's behavior became so difficult that his parents felt medication changes might be helpful, and he was admitted to a psychiatric hospital at a large urban medical school for six weeks. During his absence, the parents realized how different family life was without him and how much they needed this peace as a family. The hospital's efforts to help Frank, however, failed. Despite efforts to adjust dosages, no combination of medications made much difference in his usual behavior and he was discharged on Haldol (5 mg. four times a day). It was suggested by the psychiatric hospital that he was under too much pressure from programming efforts; he was now on a programmed schedule in school for one hour per day. The rest of the time he could choose activities within limits. It was also suggested that a group home or an institutional residential placement with firmer limits should be considered—that is, a situation in which he could not terrorize or bully the adults caring for him.

Efforts were made to find a group home placement in one of the community-based group homes for the emotionally disturbed children. When it appeared this might not be possible, application for placement in the state-operated facility for the mentally retarded was made for him by his parents. During this time the caseworker helped the family make application, toured a community-based service group home and the state facility with them, and tried to be supportive of whatever the parents decided was best for their son and themselves.

As it turned out, an opening did occur in one of the group homes, and Frank was admitted. So far he is doing quite well, although this may be the two to three month honeymoon period typical for foster children. He has tried to attack the houseparents when they wouldn't let him have his way, but they have remained firm and after a while he has calmed down. He is also reacting well to the houseparents' son, who is about his age and doesn't seem too bothered with his roommate's teasing and pinching.

Frank's parents are very much involved with this child and are encouraged to remain so. They regularly visit him at the group home, and take him home for weekends two to three times a month. They, as well as the houseparents, are involved in team meetings, parent coffees, and the like. The caseworker is trying to help them deal with the natural feelings they have of being failures as parents and trying to help them keep close contact with their son in the group home.

COMMENT.     Frank illustrates the reality type of family crisis in which parents who are adequate parents become overwhelmed by their child's complex developmental-emotional problems. It must be noted that they became overwhelmed despite their involvement, untiring efforts, and cooperation with professional caregivers. In these instances of reality-based crises the parents are in need of their own reality-based professional recommendations. If these recommendations are not provided these parents' reality-based problems with their children are sidestepped and the parents are harassed as the ones in need of the primary treatment efforts. Trying a number of definitive treatment management alternatives in a sequential basis may result, as in this instance, in a mutual decision to provide a long term residential-programmatic alternative for the child. After this mutual separation decision has been made, family involvement is a key to both preventing the disintegration of the family due to guilt, and to easing the child's difficulty in finding a new life among strangers. The presence of locally based residential services facilitates this continuing family involvement.

## CONCLUSION

One often hears the cliché that assessment should be a continuing process. From the above, it is obvious that assessment of family functioning is an integral part of the management cycle. One can thus question the rationale of the present custom of conducting the most comprehensive assessment prior to the provision of significant amounts of service. The argument for this is that it takes thorough assessment to determine the need for any type of service. The author believes this view to be erroneous. Many families are under such obvious environmental stress that needed relief measures can be identified by any intelligent citizen who has a general familiarity with available resources. Perhaps the initial evaluation should be more modest in extent, attempting to mostly ascertain the existence of novelty shock and the extent to which the child's condition warrants concern about the future. This should occur after the needs for immediate, stress-relieving services have been initiated, the crisis atmosphere has dissipated, and the parents have become more oriented toward problem-solving by means of service utilization.

Most important, the predictive function of assessment should probably be greatly de-emphasized. Instead, assessment of the child should be used more to help select the optimal developmental services and to measure the apparent response to such services. Such a reconceptualization would not only be more practical but would also help in shifting parental concern away from an unpredictable and often distorted view of the future, and toward the practical needs of their child.

## Chapter 10

# THE POTENTIAL OF COMMUNITY-BASED SERVICES FOR THE MENTALLY RETARDED: THE EXAMPLE OF ENCOR

The Eastern Nebraska Community Office of Retardation (ENCOR) was established on July 1, 1970, as a joint venture between the five counties in the eastern portion of the state of Nebraska. The purpose of this cooperation agreement was to provide a comprehensive continuum of services at the local level so that no retarded person should ever have to leave the ENCOR region to receive the services he might need. Although the ENCOR area is the smallest of the six state regions in geo-political size, the distribution of population within this area presents a relatively great challenge for service delivery. Since over two-thirds of the region's population is in one metropolitan area—while the remainder of the region is relatively sparsely populated, an unusual multi-county administrative structure was chosen to meet the challenge of maintaining the quality of both urban and rural services.

The agreement under which ENCOR was created emphasized the intention of the five counties to create a regional administration to provide services which were not or could not be provided by other agencies or organizations for their mentally retarded citizens. Accordingly, ENCOR was created as an agency designated to fill in the gaps between existing and needed services. The form of ENCOR's administrative structure is county government; elected commissioners from each of the five counties compose the government board, which maintains complete authority over all ENCOR transactions.

It is important to note that all of the initial and ongoing planning activities and service efforts that underlie ENCOR came through combined efforts of parents and professionals and have been accomplished since July 1, 1970. In its short existence, ENCOR has gained wide support from citizens, the parents of the retarded, and local and state public officials. All services within the ENCOR system operate according to the principle of normalization, which is central to the major underlying ideology of service delivery in ENCOR. The principle of normalization, as noted, states that human management practices should be such as to enable a deviant person to function in ways considered to be within the acceptable norms of his society, and that the means employed to reach this goal should be as culturally normative as possible. Actively utilizing this principle, ENCOR is to fully develop a system of services that will provide the opportunity for an optimum life for all the retarded citizens in its five counties. ENCOR currently serves approximately 1,200 individuals of all ages.

## ENCOR DIVISIONS

To accomplish the task of providing services for all ages and all needs of the mentally retarded, the following five divisions comprise the ENCOR system of services:

1. *Division of Educational and Developmental Services.* ENCOR provides developmental and educational services for all retarded children who are excluded from the public schools either because of their age or the extent of their retardation. These programs for young children are most important and are therefore staffed with highly trained individuals who are intensely developmentally oriented. Children receive services within these programs to bring their self-help skills and pre-academic abilities to a level where the public schools will accept them. Included within the developmental programs are: speech therapy, physical therapy, and social services, all closely intertwined to help the individual develop at the fastest rate possible.

2. *Division of Vocational Services.* When a child leaves the educational and developmental services of ENCOR, he may move directly into a public school program or into competitive employment; or he may need special training through ENCOR's vocational services division. Within this division many facets of vocational training are provided, depending upon the needs of the individual. After an intensive evaluation which pinpoints his strengths and weaknesses, a program is developed for each individual. He may then go into vocational and social training for employment, or he may pass into the work activities unit, which is an extended training program.

ENCOR also provides minimally supervised employment in industry through specialized work stations in various industries in the communities. In these settings, vocational training is provided right in the midst of the industry or business for which the individuals are being trained for employment. Thus the work stations in industry demonstrate the optimum of normalization.

The vocational services division also provides vocational placement and follow-up, as well as related instruction classes to provide training in those skills necessary to the world of work (basic reading, arithmetic, use of telephone, etc.). In addition, home economics and social skills training are provided in night courses, so that no interruption in the work training occurs during the day. ENCOR also collaborates with the local vocational-technical schools in providing adult basic education for those individuals wishing to further their academic skill levels.

3.  *Division of Residential Services.* Residential Services are provided for persons of all ages within the ENCOR system. The services provided include children's residences (small, family-like homes), adult residences, family living residences, adult-training residences, adult board and room homes (minimum supervision residences), co-resident apartments (staff-supervised), and supervision of independent living arrangements. In addition, the residential services provided by ENCOR include a behavior shaping residence and a developmental maximation unit.

The adult and children's residences provided by the ENCOR system operate on the belief that to allow for optimum growth, development, and acquisition of skills necessary for future independent living each resident should be accorded the opportunity of any other citizen in having a family or its surrogate substitutes and a home within the community. ENCOR attempts in every way to follow the same family patterns of living as are experienced by other citizens.

Behavioral shaping residences are provided within the ENCOR system for individuals who need short-term intensive training (24-hour service) to attain those skills and competencies necessary to return home from an institution or to be able to take better advantage of another ENCOR residential training environment. Finally, the developmental maximization unit provides for those individuals whose needs are the most complex.

4.  *Family Resource Division.* Four major services are provided in this Division of ENCOR:

a. *Community Support Services* include developmental, recreation, transportation, and volunteer services. Transportation services are coordinated and provided for retarded citizens attending ENCOR or public school programs when these clients are too severely handicapped or their families are unable to manage alone. In addition, the transportation services extend to public transportation to move about the community. Volunteer services involve the active recruitment, training, and supervision of volunteer manpower.

b. *Adult Guidance Services* include intake and referral services, as well as counseling, guidance, and follow-along services to assist families in seeking out, attaining, and coordinating needed services, whether they be generic or through the ENCOR system.

c. *Child Guidance Services* include guidance and counseling services that focus on families of retarded children: crisis assistance services and developmental home placements. Crisis assistance services are available to all clients and their families. Their major role is to provide emergency or crisis care for persons who have sudden difficulties in maintaining themselves in their homes or in independent living situations. This includes crisis relief for parents of the retarded via part-day or full-time residential care and training. The service also provides crisis counseling, homemaker services, and part-day babysitting. For example, where there is a death, divorce or major illness in the family, a mother who is having a baby, when the family is moving or attending out-of-town business, or when a parent or the entire family requires a much needed vacation, crisis assistance services may be used.

Developmental homes are similar to foster homes but differ in that long-term placements are emphasized, and training for developmental home parents is required.

d. *The Supportive Services* component of the family resource services division focuses on providing an active coordination of medical, psychological, therapy (speech, physical therapy, etc.), home training and health care needs for all clients. Once again, the programmatic rationale in this area is not the provision of services but the coordination to the highest degree possible of existing community services while teaching individuals to use what is available within the community.

5. *Division of Central Services.* The central services division of ENCOR provides not only internal operation— overall agency coordination, supervision, and program planning—but also evaluation and planning, public education and information services, and bookkeeping and accounting. The public education and information services maintain a continuous liaison with the public and active news dissemination through the communications media.

In summary, the Eastern Nebraska Community Office of Retardation provides a comprehensive system of services to meet the needs of any individual who is retarded within the five county area. Such a system is not the usual fragmented array of programs but a coordinated system capable of developing any service or series of services that is needed for any one person. This unique approach to services for the retarded has been very successful and has gained wide support from not only the general public and parents of the retarded but also from public officials who support the program's operation financially. Many individuals have passed through the ENCOR programs into public schools and into competitive employment. Similarly, many individuals who were served as adults in the vocational training center or supported through the family resource services division of ENCOR are now living independently as contributing taxpayers, leading full and happy lives, in contrast of what once was a bleak future of institutional life.

Any community-based system that intends to be comprehensive in serving the mentally retarded must follow this general structure. That is, if all retarded persons are to be served at the community level, it is necessary to develop programs that administer to their educational, developmental, vocational, residential, and counseling and support needs. To do less than this is to insure that many retarded persons will continue to live out their lives in the bleak confines of institutions.

But beyond the skeletal structure of a community service system are its particular programs; it is these, and the people who run them, which determine the quality of the system as a whole. The ENCOR system has, in its short history, been very fortunate in attracting some very dynamic and innovative administrators. These persons have not only established interesting and effective services but have seen that truly normalizing services demand more than good training programs, that normalization can occur only when the community itself is being changed and educated to accept mentally retarded persons. Thus the parents of retarded persons have been involved, and a concerted effort made to convert employers, students, and lay citizens to the idea that the mentally retarded are entitled to the normal opportunities of work, family, and community life.

## ENCOR PROGRAMS

In this section, I will describe eight innovative programs in ENCOR that bridge many of the gaps found in other community-based service systems. It is not unusual, for example, to find an area service system that has an excellent developmental program for children, but a woefully inadequate vocational system for adults. This particular failing, of course, can render the developmental program almost meaningless by undoing in the adult developmental skills he has learned by great effort. A good community-based service system must not only meet the special program needs of some individuals but should augment and enrich their programs with associations with citizens', parents', and other groups, as much as local conditions allow.

Of the following innovative programs, five are ENCOR programs designed to meet special needs of retarded persons and to foster the integration of retarded citizens into the normal community population. Two of the programs, Citizens Advocacy and Pilot Parents, are the offspring of the Greater Omaha Association for Retarded Citizens, an energetic group of parents and lay citizens who work as both friend and foe of ENCOR in monitoring the services ENCOR provides. And, finally, the SWEAT Program is operated by the Nebraska Psychiatric Institute, which has no formal ties to ENCOR at all.

My point is that the true implementation of normalization is not merely a matter of developmental and training programs run by the service agency. These special-needs programs must indeed be established, but it is important to see beyond them. We must discover ways in which retarded persons can be trained and educated in nonspecialized community programs where normalization is more apt to take place. We must reduce the stigma attached to the words "mental retardation" by encouraging people to learn about it. Finally, we must find ways to attract citizens who have something to offer retarded persons, not only in the way of job skills but in fun, friendship, and life fulfillment. The following eight programs are steps in that direction—toward true normalization.

## Developmental Maximization Unit

The Developmental Maximization Unit (DMU) serves severely and profoundly retarded persons with complex medical and developmental disorders. Ordinarily, in institutions, such persons would be given custodial care for the rest of their lives. In contrast, within the bright and colorful atmosphere of the DMU, they receive a wide variety of therapies to simulate their auditory, visual, language, motor, and social-adaptive skills. Unless medical considerations forbid it, residents of the DMU attend ENCOR developmental centers or other appropriate facilities in the community during the day. No placement in the DMU is regarded as permanent; in its two years of existence, the DMU has graduated 18 persons to more normal modes of community living.

## Coordinated Early Education Program

The Coordinated Early Education Program (CEEP) is EN-COR's most innovative approach to normalizing the early education of retarded children. CEEP places developmentally delayed children among their age-mates in normal community educational settings in order that by imitation and striving the delayed child may learn the social, self-help, and readiness skills to qualify him for public school. An ENCOR staff teacher is provided for the four to six retarded children in each preschool in order to observe their progress, enrich their daily programs, and refine their individual skills. In its two years of existence, the CEEP program has expanded to involve 56 children.

## Alternative Living Units

The Alternative Living Unit (ALU) concept is a recent innovation established by ENCOR's residential division in order to move more clients into normalizing neighborhood homes. The concept includes any living arrangement for fewer than six clients (children or adults) which is not a group training residence. Programs and services provided in the ALUs are often identical to those provided in a group home; the difference, however, is that services tend to be more individualized and are more normalizing, since the ALU is likely to be perceived as no different from any other home in a neighborhood.

The caregivers, who are simply competent individuals or couples, young or old, who wish to serve retarded persons, are called home teachers. They are trained, are considered professional staff, and are paid a salary. Thus, while the ALU concept bears a close resemblance to that of foster care, it carries none of the charity and welfare connotations of that term.

The beauty of the ALU concept is that it frees the retarded client from the stigma that is often associated with group homes. Too often, group homes develop the character of mini-institutions, particularly if the clients are adults who are not developing the skills to qualify them for more normalizing settings. Hence, neighborhoods will often resist the establishment of a group home and, if it is established, will shun its residents, thus defeating the whole intention of normalization.

The ALU, on the other hand, is easier to establish, since a client placement requires no complex zoning or licensing requirements. Unlike group homes, ALUs require no special architectural environment. The ALU appears more normal, since it conforms to certain norms of living common to our culture, such as family living or that of several adults living together. And finally, ALUs are less expensive, since the home teachers' home, apartment, or condominium entail no extra cost to the service agency.

## Structured Correctional Program

The structured correctional service is really an adaptation of the alternative living unit concept. The difference is that the clients served by this corrections service are mentally retarded persons who have demonstrated unacceptable behavior or have broken the law. This service is heavily staffed with persons experienced in both corrections and mental retardation. The method of rehabilitation, unlike the "treatment" given in prisons, is based on normalization and the belief that the client will, with supervision, work, and behavioral training, have greater opportunity to return to society as a useful citizen.

## Work Stations in Industry

The work station program places retarded persons as trainees in businesses and industries in the community. In the work stations, the clients receive training in specific skills to enable them to work in competitive employment. At present, ENCOR operates work stations in five different community industries: pet product manufacture, hotel housekeeping, urban beautification, hospital dishwashing, and the manufacture of metal furniture components. In contrast to simulated programs, all of these work stations provide reality-oriented training in the real worlds of our communities.

## Citizens Advocacy

The Citizen Advocacy program was established by the Greater Omaha Association for Retarded Citizens for the purpose of establishing relationships between retarded persons and volunteer lay citizens interested in knowing and working with retarded persons. While there are, no doubt, retarded persons who are self-sufficient and well provided with friends, it is perhaps more true that many retarded persons suffer from a lack of interpersonal contacts and experience in the community. To remedy this, GOARC conceived of citizens advocacy as a means of providing retarded persons with emotional enrichment, a friend to teach them skills for more independent living, and aid in their gaining their proper rights as citizens. The initial thrust of citizens advocacy was, however, in the direction of expressive relationships to remedy the loneliness and isolation that often afflicts the retarded person in the community. Since then, GOARC has trained a volunteer corps of instrumental advocates, whose primary purpose is to intercede, on behalf of retarded persons, with landlords, employers, teachers, police, et al. when there is a need.

Such a program gains many advantages at little cost, since the citizen advocates are volunteers. The retarded person gains the emotional enrichment of friendship and an introduction to skills and activities he might otherwise never get. Normalization, which is advantageous to both the retarded person and the community, obviously proceeds much more quickly under the tutelage of a friend. With the guidance of citizen advocates, the mentally retarded become more visible and acceptable members of the community, which is certainly a prerequisite to the necessary changes in public attitudes that will bury forever the stereotype of the retarded as dangerous deviants incapable of learning.

*Pilot Parents*

If the Citizen Advocacy program focuses on mainly the social adjustments of the retarded, the Pilot Parents program aims specifically at helping parents deal with the fact of retardation or other developmental disability in their child. For many parents the discovery that their child, newborn or otherwise, is retarded or developmentally disabled can be a devastating blow. The parents' difficulties at this point are compounded by the counsel of some family doctors to institutionalize the child, despite the existence of excellent community services that would enable the family to keep the child. Thus the need for pilot parents to allay the family's guilty and confused feelings about their child, to inform them about the developmental disabilities and the specific community services designed to help their child, and to introduce them to other persons who share their interests and concerns.

The pilot parents are volunteers but, more importantly, are themselves the parents of a child with a developmental disability, whether mental retardation, cerebral palsy, autism, learning disability, or epilepsy. To a couple with a newborn handicapped child, their voices are more credible and comforting than that of any professional.

## SWEAT (Summer Work Experience and Training Program)

The SWEAT program began in 1966 in a number of states. Its purpose was to recruit students between the ages of 16 to 21 into the field of mental retardation. Since then, with the cut-off of federal funding, most of the programs have ended. The Nebraska program, however, continues and has expanded to include the other developmental disabilities.

For the students in the Nebraska program, SWEAT is a unique combination of lectures, films, tours of institutions and other facilities for the retarded, and work experience in ENCOR facilities. SWEAT students learn of the causes and effects of developmental handicaps, the social and medical approaches to prevention and treatment, and the social and moral issues that surround the question of services for the handicapped. And finally, in actually working with handicapped persons, students gain the personal experience from which to evaluate the field as a career choice.

Approximately 50 percent of graduates of SWEAT have gone on to work in the fields of mental retardation and developmental disabilities. In short, the program has proven its excellence as a means of recruiting committed persons to the field. Beyond this, there is an influence on public attitudes as SWEAT participants educate their parents and fellow college students to a more positive approach to citizens with mental and developmental handicaps.

## NORMALIZATION

The ENCOR system derived its initial momentum from one simple motive: to bring retarded persons out of the abhorrent conditions of the state institutions and provide them with suitable programs in their communities. As noble as this sentiment was and is, it would have been insufficient to motivate the growth of ENCOR's sophisticated services had not new principles been deduced from the concept of normalization and put into practice in innovative programs. In retrospect, one can see that these are not principles that could have been developed in a vacuum or cast in stone tablets in the absence of services. Rather, they are organic principles that grew out of the failures and successes of programs and clients, and they represent the most solid of principles on which to base the human services—that is, high ideals tempered with practical experience.

The most prominent of ENCOR's principles is, of course, normalization—an overarching concept that implies the dignity and worth of retarded persons. Normalization implies the integration of retarded persons into the community, and thus the ideal supplies a means of measuring a program's effectiveness.

It is surprising to consider how unsophisticated was our understanding of normalization in the early days of ENCOR. It was felt, for example, that any alternative to the institution was an improvement, that a new facility location in the community was ipso facto normalizing. In that spirit, it was easy to overlook the extent to which group homes can become mini-institutions; we could fail to see the less restrictive alternative now available within the ALU concept. It was easy to make the error of institutions; to assume that because the clients were mentally retarded, they were not diverse and multifaceted individuals. Thus, ENCOR's initial program offering was lean, and only experience could lead ENCOR to such innovations as the DMU, the Behavior Shaping Unit, Work Stations in Industry, and the Structured Corrections Program. It was necessary, too, to learn to respect a retarded person's desire to be unaffiliated with ENCOR. This is the hard lesson every service agency must learn—that occasionally, its services are not wanted.

In many service agencies there is a great deal of futile discussion of goals and objectives. In ENCOR, however, this clarification process has greatly accelerated the process of streamlining its services and approximating more closely its major goal of normalization for retarded citizens. Instead of "serving retarded persons," the initial goal, ENCOR's purpose became "moving retarded persons to more normal settings." From this clarification of purpose came a number of changes. The CEEP program and work stations were inaugurated, for it was recognized that these forms of training and education for retarded persons could be accomplished more effectively, with no great administrative difficulty, in the less restrictive, more normal community settings of preschool and industry. Thus, existing community facilities could be used. Certain programs and facilities, such as the Behavior Shaping Unit, were phased out, for it was now recognized that they were failing in the purpose of moving retarded persons to more normal settings, and were being perceived as mini-institutions.

In short, the criterion for judging the adequacy of programs became more clear; no longer was it the vague standard of "service," but the more dynamic and easily recognizable one of "movement."

## Alternate Living Units

By way of summarizing the dominant principles that motivate the growth and improvement of ENCOR's services,
one should consider the alternative living unit concept. For
this program, the alternative to group homes, any client
who cannot live with his natural parents or cannot live
independently is immediately qualified. An alternative living unit is obviously superior to a group home; the ALU is
less restrictive; it is more individualized, since it conforms
to a small family setting; the setting appears more normal
and hence is more likely to result in the retarded client's
integration into that neighborhood; and because of its
name and its form, the ALU is more immune to labels such
as "group home," "institution," "reformatory," or "foster
home," all of which tend to connote charity, welfare, and
nonvalued individuals. Finally, natural parents, when possible, are closely involved in the training given their son or
daughter; contracts between ENCOR and the parents specify that, when certain behavior training and education conditions are achieved, the parents will resume their
responsibility. Thus is the criterion for "movement to more
normal settings" fulfilled.

The ALU concept is, of course, much more difficult to
administer than a group home, and this brings to mind a
final point. In the past it was necessary for clients to "qualify" to live in a less restrictive setting by having certain
necessary skills. Thus if a client failed to develop, one could
blame the client. Under the new ALU system, the client's
movement is the staff's responsibility. If a given client is
autistic, acting-out, or not toilet trained, it is the ENCOR
staff's responsibility to find a person willing to be that
client's home teacher.

While one must recognize that teachers and caregivers
are human and that there may be insoluble difficulties, the
idea is a vital and necessary innovation. For too long we

have blamed retarded persons for not letting us help them develop, when the real problem is our lack of skill and creativity. "Don't ride the client's back," is the injunction of one ENCOR administrator, and this is an entirely appropriate reminder of our own responsibilities.

## Conclusion

Normalization is a noble ideal for retarded persons, and, as certain ENCOR programs demonstrate, a guide to what is practical and possible. What is necessary is further innovation in services, and program evaluation and self-criticism to remind us of our purpose: to move retarded persons to the normal life of work, community, and personal fulfillment that is the right of us all.

*Chapter 11*

# DE-INSTITUTIONALIZATION

The many issues and trends which currently surround the large public institutions for the retarded have been discussed in other sections of this book. A major trend of decreasing the population of retarded citizens in institutions has become even more focused in the recent past, and has generated a distinct new federal program. This program is seeking to develop planning strategies to reduce by one-third the number of mentally retarded citizens in public institutions by 1980. This new federal program has been referred to as the "de-institutionalization program," and the challenges it faces will be reviewed in this section.

In an address now called "the de-institutionalization statement," President Richard Nixon announced on November 16, 1971, that "The cruel bane of mental retardation can be sharply reduced." He pledged his support for two major goals: to reduce by one-half the occurrence of mental retardation; and, more pertinent to our purposes here, to enable one-third of the more than 200,000 retarded persons in public institutions to return to useful lives in the community.

In the four years since President Nixon's "de-institutionalization statement," a number of factors have added momentum to the moral imperative of de-institutionalization. Action in the courts on behalf of retarded persons has come closer to the inevitable recognition of the retarded person's right to treatment (instead of the traditional institutional inactivity) in a milieu which offers the fewest necessary restrictions. Although the courts have not fully recognized the impact of their recent decisions, these concepts have accelerated institutional reform and bolstered the growth of community-based service systems as an alternative to the institutions.

Presently, there is little professional doubt that mildly and moderately retarded individuals can profit from the life of work, home, and community that community-based services offer. But even more, it is becoming clear that community-based programs can provide effective and normalizing services for even the severely retarded-multiply handicapped now in the institutions. This is the practical proof: a number of the community-based systems now existing have indeed provided for all types of mentally retarded persons the milieu of growth, learning, and societal membership that is rightfully theirs.

A review of the costs of institutions likewise favors de-institutionalization, although, lest one be too sanguine, one should be aware of the vested interests implied by the following figures:

> Public institutional care is a major industry. A recent evaluation of 76 of the current facilities for the retarded noted that their program expenses were $709,481,000, and their total assets were valued at $1,001,827,000. Since these figures represent only one-third of such facilities, the projections for the

staffing, expenditures, and assets of all public institutions would be three times as high.

The economic and technical problems of converting from an institutional to a community mode of serving the mentally retarded would equal in magnitude the shifting the elements of one major industry (for example, the railroads) to another major industry (for example, the airlines).

The present per diem cost of institutional care for the mentally retarded ranges from $11.46 to $79.29 per resident per day with a median of $26.02. Thus, annual costs are between $4,200 and $16,000 per resident, with a median of $10,200.

Construction is reported to cost up to $50,000 per bed at the present time. Over the past twenty years, there has been marked inflation in the costs of construction and operation of public institutions; in today's wildly inflationary economy, this trend will no doubt worsen.

All of these figures raise serious questions about the feasibility of supporting the present number of public institutions, especially when these high costs do not prevent conditions of great neglect. In this regard it is worth noting that Willowbrook, the scandal of public institutions, charges $72.00 per day, per resident.

There are a number of community-based systems for the mentally retarded across the country which focus on providing contemporary services within the framework of normalization, the developmental model, and a backdrop of modern financial approaches to providing comprehensive services. One example of such a community-based system is the Eastern Nebraska Community Office of Retardation (ENCOR). It is equipped to provide whatever services are necessary to a retarded person from his birth to his death, and thus can serve as a prototype alternative to institutions. For this reason, I will refer to ENCOR's costs in comparison to the traditional institution. Both logic and certain rules built into ENCOR's charter make it likely that the ENCOR system will be more economical than the institution. ENCOR does not build; it rents, leases, and occasionally buys existing facilities—a policy that obviates the need for huge capital construction budgets. The principle of using generic community services is paramount to ENCOR's ideology; thus, much of ENCOR's energy is used to procure for retarded persons the services deemed normal by the general populace (family care and living, the use of public schools, community physicians, public transportation, etc.). Only where retarded persons are excluded from "normal" services does ENCOR serve them directly. The savings entailed by the use of generic services should be obvious: In this way, ENCOR *saves the cost* of school buildings, teachers, staff doctors, psychiatrists, and so on. In the fiscal year 1973–1974, ENCOR's budget was $3,375,460; with this budget the agency served 1,242 unduplicated individuals, for an average cost of $3,009 per client, which is less than one-third of the median cost of institutional care. These 1,242 individuals have the same variety of levels of retardation, complexity of associated handicaps, and allied treatment challenges as one could find in a randomly selected group of retarded citizens in an institution. That is, the number of individuals who are severely retarded or multiply handicapped, who have seizures or behavioral problems is *not* significantly different from an institutionalized group of retarded citizens!

## BARRIERS TO DE-INSTITUTIONALIZATION

De-institutionalization depends on the achievement of three interrelated processes:

1. The prevention of admissions to institutions through the development and utilization of alternative methods of care
2. The return to community life of all residents who have been prepared and trained for this adjustment
3. The establishment and maintenance of a responsive residential environment which protects the human and civil rights of the mentally retarded.

Until the present time, the lack of community service systems which could offer alternative services to retarded persons was the general justification for the high rate of institutionalization in this country. In Britain, for example, the rate of institutional bed utilization for children is 22 per 100,000 population, compared to 30 per 100,000 in the United States. The reason for the difference is the provision of day-care and work centers for the severely retarded in British communities. It is generally agreed that the first step in limiting institutional costs is limiting the rate of bed use to appropriate cases only, thereby preventing new unnecessary admissions. The second step is developing community alternatives which will serve persons previously viewed as candidates who could live in public communities if quality services were more generally available (128).

There are, however, a number of barriers to de-institutionalization. Even if institutions comply with changes that will diminish their size and importance, two important early reforms are clearly needed: 1) adequate retraining and habilitation programs to prepare retarded persons for community life, and 2) comprehensive community-based service systems. Adequate solution to these problems on the state and local levels will determine the success or the foundering of the de-institutionalization challenge.

De-institutionalization has engendered the strong opposition of organized institutional employees to the process, (129) which threatens to cut institutional budgets and employee rolls. To overcome this barrier, it will be necessary to devise meaningful employment alternatives through re-training and subsequent high priority for re-location of these employees.

There is an obvious need for renovation and repairs in many public institutions. Community programs to benefit retarded persons must not overlook the necessity of rendering institutional conditions consonant with health and safety standards. Nevertheless, budgetary limits in the inflationary 1970's demand that national, state, and local authorities clarify their goals for all developmentally handicapped persons and that they make clear cost-effective and care-effective choices in their commitment of funds. Whether it makes sense to invest in major institutional renovation should be decided on grounds that clearly define the kinds of services needed.

The Joint Commission on Accreditation of Hospitals/Accreditation Committee on Facilities for the Mentally Retarded report of March 1975 (130) demonstrated the custodial nature of most institutions by approving accreditation for only 22 of the 88 institutions surveyed. One may doubt seriously the capacity of non-accredited institutions to prepare retarded individuals for the return to community life. Since the traditional institutional emphasis is on custodial care and administration, the staff at institutions need additional training in vocational, motor, and language habilitation techniques. While the present deficiencies may be due to institutional understaffing and consequent lack of time for individual programming, it is evident that future habilitation programs in the institutions must receive high priority in de-institutionalization. The upgrading of staff skills is a necessary element of that process.

It is unlikely that community-based facilities are currently sufficiently developed or widespread to accept the many candidates for community living identified by superintendents of institutions. Nationally, not many comprehensive community-based systems are ready for a substantial number of de-institutionalized clients, although there are many community programs in the developing stage with many excellent program components.

Zoning restrictions may present a serious stumbling block to creating normalizing and appropriately located group homes for retarded persons in the rapidly evolving community-based systems. The education of fire and safety officials in the modern concepts of residential care is long overdue.

Approximately 30 - 35 percent of mentally retarded persons have emotional problems that require mental health services (131). Community mental health services are often closed to the retarded; private psychiatry services tend to be prohibitive in cost, and too often the retarded person with emotional problems is merely referred back to the institution. Recent federal legislation has mandated services for these individuals through Community Mental Health Center guidelines.

Parents of institutionalized persons frequently resist the return of their offspring to the community and evidence an overconcern for their safety with an unrealistically low appraisal of their abilities.

A most difficult barrier is the lack of administrative or legal linkages between the institutional and community service system. This lack impedes the free flow of persons between facilities, fosters competition and dissension between the two systems, and prevents the kind of cooperative planning that is at the core of the de-institutionalization process.

Of all these obstacles to de-institutionalization, the major current problem is the lack of administrative linkages between the two systems of institutional and community-based services. The result has been the growth of wide differences between two systems which ought to complement, not compete with, each other. Institutions cling to the view of retarded persons as helpless and unable to learn, a prophecy which becomes self-fulfilling in the custodial atmosphere of most institutions. Community-based programs may, at times, be guilty of excessive optimism, and yet, it has been just this idealistic spirit which has led "hopeless" retarded persons to gain skills that no one else had thought possible!

There is a similar gap in the staff skills in the two systems; in one, skills stagnate because custodial care does not stimulate on-the-job learning, while in the other, the fluid nature and unpredictable demands of community life can foster staff skills one would have no right to expect.

Finally, in the situation of funding, the political power and vested interests of the institution usually win the largest part of the available monies. Despite the demonstrable cost-benefit of community-based services, the hope that they represent to many families and retarded persons, and the dignified comprehensive solution to the problem of mental retardation that community services offer to our society, this alternative to institutions is often ignored or underfunded. One may hope that the federal mandate of deinstitutionalization may compel the kind of cooperation required for the policy to succeed.

## Facilitating Factors

Despite the obstacles to de-institutionalization, the legislative means for implementing the program are many. Since the passage in 1963 of Public Law 88–156 (which authorized grants for comprehensive state planning in mental retardation) and Public Law 88–164 (which authorized federal funding for construction of facilities for the mentally retarded with the sponsorship of a voluntary or public organization), there have come into law many federal legislative bills whose funding may be applied to the process of de-institutionalization. These legislative supports include:

> Title XX of the Social Security Act authorizes the states to utilize such funds to provide services to retarded persons in institutions.
>
> The Medicaid program provides an intermediate care facilities component under which $500 million are available nationwide for services to retarded persons.
>
> Under the Supplemental Security Income program, institutionalized persons may qualify for vocational rehabilitation services.
>
> The Elementary and Secondary Education Act (Public Law 89–313, later amended by Public Law 88–330) provides funds for the education of children in institutions. These funds are transferable to the local school agency when the retarded or handicapped child returns to a community residence.
>
> The Hill-Burton Act provides funds for the construction of medical surgical facilities on the grounds of institutions.
>
> The Hospital Inservice Training Program (in Section 303 of the Public Health Service Act) provides funds for training institutional personnel. The Hospital

Improvement Project of the same act funds demonstration service programs in institutions.

The Foster Grandparent Program (administered by ACTION under Section III of the Domestic Volunteer Services Act of 1973, Public Law 93–113) pays low-income elderly persons for part-time work in institutions as companions to the residents.

The Vocational Rehabilitation Act (Public Law 93–112) provides for the counseling and training of institutionalized persons. The 1973 amendment removes the one-year limitation previously placed on follow-up for persons who need additional ongoing support.

The Developmental Disabilities Program provides funds for the planning and demonstration of service to persons who are developmentally disabled, and includes a special project authority for planning funds to assist in the integration of institutional services with larger service systems. This program is a focus for the coordination of de-institutionalization and the establishment of community-based services for those who have developmental disabilities.

The Fair Labor Standards Act assures minimum wages for those institutional residents who work. This act has been more actively implemented in light of the recent court decisions on the peonage issue.

### SUMMARY

In summary, then, there are factors that work for and against the success of de-institutionalization. The primary positive factor is the federal government's advocacy of that policy, and the many pieces of legislation that can be used to fund it.

However, in order to implement de-institutionalization fully, some first steps in creating ideological agreement and service cooperation between institution and
community-based systems must be initiated. For example,
both systems could agree on the ideological wisdom and
the service possibilities flowing from the concept of normalization. Both could agree on standards in evaluating
client potential and performance, program content, and
staff quality. At present, there are wide disparities between
the two systems on these issues, and the very real possibility
exists that the retarded client will be stuck between an
institution that is too protective, too custodial, and too
unstimulating, and a community-based program that is too
open, unstructured, and threatening. Thus, it appears that
we are presently in a transitional state—between the traditional models of care and custodial philosophies of the
past, and the burgeoning philosophical bases and service
components of the community-based approach. The latter
approach *is* consistent with the increasing legal precedents
to provide a meaningful right to treatment for retarded
citizens. The aftermath of these federal court decisions has
produced much "gnashing of teeth" among state government and institutional personnel alike. The due process
findings of the legal decisions have clearly documented the
need to provide treatment modalities, thus acting as a spur
to the states to try even harder to deliver services. I would
stress that many of the states *have* committed themselves to
actually meeting this set of unmet needs. The issue really
becomes one of *further* accomplishments over a specific
timetable of implementation. In other words, the legislatures must try harder, the organized advocate movement
must work more diligently (both to provide and then monitor the extended or new services), and societal interest
must remain high via specific public information strategies.
In brief, we are at a time in the historical evolution of
providing services to the retarded when the reality-based

challenges of actually providing normalized services for the retarded citizens can give them the equal rights and opportunities to which they are entitled. Since the mentally retarded as a group have for so long been deemed unequal by our negative attitudes, our overriding concern must be the re-affirmation of their rights to as full a life as possible. Though it will be difficult to implement this societal ideal, it can be done if we trust and work together to spur local-state-federal political groups to be more creative in seeking alternatives in delivery of effective human services.

## COMMUNITY-BASED SERVICES AND THE PERSONS TO BE SERVED

A major section of this book has been devoted to describing a viable and successful alternative to the institution: community-based services. As previously indicated, a noteworthy feature of the ENCOR system is its comprehensiveness: the system can provide services in a normalizing setting for persons with all levels of retardation and handicaps. The community setting for these services provides convincing proof, as well, that retarded persons are varied individuals and do not uniformly fit the pejorative stereotypes of the retarded as "sick," "dangerous," "unable to learn," "hopeless," or "helpless" that have historically provided the rationale for excluding them from society. This is, I think, an important point, for only through real contact with retarded persons—contact that community-based programs provide—will the public recognize them as individuals capable of growth.

The experience of community-based services has proven the fallacy of the many myths regarding the mentally retarded and services for them. The following myths were, and continue to be, the justification for institutions: (1) the retarded are hopeless, unable to learn, dangerous, etc.; (2) the retarded cannot be rehabilitated to work and live in community settings; (3) more than custodial care is exorbitantly expensive; and (4) institutions will always be necessary.

It is important to remember that community-based services are an evolving and dynamic system, not a structure that is built overnight, or that suddenly appears by magic or administrative fiat. The ENCOR system began with little more than one child development center, one group home, and one sheltered workshop. From this modest beginning has grown a system which offers components as specialized as their names connote: "Developmental Maximization Unit," "Behavior Shaping Unit," and "Structured Correctional Unit." In short, this particular system has grown to the point where it can serve persons it was not expected to serve. The same or similar systems can, I believe, serve those severely handicapped individuals now in institutions.

Among those mentally retarded persons still institutionalized are three classes of individuals whose handicaps and personality characteristics may present problems to the community-based service system: the severely physically handicapped, the emotionally disturbed, and the mentally retarded offender. I stress the word "may," for it is indeed possible to serve these persons in a community setting, as the ENCOR system has done. There is a belief now current that these three classes of persons are the "worst," the "most difficult" cases, and that they comprise the majority of the present institutionalized population. This notion is a myth, used frequently to justify the existence of institutions and impugn the capacity of community systems to serve all retarded persons. Community systems such as ENCOR serve and have served a retarded population with a severity and frequency of these handicaps comparable to an institution. While the numbers of such "hard-to-serve" persons in institutions have been exaggerated, it is nevertheless true that community-based systems should begin to conceptualize services to aid these individuals.

The first group are persons afflicted by cerebral palsy or epilepsy, or who are so severely afflicted physically as to make their mental retardation secondary and their physical limitations the primary issue. Often the complexities of their problems prompt professionals to refer them elsewhere since the broad-gauged treatment program is difficult to conceptualize and implement. It is my impression that the medical symptoms present in these persons tend to be secondary to non-progressive bodily disorders, and hence can be treated effectively the first time around. Focus must then shift to the developmental skills and physical development, which change and thus need the most professional interest and largest investments of time and personnel.

The secondary category of "hard-to-serve" persons are those with severe emotional problems. Psychiatrists and psychologists have long argued about which is the more important of such an individual's twin handicaps—his mental retardation or his emotional disturbance. For the community-based professional, it makes very little difference; he is confronted with an individual whose behavior is difficult to adjust to the norms of community life and even to those more tolerant parameters of service programs. In short, it is the person's *behavior,* regardless of causes, which must be adjusted in the direction of the social norm.

The same attitude should guide a service system's approach to the third category, the mentally retarded offender, discussed in Chapter 5. There is a real lack of services for these neglected individuals. Correctional institutions fail the mentally retarded offender completely in his rehabilitation for even if they offer work and academic rehabilitation skills, correctional facilities seldom provide the meaningfully structured setting and interpersonal context that the retarded offender needs. The retarded offender, who has usually committed rather minor crimes, may do well in prison. But his problem is coping in society with a very limited repertoire of social skills. Once out of prison, he has the same problem and the same paucity of skills in dealing with it.

Serving the physically handicapped person in the community setting is difficult only in the organizational sense: one must choose the proper setting, prosthetic devices, therapists and trainers to maximize that person's development. As in the case of clients in ENCOR's Developmental Maximization Unit, a physically handicapped person may begin receiving such services in a hospital setting, and move to a more normal living environment as his skills enlarge and the need for medical intervention decreases. The value of the developmental physical therapy is beyond dispute, and a client's progress in an intensive program is indeed dramatic.

With the emotionally disturbed retarded person and the retarded offender, there are no infallible methods or therapies. Nevertheless certain behavioral characteristics of these two classes of individuals suggest approaches to treating them. In both, one often sees evidence of 'affect hunger': the lack of meaningful relationships through which affection and trust can develop. In the emotionally disturbed person, this is often the result of institutional living from his early years; in the retarded offender, who is usually only mildly retarded, "affect hunger" stems from the frequently unstable, disorganized and loveless home life in which he was raised. Hence both the disturbed retarded person and the retarded offender share an inability to trust, and relate to, other persons; inappropriate behaviors; and environments in which normal behavior is seldom rewarded. These deficits suggest certain necessary elements in treatment approaches: a structured setting that permits close and stable interpersonal relationships; a behavior modification program to eliminate inappropriate behaviors and program in new behaviors (i.e., education); supervision that will permit the individual to enjoy the opportunities of community life and yet support him and protect him from failure.

Serving these three groups of persons in a community-based system, while observing the guidelines of normalization and least restrictive settings, will not be an easy task. The remedy to the narrow, isolating life of the institution is the community, but the shape of the services that can simultaneously meet their needs and normalize their behavior is not so obvious. Severely handicapped persons with medical problems must be served in a context that gives them ready access to both special services and the general ambience of community life. The emotionally disturbed retarded person and the potential offender must be sheltered and supervised in order to protect community rights, and yet must not be prevented from participating in those enriching activities and contacts with people which are the major key to their rehabilitation.

The problem here may be somewhat illusory: the needed services that can balance on such a tightrope may elude definition, but they are indeed possible if they remain fluid, dynamic, and responsive to their clients' needs and the ideal of normalization. ENCOR's Developmental Maximization Unit, described earlier, is a good example. Though the DMU is located in a hospital wing in order to provide medical supervision for its clients, the atmosphere is more like home than hospital, and its clients partake of education and recreation in the community. The crucial point here is that services to retarded persons must be conceptualized with their integration into normal community patterns in mind. Developmental centers are now being diverted into two areas, public schools and community day care centers, since there is no reason why handicapped and non-handicapped children cannot be educated side by side. Again, the important point is to refuse to let services be bound by the traditional, narrow definitions of them.

Perhaps the most important concept for preparing services for de-institutionalization is the "Alternative Living Unit." Under this neutral residential rubric are served all retarded persons, regardless of handicap, who can live neither with parents nor independently. Staff persons are matched with 1 to 3 clients according to the latter's needs; the extent of supervision, the need for behavior modification, as well as the particulars of the clients' work and recreation are decided on the basis of the individual's program plan. ENCOR has used Alternative Living Units for behavior shaping of disturbed individuals, rehabilitation of retarded offenders and as a normal stage of a client's growth toward independent living. Thus, a primary advantage of the ALU concept is that it permits adjustment of the mode of support to the needs of any individual, and that it appears more normal, thus freeing the client from the stigma often attached to him by a group home. Although the DMU and group home concept are subsumed under this term, the ALU concept is, in its most useful and flexible form, a highly individualized way of serving retarded persons who live in the community.

## PREPARING THE RETARDED CITIZEN, THE PROGRAM, AND THE PUBLIC

When the retarded person actually returns to the community, it is vitally important to his success that three areas have been well prepared: the client himself, the service program, and the public mind. In the past, much of this preparation has been inadequate, and the result has often been the prompt return of the client to the institution. But this need not be. An excellent system of de-institutionalization components will be sensitive to the particular citizen's needs and will provide the service components necessary to facilitate his return to community life.

## Preparation of the Retarded Person

The retarded citizen's preparation for community life must encompass the fundamental activities of developing a series of self-help skills, motor and communication faculties, and usable vocational skills—preparatory considerations which should be a part of his daily institutional programming. For those preparing for community life, these programs would be accelerated. But beyond these basic habilitation and readiness programs, an abundance of measures could be taken to facilitate their adjustment to the new milieu of community life. Consider the many aspects of community life from which the institutionalized person may have been excluded: the integration of the sexes in work and recreational activity; education in areas of sex, behavior, and socially acceptable uses of alcohol; firm expectations on the appropriateness of his behavior in a variety of settings; contemporary notions of fashion and grooming, and so on. Classes should be given in the institution on those many aspects of personal behavior on which the institutionalized individual will be judged in community life.

Or consider other skills he may have failed to develop in the sheltered environment of the institution: care for his money, and responsible and meaningful ways of spending it; meaningful use of his leisure time; appropriate ways of dealing with unfamiliar persons and situations; the ability to shop for food and then to prepare it; the ability to cross the street in busy traffic. In short, the retarded person's return to community life will necessitate many training challenges which will have to be rehearsed prior to his return.

As much as possible, the individual's self-image ought to be improved and his sense of self amplified, for this is probably his most basic and valuable resource in dealing with the competition, the expectations, and the learning challenges of community life. He should be provided with personal clothes, personal belongings, and a private place he can call his own and learn to care for. The lack of privacy and the communal "ownership" of clothing, facilities, toys, tools, books, and space—long the hallmarks of institutional care—discourage the development of self and individual distinctiveness that is the root of learning. Yet, on the grounds of many institutions, there are buildings and structures that could be used to provide private rooms for persons prior to their returning to the community. A citizen advocate (a volunteer friend) and community-based services counselor should meet the individual on a regular basis while his de-institutionalization training is going on. Similarly, ties to his family and relatives should be discovered and encouraged to grow.

While it is unlikely that the institution will succeed in perfectly simulating the challenges of community life, frequent weekend sojourns to the community will provide opportunities to test the work, living, and recreational possibilities to which retarded individuals aspire. "Testing the waters" will probably set their fears to rest and greatly motivate their preparation for leaving the institution. Finally, it will give their teachers and other helpers a chance to observe their behavior and note weak and strong points that may not show up in the control situation of the institution.

## Preparation of the Program

The community-based program's readiness for de-institutionalization is, of course, vital to that policy's success. Were the service system not ready to provide its clients with

full support, it would be better to postpone de-institutionalization until a viable structure of services is ready to accept clients. If clients "fail" in community life and are
re-institutionalized because of inadequate services, it is
likely that their chances for a second return to community
life would be considerably diminished.

To demand that all community-based systems of services achieve an advanced state of readiness prior to initiating an active de-institutionalization thrust is to deny these
systems the opportunity to grow and change according to
individual needs and local conditions. A full blown system
with all its rigidities and pre-conceptions is not necessary.
But the following features are minimally necessary:

1.   Each retarded person returning to community
life should have a counselor. The counselor's responsibility
is to be the primary advocate for his client, and since he
theoretically will know the client better than any other service giver, he should insist on appropriate services.

2.   The provision of age-appropriate training and
education services for returning individuals is an obvious
necessity. In addition to developmental centers and vocational centers, serious thought must be given to insuring
that the individual will move from these "special" (not
normal) settings to the more integrated and normalizing
settings of community life (e.g., public schools, integrated
early education, work stations in industry, independent
work).

3.   Small group homes are a necessary first step for
de-institutionalized retarded persons. No individual returning from the institutional life should be permitted to
live independently until the service agency (the counselor)
has assessed that person's abilities, needs, and aptitude for
independent living. Indeed, I strongly feel that the de-
institutionalized retarded citizen is routinely in need of a
community setting in which he can be "decompressed"

from the overly restrictive setting where he has spent many of his formative years. This residential setting also permits close observation so that the counselor and service staff can more fully understand the retarded citizen in totality. A group home should be small enough (no more than six clients) to avoid being perceived as a mini-institution. Although group homes are sufficient residential provision to begin de-institutionalization, preliminary planning at the time of entry in the community-based system should at the least identify the agency's goal of providing a continuum of less structured and more normal modes of living.

The above is a minimum outline of services necessary to implement de-institutionalization with some hope for success. But planning for more specialized services must go on, lest an emergency catch the service system unaware. ENCOR, it should be remembered, found it necessary to "invent" the Developmental Maximization Unit, the Behavior Shaping Unit, and the Structured Correctional Program in order to serve the very real problems which a small proportion of the mentally retarded population present: medical complexities, emotional disorders, and asocial behavior. A community-based system that intends to be a true and comprehensive alternative to institutions must consider the possible need for these and other services and actively plan for them.

### Preparation of the Public

A recent public service announcement succinctly conveyed the third necessity of de-institutionalization: preparing the public. A young man, retarded, tells of his life in the community and his work; he ends by saying, "My biggest problem is your attitude." If compassion, understanding, and patience were a common public attitude toward retarded persons, the normalization that community-based programs promise would be a reality, not a goal. Institutions are in many ways proof that public attitudes tend instead to be fearful, hostile, or ignorant. Thus a continuing public education program should be considered, not as frill and luxury, but as a necessary part of the de-institutionalization process. Retarded persons in community life need tolerance and support, and it should not be blithely assumed that they will get it.

Radio, newspaper, and television are the most effective means of reaching the general public, first with news stories about individual retarded citizens with human adjustment challenges and about de-institutionalization and the available alternative systems, secondly with information about mental retardation. There is evidence that the media is eager for interesting and informative material to use in a broad number of formats - radio spots, interviews, and human interest articles. The service program that satisfies the media's needs can further its own ends of educating the public. For this reason, a public information specialist with media contacts is a small investment in obtaining what no service programs can give the retarded person: supportive community attitudes.

Similarly, various professional groups—teachers, doctors, lawyers, and judges—often have contact with retarded persons, and have a definite influence on public attitudinal change. The police should be given a short course on mental retardation and urged to be tolerant of "deviant" but harmless behavior. Fire and safety officials should be instructed in the modern concepts in residential care. Students in professional programs of psychology, social work, and nursing should incorporate mental retardation into their respective specialities. Architects and builders should be impressed with the importance of barrier-free environments. Factory owners and industrial supervisors should be made aware of the advantages retarded persons can offer as employees at small cost of convenience.

The purpose of such a public information campaign (which is continuing, not merely preliminary) is twofold. One goal is to act quickly to counter the various stereotypes of retarded persons by an accurate portrayal of their capabilities, limitations, and problems. Most people, one must remember, have had little experience with retarded persons, and hence are likely to perceive the mentally retarded clothed in stereotypes they learned in their early years. One must believe that a little knowledge and an accurate portrayal of retardation will go a long way. Secondly, the professional groups mentioned do have contact with the retarded in their roles as teachers, doctors, and police, and their attitudes will have important consequences on their actions toward the retarded. Aside from their direct contacts with retarded persons, their professional voices will do much to create supportive, or at least non-hostile attitudes which retarded persons need in their adjustment to community life.

## DISQUIETING VOICES ON DE-INSTITUTIONALIZATION

### Employees

As de-institutionalization becomes less a futuristic slogan and more a policy resulting in real reductions in the institutional population, a strong opposition has emerged. Much of the motive for this resistance is economic, for as retarded persons leave the institutions, there is less reason for the large budgets and employment rolls that institutions usually command. One would hope that this problem would be amicably resolved; alternative employment should be offered where possible. It is likely that many institutional personnel would be hired in community-based systems. While the anxieties of institutional personnel are understandable, it is clear that the civil and human rights of retarded persons are at stake here, and such narrow interests should not be used to abridge those rights.

More dangerous are the "scare stories" being circulated by opponents of de-institutionalization in order to discredit the idea of normalization and community-based service systems. A publication of the American Federation of State, County, and Municipal Employees, *Out of Their Beds and Into the Streets,* for example, paints de-institutionalization as a policy of neglect and abandonment, as well as a source of enrichment of the private nursing home and halfway house industry. The author, Henry Santiestevan, tends to avoid mentioning the existence of community-based service systems that can offer as much protection and support as their clients require (132).

## Researchers

A not so distant cousin to the opposition of the unions is that of academic researchers in the field, whose subjects for research have almost always been the residents of institutions for the mentally retarded. In the past and even the present, researchers have had relatively unfettered access to "subjects." Parents of institutionalized residents have only infrequently opposed their childrens' use as subjects for research. In the case of residents without parents, wards of the state, it has usually been a simple matter to obtain the permission of the superintendent of the institution, who is that person's guardian. The retarded person himself, the "subject," has had no say in the matter.

Some of this research, of course, has been very helpful, particularly in the areas of learning and in the delineation of causes and syndromes of mental retardation. But this does not justify the dubious ethics of performing research on persons who have not given their consent. Some researchers justify this violation of retarded persons on grounds of the compelling need for such research, which has indeed led to breakthroughs in treatment and prevention. In the case of those severely retarded persons who may be able to neither understand the experiment nor give their consent, such a violation may be justified if the need is compelling, and the tests or conditions to which they must submit are not extraordinary. But some research done recently can hardly be so justified. Experiments involving painful aversion therapies have been numerous. Retarded persons have been injected with viral hepatitis to test the effects of certain drugs on their kidney functions. Indeed the harmful effects of many psychotropic drugs have long been tested on retarded persons. That this sort of experimentation is repellent is proven by the protest against such research performed on willing inmates in prisons. Is it not even worse to use persons who do not have the right to say "no"? It is a short step from such practices to wholesale experimentation justified on "larger grounds" that ignore the value and rights of that particular person.

De-institutionalization and the recognition of the legal rights of retarded persons thus will deprive researchers of captive subjects, and that, I think, is all to the good. Research will not stop; its exponents will simply have to recognize the humanity of the potential subject, that is, his right to refuse, or be protected from, experiments that may be harmful, painful, or dangerous to him. Progress in treatment and prevention of mental retardation depends, to a great extent, on research. Nevertheless, that end does not permit the use of means that deny the central idea that motivates advocacy for the mentally retarded: the human rights and dignity of retarded persons.

## Parents

As de-institutionalization progresses in various regions from plan to process, another opposing voice has been raised, that of advocacy groups whose members are parents of institutionalized persons. Although these rather small parental groups claim to support good community programs as well as institutional programs, their primary purpose seems to be to maintain the principle of parents' right to decide what constitutes appropriate care for their retarded children (whatever their ages). A basic premise of de-institutionalization is the superiority of the community setting to the institution in providing the stimuli and opportunities for growth, learning, and fulfillment. Hence it is mandated that those institutionalized persons who can be cared for in the community setting be placed in community-based programs. At this point, the parents of a retarded adult may oppose his leaving the shelter of the institution. The parents may feel that the community-based services are inadequate and the institutional care excellent. Or, as I have seen frequently, the parents develop an intense loyalty to the institution, regardless of the quality of its services. Parents of a retarded person also tend to underestimate their offspring's abilities and learning potential; hence they may oppose his placement in programs and settings that will demand more of him.

Thus these same parents, for the several reasons cited above, are strongly opposed to de-institutionalization, believing that their wishes for their children are being disregarded and their presumed rights as parents being erased. For these reasons, many of them have organized with groups to provide a voice against the current national de-institutionalization thrust. An example of such a group is the Mental Retardation Association of America (MRAA), a recently formed organization whose members are parents of institutionalized retarded citizens. In a fair statement of the MRAA's position, its Utah component expressed its editorial disagreement with the recent (1975) Federal Court Consent Decree that sets a new timetable of de-institutionalization in motion in Nebraska:

In this court case, which was lost by the Beatrice State Home, parents' rights were stripped throughout the agreement to where they have no right to make any decision regarding their child. Thus the person who may care the most about the mentally retarded family member is to be silenced (133).

The MRAA's philosophy is based on the premise that a parent's rights are absolute, and this, I believe, is a false premise. All rights, in fact, assume a balance between one person's freedom to act in a certain way and another person's need to be protected from harm that might arise from the wrongful expression of that freedom. I have freedom of speech, but as in Justice Holmes' famous example, I do not have the right to shout "Fire!" in a crowded theatre. In the same sense, a parent does not have absolute rights over his child; child labor laws, mandatory education, and child protection laws are effective and necessary abridgements of the parent's rights. Although it is usually assumed that the parents will act in the best interests of the child, the parents' rights are legally subordinate to the consideration of the child's welfare.

The parents' right, or lack of right, to keep their retarded child or adult retarded person institutionalized has not yet received appropriate legal review. But I believe that the courts will eventually decide, for several reasons, against the parents' "right" to keep their child (or adult) institutionalized, and will recognize that the retarded person's right to treatment (in the least restrictive setting possible) is the paramount consideration. First, the repeated abuses of institutional life have been clearly documented in benchmark Federal Court legal decisions in Alabama, New York, Minnesota, etc., and the inferiority of institutions to the community setting is implied in the current de-institutionalization policy that is mandated by federal policy. Second, the supremacy of the child's welfare to the parents' right to decide on his behalf, has solid legal precedent (note the recent Juvenile Court decisions concerning sterilization of adolescents), and necessarily extends to adults. Third, in the area of mental health, persons who are committed to state hospitals for mental disorders are shifted to less restrictive community settings when that is deemed proper treatment *without reference to the person who has taken the legal responsibility for the commitment;* since state officials are the treators, *they* decide what is proper treatment. One may draw the reasonable inference that, since "institutional care" is presumably treatment, the treators of mental retardation may similarly decide, free from parental influence, on what is proper treatment for that person.

## Competence and Individual Rights

The issues of parents' rights raised by de-institutionalization brings to the fore another question not yet settled by the courts: the legal competence of mentally retarded adults. Among the general public, an adult is assumed to be legally competent unless proven incompetent. With mentally retarded persons, the same assumption should be operative. A good community-based system should, in effecting normalization, treating its clients as competent and should insist that the community do likewise, excepting only those persons who have court appointed guardians and those declared incompetent in a court of law. With retarded persons who are institutionalized, however, the assumption is often the reverse. This denial of the retarded person's right shows up clearly in instances where the institutionalized resident has shown a competence or desire to move to a less restrictive setting, but is opposed by his parents. In few such cases does the institution oppose the parents, but rather assumes that the parents have the right to decide the fate of an adult who may indeed have the capacity for more independent living arrangements and opportunities. There are, in fact, many such persons in the ENCOR system who, despite their capabilities, languished in the state institution, until ENCOR petitioned the Department of Public Institutions for their release to the community program on the grounds of their legal right to decide. To date, in all such conflicts that have gone through the legal appeal process, the state has decided against the parents on grounds that the retarded adult's right to non-institutional living and right to decide were superior to his parents' right to control an individual they had surrendered to state institutional care. Unfortunately, such appeals have taken as long as two years, during which time the retarded persons remained in the institution, waiting for vindication of a human right they should have possessed by constitutional mandate as fellow citizens. What is needed are state laws which specifically state the legal competence of retarded persons unless they are pronounced incompetent by a court. If this is not achieved, state officials should adopt a uniform policy to prevent this frequent abuse at institutions for the mentally retarded. Too often the retarded person is merely a pawn used at the expense of the coincident interests of his parents and institutional officials: the parents do not wish to care for their offspring at home or have him embarrass or discomfort them by his presence in their home community, and thus seek to keep him institutionalized; institution officials are eager for the often public praise of such parents for the institutional services, and use it in the political struggle against community-based programs. This may seem a harsh judgment of parents; but in fact, institutional visitation and payment records indicate their low esteem for their mentally retarded children. At the Beatrice State Home in Nebraska, for example, only 15 percent of parents of institutionalized persons contribute financially to their care, and only 22 percent visit as often as once per year. Thus the physical isolation of retarded persons can be compounded by the diminution of their legal rights by parents and institution officials. Recognition in law, or at least in the form of state policy, of the right of those retarded persons not legally declared incompetent would give many institutionalized persons the leverage they need for exercising their varying levels of personal-social-vocational developmental abilities.

Finally, it is necessary that the community-based service agency assume an advocacy posture on behalf of each of their clients. The service agency's counselor-advocate is both a guide to the client through the community's service programs, and a protector (when necessary) of the client's right to appropriate and worthy services. As much as possible, the client must be kept from becoming a prisoner of the service system, a status that is an unhappily apt description of the institutionalized person. Thus the ideology of normalization demands that service-givers treat clients as competent, unless proven otherwise, and create and support conditions where they may exercise that competence. Hence, the counselor-advocate and the service system itself must support the principle of the assumption of legal competence, and should work with parents, legislators, and institutions so that they may recognize this right of retarded persons, if not in law, at least in fact.

## Professional Resistance

Some of the professionals in the field of mental retardation, who are opponents of de-institutionalization, seem determined to revive the moribund stereotypes of the retarded person as sick, unable to learn, dangerous to others and himself. At a recent professional conference recently, I was stunned to hear the same distorted stereotypes brought out to discredit de-institutionalization. I give these examples at length, first because the conclusion drawn from the case histories are testimony to the myopic and biased view of those who oppose de-institutionalization, and second because they point to aspects in the process which must be attended to if de-institutionalization is to work.

A. Joan, a mildly retarded, 24-year-old girl with good vocational skills, was released from an institution for the mentally retarded after 14 years. She rented an apartment in her native city and found a job. With her first paycheck, she bought a week's supply of groceries, including a substantial amount of hamburger, and put it all in the small freezer. Subsequently, she would thaw the hamburger, cook some, and then re-freeze the meat. As a result, she contracted food poisoning and nearly died.

B. Albert, mildly retarded, was a 22-year-old man released from an institution to a community-based program. Since he was verbal, had good job skills, and succeeded in quickly getting a job, his counselor made no follow-up visits. A month later, Albert was living with a homosexual co-worker who appeared to help Albert with his work situation, personal decisions, and money management. Two months later, they both quit their jobs and left town. Albert returned alone shortly afterward with no money, job, or place to live.

C. Estelle, a rather vivacious, moderately retarded adolescent, was placed upon her release from an institution, in a regular public school class for the educable retarded with a skilled teacher. She had difficulty adjusting to the competition at school, had a number of arguments with her roommate at the group home, and gradually became quiet, lonely, and sullen. Soon, she refused to attend school at all because she felt that she was the object of her classmate's ridicule. Her overall uncooperative behavior led to dismissal from school, and shortly thereafter she was returned to the institution as "an emotionally disturbed and troublesome individual."

The conclusion of the speaker who gave these examples was that these were the "horrors" of de-institutionalization: people left alone, abused, and mistreated in a world too complex for them to understand.

In dealing with such scare stories, one must ask first: Is the total absence of concern and support services for the persons portrayed a fair picture of community-based services? The opponents of de-institutionalization almost invariably picture the process as one which abandons retarded persons to poverty, exploitation, insensitivity, and isolation. De-institutionalization need not abandon people in need; in Nebraska, for example, the process places them in a system of services which offers as much certainty of service as the best of the many institutions that I have visited.

The above examples are hardly sufficient reasons for rejecting community-based programs *in toto,* as the speaker did. The above incidents could probably have been avoided, had each client been assigned to a conscientious counselor or social worker who would understand the client's limitations and prepare the way for the transition from institutional to community life, who would closely monitor this transition and follow the client through increasingly autonomous life adjustments. In ENCOR, for example, each client is assigned a *permanent* counselor, and even the most independent client returning to the community spends a transitional period in a group home before entering into more independent living.

The institution, which is relegated to the background in the above vignettes, is meant to be seen as the safe and secure home from which these persons were evicted. One may, however, have a different impression. Why was Joan, in example A, left to remain ignorant of food care for 14 years? Why was she permitted to leave the institution without extended lessons in independent living, including food preparation? In example B, is it so unlikely that Albert engaged in homosexual activity in the institution? Sex segregation is, of course, *de rigueur* in institutions, and boredom is common. In that context it would be quite expected for a young man to satisfy his sexual drives in whatever way he could. And, to take a less hysterical look at these two examples, both Joan's and Albert's experiences will undoubtedly be the motive for their personal growth. Joan, though she came perilously close to an unfortunate death, will be doubly motivated to learn about food preparation. Albert will learn a healthy distrust for the benevolence of strangers. As for Estelle, in example C, one might ask: How much of her poor self-image and inability to meet the demands of school are due to the poor educational programs for which institutions are justly notorious? Certainly, no proponent of community-based programs would try to justify her classmates' abuse of her; the "skilled teacher" in the vignette should use her skills to educate Estelle's fellow pupils and to raise her self-image. But is it not the institutionalization, the hiding away, of such persons as the educable Estelle that makes her an exotic, strange subject to be ridiculed by her classmates? When people who are "different" are integrated into general society, the rationale for fear, hostility, and ridicule disappears; this certainly is an obvious effect in the American melting pot. The same can be true for retarded and handicapped persons; when they are no longer "protected" from society, they will be merely one more kind of person society will adapt to.

## CONCLUSION

Less than a home, the institution, in its present form and with its present ideology, more resembles a lifelong womb which holds its retarded residents in a state of dependence and sameness which precludes any meaningful or accumulative developmental growth. The last decade has shown, via documented Federal Court cases, that many institutions for the mentally retarded have fostered abuse and neglect. Even if we assume that such situations will never again recur, the over-protection and boring sameness of institutional life condemns retarded persons to a life far short of their developmental potentials. In the past, it has been assumed that society's highest duty to retarded persons was to make them "content." Usually, this has meant, at best, the bland fare of three meals, a bed, and a life within narrow limits. Is it any wonder they are "content" when institutional life has taught them there is no alternative? And is it any wonder they have so long been denied human status when they have been denied the challenge and striving that earn us the dignity and respect of others? In his warm and thoughtful book, *New Directions for Parents of Persons Who Are Retarded,* Robert Perske speaks of "the dignity of risk," which is, I think, the primary reason for bringing retarded persons back to community life: only in this way can retarded persons become, and be recognized as, fellow members of society worthy of respect:

> It is tempting to build virtually total avoidance of risk into the lives of persons who are mentally retarded by limiting their sphere of behavior and interaction in the community, jobs, recreation, relationships with the opposite sex, and so forth. This is especially true in institutions where overpopulation and understaffing is a problem. Even buildings, constructed supposedly for the benefit of the retarded, were designed to help avoid the risk. Fortunately, there is a growing awareness that persons who are retarded must assume their fair and prudent share of risk, commensurate with their level of functioning. . . . Acting on the impulse to protect at the right time can be kind. But it is not kind to so overprotect a person that he is emotionally smothered. It diminishes his dignity as a human and keeps him from experiencing the

risks in life necessary for formal human growth and development (134).

In conclusion, the current national focus on de-institutionalization presents many complex challenges in the continuing effort to enhance the horizons of help and hope for our retarded citizens. The de-institutionalization process of the 1970s represents the culmination of evolving professional, advocate, and judicial thrusts over the last two decades. It is significantly altering the nature of human service systems to give the right to treatment in the least restrictive settings to a group of citizens who have for too long been viewed as unequal.

# EPILOGUE

# TO REDEEM THE PRESENT: REFLECTIONS ON PROGRESSIVE CHANGE IN SERVICES FOR THE MENTALLY RETARDED

A global review of the field of mental retardation during the last ten years demonstrates promising change. After the major exposés of the sordid and dehumanizing conditions that existed in many institutions for the retarded, a period of reform set in. And while community-based service programs were the primary antidote to the disgraceful treatment of retarded persons in institutions, one should recognize that institutions have improved themselves in some ways. Minimum programming for residents has begun. Unsanitary and hazardous conditions, the hallmark of institutions, are less noticeable. The exploitation of residents for the purpose of work without pay (the peonage issue) has, or will soon be, ended.

But, if the conditions of institutions are no longer abhorrent, they are still abnormal. Institutions are inherently inward-looking and self-contained and thereby make it more difficult for residents to return to community life.

Institutions encourage dependency, submissiveness, and apathy, and often reinforce these tendencies with excessive use of sedative drugs. And finally, institutions enforce dull, dehumanizing idleness. These damaging tendencies are, I think, in the nature of institutions; all run counter to the idea I regard as the moral imperative in the field of mental retardation, the concept of normalization.

Normalization, as was discussed elsewhere, has five consequences for programming in residential services:

1. The principle of *integration,* which means that residential services should be community oriented
2. The principle of *smallness,* by which institutional management and congregate-care regimentation are avoided
3. The principle of *separation of domicile* from other functions such as work and play, the normative pattern in our society
4. The principle of *specialization,* which states essentially that services be designed to foster homogeneous groupings
5. The principle of *continuity,* or the ease with which clients can move from one service to the next, in the direction of the least restrictive model available

A striking development of the last few years, and in many ways a corollary to normalization, is the advocacy movement on behalf of the retarded. The first tentative efforts of parents of the retarded to procure better services for their children by forming NARC in 1950 has grown into a movement dedicated to improving services and guaranteeing the full legal and human rights of retarded persons. Advocates are involved in the key processes of planning, decision-making, and monitoring and evaluating programs for the retarded; they are also in the forefront of efforts to gain for the retarded their full rights as citizens.

The change in the field of mental retardation in the last ten years is unmistakably progressive. But what I wish to stress here is the moral nature of the impetus behind this progress. Without the moral commitment of parents to stand up to institutional superintendents, or journalists to uncover the medieval degradation of institutions for the retarded, or of lawyers, doctors, and other professionals to risk their professional security, this progress would have come to nothing. What is as necessary today as it was ten years ago is that same moral commitment. We must see through the rationalizations and the halfway solutions and work through the knotty financial problems and the bureaucratic fumblings to a society where the retarded are considered persons and citizens as valuable as you and I.

Not long ago I attended a national meeting of an organization of professionals whose major vocational endeavor is to provide services for the mentally retarded. Historically this organization stems from the early meetings of superintendents of institutions for the retarded, and to this day it remains packed with these old guard professional personnel. I had been invited to present a paper as part of a panel on behavior problems in the retarded. Since studying the behavioral dimensions of the retarded is my favorite vocation-avocation, I readily agreed to attend and to present.

The first speaker was a psychologist, whose paper was listed in the program as "Psychological Issues in Institutionalization of the Mentally Retarded." He prefaced his presentation by remarking that he had just changed jobs from a Midwestern institution for the retarded to a university setting in another region of our country. He stated that during the interval between the time he agreed to present the paper and the day of the presentation, he had searched deeply his reasons for staying at this institution for the last six years and his service value to his retarded clients; wondered why the community programs which he had both visited and studied were not more actively accepted by his institutional colleagues; decided to leave his institutional position; and rewritten his paper. His gut-level presentation succinctly questioned both the validity and the morality of professionals who staff traditional institutional settings for the retarded, institutions which have lost their ideological underpinnings and are of minimal value to their retarded residents, preparing them for a life of personal oblivion in a human wasteland. He strongly recommended that institutions for the retarded be rapidly phased out while, at the same time, a wide array of community-based programs be started, elaborated, and brought to fruition. It was an excellent paper, presented with a flair and conviction that was no doubt a little upsetting to his institutional colleagues.

That afternoon there was a symposium on architectural challenges in providing residential settings for the retarded. The opening speaker began by discussing normalization, the nonmedical model, specialization of services, and so on. This meeting sounded like the fulfillment of the promise of the morning session. Then a document pertaining to the speaker's topic was distributed to the audience. The document contained the plan for a 400-bed institution to be built in the countryside in one of our states. Like some cruel parody, the document used modern concepts primarily as a means of disguising and selling an obsolete idea, another isolated institution! The preface started as follows:

> It is the belief of the mental health experts in [name of state] that residents of state facilities for the mentally retarded have often been relegated to the status of second class citizens, have been subjected to a dehumanizing process and have been denied their basic human and civil rights. Too often, state facilities have been "make-believe hospitals" in their structure, staffing, and administration, when in fact, a

large percentage of their patients do not require medical care. The important needs of the mentally retarded, i.e., aid in developing language skills as well as social, emotional and basic behavioral training, have been severely neglected.

Following the preface there were a number of line drawings which depicted mentally retarded individuals in a variety of "home-like settings." The drawings were captioned; "Come with me to touch, to taste, to feel the world: for this is what is real." "Clustered homes amid the green of grass and trees. Walk with me. Enjoy the gentle breeze." "Drink in the warm, the love, the sound you hear; where life is full of hope without fear"—and so on. Are these the realities of life which you and I, presumably part of the "normal" population, experience in the mainstream of our urban communities?

More disturbing was the architectural rendering and its accompanying title narratives which commenced with the heading "A Planned Community": "Clusters of single story condominiums set among green belts, playgrounds, winding walkways, overlooking a crystal lagoon ..." "A complete community with medical, religious, educational and recreational facilities ..." "A community environment where the mentally retarded can experience the same rights and privileges as due all citizens ... where the exceptional are not an exception." Are these the standards of mainstream society? Who has the everyday luxury of a "crystal lagoon"? Doesn't a "complete community" sound like the old wine of the large institutional setting for the retarded in a new bottle—in a smaller but still self-contained entity? The phrase "where the exceptional are not an exception" sounds like a modern-day rationalization for a colony for the deviants, whether they be exceptional via tuberculosis, leprosy, epilepsy, or mental retardation!

Increasingly, when I attend such conventions, I abstract them into antitheses. On one hand, the dream, the promise, the idealism, the hard and clean moral decision of the man whose conscience demands that he use his knowledge to improve the lot of retarded citizens as much as he knows how. On the other hand, the status quo, the frozen negative attitudes, and, increasingly today, the slick Madison Avenue packaging of the same old, dreary, institutional story. There was a time, perhaps, when this dichotomy between morality and indifference was not so sharp. The earliest institutions for the mentally retarded in this country were, in fact, training schools, and those who entered returned to society better trained and more fully developed individuals. That day certainly is past. Today, institutions for the retarded are too often a one-way street to squalor and oblivion. Not all institutions for the retarded compare with the abomination of the infamous Willowbrook of New York, but I can recommend few of the many I have visited as humane places where a retarded person can develop as a growing, learning individual. Institutions for the retarded per se are overcrowded, understaffed, dehumanizing, and incapable of delivering a fraction of the opportunity and enrichment of normal society.

But these are retarded people, says the institutional superintendent. This is where society sends them. We are understaffed and overworked. But we do the best we can, he adds.

It is not, I would contend, that such men are immoral —they are simply immune to the demands of morality. Institutional blinders are indeed restrictive, and in time the rock-bottom dehumanizing minimum of custodial care begins to look like "the best we can do." A shocked public may demand entrance to view this affront to our ideals, but the fortress walls are up; visitors' passes are necessary; no cameras, thank you. At this point, an appeal to the morality of the institution-keepers, to their ideals and their presumed knowledge, is seen by them as irrelevant. The effect of the institution is to make them as blind to the needs and human potential of the retarded individual as the fearful parents who first placed their child within its walls.

Is there an alternative? This ubiquitous question is testimony to our own blindness to the capabilities of the retarded. The alternative, of course, is outside the institution, in the society of home and community that nourishes us, challenges us, forces us to grow, and fulfills us. Every member of our society has varying medical, psychiatric, counseling, educational, and vocational needs. These needs we deal with in many ways, none of which separate us from home and community. Why then not administer to the needs of the retarded in the same fashion? The success of community-based services for the retarded are persuasive proof of the capabilities of retarded persons; these programs are also a validation of a moral attitude that perceives an ideal and strives to make it real. He who dismisses the promise of community service programs as "lies" and "distortions" is guilty of a double blindness; an inability to see not only what is but what should be.

What, then, is the moral duty of the professional in human services? The physician takes a Hippocratic oath to heal the sick; but there is no counterpart in human services. There is, however, in the analogy of the physician, a clue to what should be the moral oath of the professional in human services and specifically in the field of mental retardation. It is not culturally normal for one to spend his life in any institution, much less in a warehouse that calls itself a therapeutic center. It is, in fact, horrendous that anyone does. Cultural norms cannot be learned in an abnormal milieu. This is a truism today, and if the professionals of 25 years ago could plead ignorance of an alternative to warehousing as an excuse, no such plea is possible today. Community service programs exist, and their value and workability is proven. The knowledge on which these service systems are based is readily accessible to those who recognize that a life based on cultural norms of home, work, and community is not only a possibility for retarded persons, but a moral necessity.

Finally, there is knowledge itself, and the moral demands it creates. The social services are presumably "helping" professions, and, unless the practitioners are morally bankrupt, they must use what is known to help their clients to attain cultural norms as far as is possible. The pioneering efforts of Itard, Séguin, and Howe proved that retarded persons could learn; the mountain of data compiled since then has proven how much they could learn. These are inconvenient facts for the defenders of institutions, and one can only conclude that by denying these realities, this data, these facts, they are confirming their own moral bankruptcy as contributing professionals.

To work in community-based services for the retarded is not a total divorce from the "system." The radical posture may be temping, but ultimately it is isolating and self-defeating. I would advise against it. In my experience, the system that fosters and supports the institutions for the retarded can be persuaded to support the community-based alternatives to it. In fact, if one is serious about change, the system must be dealt with and persuaded, for its components are parents, professionals, legislators, and institutional personnel whose support is necessary to a true alternative to institutional care. The community-based system, once established, then depends upon the institution to release clients into the community, and may find that former institutional personnel are early and valuable applicants for work in the alternative system. Thus, while an arm-in-arm or hand-in-hand relationship with the institution may be uncomfortable, communication between the two systems is vital. This the rigid and isolated radical cannot facilitate.

The dichotomy of the two systems is an unnatural one, and the political competition between them can be a distraction from, and detriment to, the proper goal of serving retarded persons. There is evidence, however, that systems of care that utilize both institutional and community resources are evolving. As the 1976 report of the President's Committee on Mental Retardation (135) states, there appears to be a major reorientation of the role of certain public institutions. The report points to three models of services, all of which differ significantly, at least in theory, from the traditional model of the isolated institution. The first of these is the urban residential center which provides services to residents and day services to clients living in the community. An example of the second model is the State of California's effort to convert institutions into speciality residential facilities which prepare clients for community living, where they are served by community based programs. The third model is the regional service delivery system in which the institution is the central facility connected by communication, outreach activities, and the flow of clients to the community based components of the system. One should note that these are fluid, not final, models; but they are extremely hopeful signs that institutions and community based services can work together to provide normalizing services for retarded citizens.

The question of morality, then, is not "us" against "them," or community-based programs versus institutions. It is more a matter of the individual professional's perception of what we all, as human beings, deserve, and his assessment of his own knowledge, power, and vision to effect the necessary changes. I would stress that service providers must focus on the need for individual programming for each and every retarded citizen, regardless of where they reside. If that attitude were common to professionals in mental retardation, the results would vary, for morality leads men in many directions. I do not doubt, however, that the futures of retarded persons would be a hundredfold brighter; that there would be many shapes and forms of service models; and that more young and dedicated professionals would join, anxious to use their knowledge and enthusiasm in the service of persons so long denied the normal life experiences we take for granted.

The legal rights of mentally retarded persons are, at present, being affirmed in the courts. What is crucial now is the affirmation of their human rights by society, the recognition of them as learning, growing persons who deserve the opportunities for self-fulfillment as much as you and I. From my own experience with community-based program in Nebraska, I can say that, when the professionals can embrace this ideal as the proper moral expression of their knowledge, the acceptance of mentally retarded persons by our society will not be far behind.

# NOTES

## INTRODUCTION

1. Doll, E. A. The essentials of an inclusive concept of mental deficiency. *American Journal of Mental Deficiency* 46 (1941): 214–219.
2. Benda, C. E. *Developmental disorders of mentation and cerebral palsies.* New York: Grune & Stratton, 1952.
3. Masland, R. L., Sarason, S. B., and Gladwin, T. *Mental Subnormality: Biological, psychological and cultural factors.* New York: Basic Books, 1958.
4. Grossman, H. J., ed. *Manual on terminology and classification in mental retardation.* Washington: American Association on Mental Deficiency, 1973, p. 11.
5. Ibid., pp. 12–13.
6. Carter, C. H. *Medical aspects of mental retardation.* Springfield, Ill.: C. C. Thomas, 1965.
7. Hillard, L. T., and Kirman, B. H. *Mental deficiency.* Boston: Little, Brown, 1965.
8. Grossman, op. cit.
9. Denhoff, E. *Cerebral palsy: The preschool years.* Springfield, Ill.: C. C. Thomas, 1967.

10. Pearson, P. H. The physician's role in diagnosis and management of the mentally retarded. *Pediatric Clinics of North America* 15 (1968): 835–841.

11. Wolfensberger, W. Embarrassments in the diagnostic process. *Mental Retardation* 3 (1965): 29–31.

12. President's Committee on Mental Retardation. *MR-72: Islands of Excellence.* Washington: Government Printing Office, 1973.

13. Menolascino, F. J. Changing developmental perspectives in Down's syndrome. *Child Psychiatry and Human Development* 4 (1974): 205–215.

14. Crocker, A. C., and Cushna, B. Pediatric decisions in children with serious mental retardation. *Pediatric Clinics of North America* 19 (1972): 413–418.

15. Menolascino, F. J. Primitive, atypical and abnormal behavior in institutionalized mentally retarded children. *Journal of Autism and Child Schizophrenia* 3 (1972): 49–64.

16. Freeman, R. D. Psychopharmacology and the retarded child. In Menolascino, F. J., ed. *Psychiatric Approaches to Mental Retardation.* New York: Basic Books, 1970.

17. U.S. Department of Labor. *Annual Report.* Washington: Government Printing Office, 1972.

# CHAPTER 1

18. Itard, J. *The wild boy of Aveyron.* (Translated by G. & M. Humphrey). New York: Appleton-Century-Crofts, 1962.

19. Seguin, E. *The moral treatment, hygiene, and education of idiots and other backward children.* New York: Columbia University Press, 1846.

20. Goddard, H. *The Kallikak Family.* New York: MacMillan, 1912.

21. Davenport, C. *Heredity in relation to eugenics.* New York: Holt, 1911.

22. Fernald, W. E. *Annual report of the Massachusetts state school for the feebleminded.* Springfield, Mass.: 1922.

23. Vail, D. J. *Dehumanization and the institutional career.* Springfield, Ill.: C. C. Thomas, 1966.

24. Blatt, B., and Kaplan, F. *Christmas in purgatory.* Boston: Allyn & Bacon, 1966.

25. Edgerton, R. B. *The cloak of competence.* Berkeley: University of California Press, 1967.

26. Hunt, N. *The world of Nigel Hunt: The diary of a mongoloid youth.* New York: Taplinger, 1967.

27. Bernstein, N. R., ed. *Diminished people.* Boston: Little, Brown, 1970.
28. Tizard, J. *Community services for the mentally handicapped.* Oxford: Oxford University Press, 1964.
29. Blatt, B. Empty revolution beyond the mental. In Menolascino, F. J., ed. *Psychiatric approaches to mental retardation.* New York: Basic Books, 1970.
30. Menolascino, F. J. The facade of mental retardation: Its challenges to child psychiatry. *American Journal of Psychiatry* 122 (1966): 1227–1235.
31. Wolfensberger, W. *The principle of normalization in human services.* Toronto: National Institute for Mental Retardation, 1972.
32. Potter, H. M. Human values as guides to the administration of residential facilities for the mentally retarded. In Menolascino, F. J. ed., *Psychiatric approaches to mental retardation.* New York: Basic Books, 1970.

## CHAPTER 2

33. President's Committee on Mental Retardation. *MR '68: The Edge of Change.* Washington: Government Printing Office, 1969.
34. Nirje, B. The normalization principle and its human management implications. In Kugel, R. B., and Wolfensberger, W., eds. *Changing patterns in residential services for the mentally retarded.* Washington: President's Committee on Mental Retardation, 1969.
35. Wolfensberger, W. *The principle of normalization in human services.* Toronto: National Institute for Mental Retardation, 1972.
36. Perske, R. The dignity of risk and the mentally retarded. *Mental Retardation* 10 (1972): 24–27.
37. President's Committee on Mental Retardation. *MR '72: Islands of Excellence.* Washington: Government Printing Office, 1973.
38. Masland, R. L., Sarason, S. B., and Gladwin, T. *Mental Subnormality: Biological, psychological and cultural factors.* New York: Basic Books, 1958.
39. Hurley, R. L. *Poverty and mental retardation: A causal relationship.* New York: Random House, 1969.
40. Menolascino, F. J. The facade of mental retardation: Its challenge to child psychiatry. *American Journal of Psychiatry* 122 (1966): 1221–1235.

41. Gardner, W. I. The use of behavior therapy with the mentally retarded. In Menolascino, F. J., ed. *Psychiatric approaches to mental retardation.* New York: Basic Books, 1970.

## CHAPTER 3

42. Cramond, W. A. One step at a time: A review of some aspects of the recent literature on mental retardation. *The Australian Journal of Mental Retardation* 1 (1970): 101–114.
43. Koch, R. The multidisciplinary approach to mental retardation. In Baumeister, A. A., ed. *Mental Retardation.* Chicago: Aldine Publishing, 1967.
44. President's Committee on Mental Retardation. *MR '71: Entering the era of human ecology.* Washington: Government Printing Office, 1972.
45. National Association for Retarded Citizens. *1972 Annual Report.* Arlington, Texas: 1973.

## CHAPTER 4

46. Chess, S. *An introduction to child psychiatry,* 2nd ed. New York: Grune & Stratton, 1969.
47. Woodward, K. F., Jaffe, N., and Brown, D. Early psychiatric intervention for young mentally retarded children. In Menolascino, F. J., ed. *Psychiatric approaches to mental retardation.* New York: Basic Books, 1970.
48. Joint Commission on Mental Health in Children. *Crisis in child mental health: Challenge for the 1970's.* New York: Harper & Row, 1969.
49. Chess, S., Korn, S., and Fernandez, P. B. *Psychiatric disorders of children with congenital rubella.* New York: Brunner/Mazel, 1971.
50. Grunewald, K. International trends in the care of the severely and profoundly retarded and multiply handicapped. In Menolascino, F. J., and Pearson, P. H., eds. *Beyond the limits: Innovations in services for the severely and profoundly retarded.* Seattle: Special Child Publications, 1974.
51. Menolascino, F. J. Emotional disturbance in institutionalized retardates. Primitive, atypical and abnormal behaviors. *Mental Retardation* 10 (1972): 3–8.
52. Webster, T. G. Unique aspects of emotional development in mentally retarded children. In Menolascino, F. J., ed. *Psychiatric approaches to mental retardation.* New York: Basic Books, 1970.

53. Eisenberg, L. Caste, class, and intelligence. In Murray, R. F., and Rosser, P. L. *The genetic and developmental aspects of mental retardation.* Springfield, Ill.: C. C. Thomas, 1972.
54. Kanner, L. Problems of nosology and psychodynamics of early infantile autism. *American Journal of Orthopsychiatry* 19 (1949): 416–426, 422.
55. Kanner, L. Feeblemindedness: Absolute, relative and apparent. *Nervous Child* 7 (1948): 365–397.
56. Schain, R. J., and Yannet, H. Infantile autism. *Journal of Pediatrics* 57 (1960): 560–567.
57. Rutter, M., Graham, P., and Yule, W. *A neuropsychiatric study in childhood.* (Clinics in Developmental Medicine, Nos. 35 and 36) Philadelphia: Lippincott, 1970.
58. Kanner, 1949, op. cit.
59. Bender, L. Autism in children with mental deficiency. *American Journal of Mental Deficiency* 63 (1959): 81–86.
60. Wing, J. K. Epidemiology of early childhood autism. *Developmental Medicine and Child Neurology* 5 (1963): 646–647.
61. Rutter, Graham, and Yule, op. cit.
62. Menolascino, F. J. Emotional disturbance in mentally retarded children. *American Journal of Psychiatry* 126 (1969): 54–62.
63. Creak, E. M. Childhood psychosis: A review of 100 cases. *British Journal of Psychiatry* 109 (1963): 84–89.
64. Finley, K. H. Behavioral disorders and brain dysfunction. *Medical Clinics of North America* 17 (1963): 1691–1710.
65. Piaget, J. *The origin of intelligence in the child.* New York: International Universities Press, 1952.
66. Cleckley, H. *The mask of sanity.* St. Louis: C. V. Mosby, 1941.
67. Humphreys, E. J. Psychopathic personality among mental defectives. *Psychiatric Quarterly* 14 (1940): 231–247.
68. Tarjan, G. Current thinking regarding psychopaths. *American Journal of Mental Deficiency* 53 (1948): 302–312.
69. American Psychiatric Association. *Diagnostic and statistical manual of mental disorders,* 2nd ed. Washington: 1968.
70. Chess, S. Emotional problems in mentally retarded children. In Menolascino, F. J., ed. *Psychiatric approaches to mental retardation.* New York: Basic Books, 1970.
71. Webster, op. cit.
72. American Psychiatric Association, op. cit.
73. Menolascino, F. J. Psychiatric aspects of mongolism. *American Journal of Mental Deficiency* 69 (1965): 653–660.
74. Caplan, G. *Community support systems.* New York: Behavioral Publications, 1973.

75. Gardner, W. I. *Behavior modification in mental retardation: The education and rehabilitation of the mentally retarded adolescent and adult.* Chicago: Aldine-Atherton, 1971.

76. Rogers, C. R., and Dyamond, R. F. *Psychotherapy and personality change.* Chicago: University of Chicago Press, 1954.

76a. Wolfensberger, W. Diagnosis diagnosed. *Journal of Mental Subnormality* 11 (1965): 62–70.

77. Lindsley, O. R. Direct measurement and prosthesis of retarded behavior. *Journal of Education* 147 (1964): 62–81.

78. Ullman, L. P., and Krasner, L., eds. *Case studies in behavior modification.* New York: Academic Press, 1969.

79. Baumeister, A. A. More ado about operant conditioning—or nothing? *Mental Retardation* 7 (1969): 49–51.

80. Fish, B. Drug therapy in child psychiatry: Psychological aspects. *Comprehensive Psychiatry* 1 (1960): 55–61.

81. Freeman, R. D. Psychopharmacology and the retarded child. In Menolascino, F. J., ed. *Psychiatric approaches to mental retardation.* New York: Basic Books, 1970.

82. Colodny, D., and Kurlander, L. F. Psychopharmacology as a treatment adjunct for the mentally retarded: Problems and issues. In Menolascino, F. J., ed. *Psychiatric approaches to mental retardation.* New York: Basic Books, 1970.

83. Lipman, R. S. The use of psychopharmacological agents in residential facilities for the retarded. In Menolascino, F. J., ed. *Psychiatric approaches to mental retardation.* New York: Basic Books, 1970.

84. Menolascino, 1965, op. cit.

85. Menolascino, F. J. Changing development perspectives in Down's syndrome. *Child Psychiatry and Human Development* 4 (1974): 205–215.

86. President's Committee on Mental Retardation. *MR '72: Islands of excellence.* Washington: Government Printing Office, 1973.

## CHAPTER 5

87. Sumner, W. *Folkways.* Boston: Ginn, 1906.

88. Allen, R. The mentally retarded in penal and correctional institutions. *American Journal of Psychiatry* 124 (1968): 9–13.

89. Holmes, O. W. *The common law.* (Edited by M. D. Howe). Boston: Little, Brown, 1963.

90. Kugel, R., Trembath, J., and Sugar, S. Some characteristics of patients, legally committed to a state institution for the mentally retarded. *Mental Retardation* 6 (1968): 9–12.

91. Bazelon, D. L., Boggs, E. M., Hilleboe, H. D., and Tudor, W. W. *Report of the task force on law: The president's panel on mental retardation.* Washington: Government Printing Office, 1963.

92. Allen, R. C. The law and the mentally retarded. In Menolascino, F. J., ed. *Psychiatric approaches to mental retardation.* New York: Basic Books, 1970.

93. Keller, O. J., and Alper, B. S. *Halfway Houses: Community centered correction and treatment.* Lexington, Mass.: Health, 1970.

94. *Sas* v. *Maryland,* 334 F. 2d 506, 4th Cir. 1964.

95. Brown, B., and Courtless, T. *The mentally retarded offender.* Washington: The President's Commission on Law Enforcement and Administration of Justice, 1967.

96. Fernald, W. E. *Annual report of the Massachusetts state school for the feebleminded.* Springfield: State of Massachusetts, 1922.

97. Krause, F. J. Juvenile justice deficiencies are multiplied for retarded. *PCMR Message* 32 (1972).

## CHAPTER 6

98. De la Cruz, F. F., and LaVeck, G. D., eds. *Human Sexuality and the mentally retarded.* New York: Brunner/Mazel, 1973.

99. International League of Societies for the Mentally Handicapped. *Declaration of general and specific rights of the mentally retarded.* Brussels: 1969.

100. President's Committee on Mental Retardation. *MR '69: Toward progress—the story of a decade.* Washington: Government Printing Office, 1970.

101. Nirje, B. The normalization principle and its human management implications. In Kugel, R. B., and Wolfensberger, W., eds. *Changing patterns in residential services for the mentally retarded.* Washington: President's Committee on Mental Retardation, 1969.

102. Perske, R. About sexual development: An attempt to be human with the mentally retarded. *Mental Retardation* 11 (1973): 6–8.

## CHAPTER 7

103. Jordon, J. B., and Robbins, L. S., eds. *Let's try doing something else kind of thing: Behavioral principles and the exceptional child.* Arlington: Council for Exceptional Children, 1972.

104. Wolfensberger, W. *The principle of normalization in human services.* Toronto: National Institute for Mental Retardation, 1972.

## CHAPTER 8

105. Lindsley, O. R. Precision teaching in perspective: An interview with Ogden R. Lindsley. *Teaching Exceptional Children* 3 (1971): 114–119.

## CHAPTER 9

106. Solomons, G. Counseling parents of the retarded: The interpretation interview. In Menolascino, F. J., ed. *Psychiatric approaches to Mental Retardation.* New York: Basic Books, 1970.

107. Menolascino, F. J. Psychiatric aspects of mental retardation in children under eight. *American Journal of Orthopsychiatry* 35 (1965): 852–861.

108. Wolfensberger, W., and Menolascino, F. J. Methodological considerations in evaluating the intelligence enhancing properties of drugs. In Menolascino, F. J., ed. *Psychiatric approaches to mental retardation.* New York: Basic Books, 1970.

109. Ross, A. O. *The exceptional child in the family.* New York: Grune & Stratton, 1964.

110. Beddie, A., and Osmond, H. Mothers, mongols, and mores. *Canadian Medical Association Journal* 73 (1955): 167–170.

111. Solnit, A. J., and Stark, M. H. Mourning and the birth of a defective child. *Psychoanalytical Study of Childhood* 16 (1961): 523–537.

112. Olshansky, S. Parent response to mentally defective children. *Mental Retardation* 4 (1966): 21–23.

113. Farber, B. Effects of a severely mentally retarded child on family integration. *Monographs of the Society of Research in Child Development* 24 (1959).

114. Solnit and Stark, op. cit.

115. McDonald, E. T. *Understanding those feelings.* Pittsburgh: Stanwix House, 1962.

116. Kramm, E. R. *Families of mongoloid children.* Washington: Government Printing Office, 1963.

117. Wolfensberger, W. Diagnosis diagnosed. *Journal of Mental Subnormality* 11 (1965): 62–70.

118.  Kugel, R. B., and Wolfensberger, W., eds. *Changing patterns in residential services for the mentally retarded.* Washington: President's Committee on Mental Retardation, 1969.

119.  Eaton, J. W., and Weil, R. J. *Cultural and mental disorders. A comparative study of Hutterites and other populations.* Glencoe, Ill.: Free Press, 1955.

120.  Farber, op. cit.

121.  Kramm, op. cit.

122.  Buck, P. *The child who never grew.* New York: John Day, 1950.

123.  Frank, J. P. *My son's story.* New York: Knopf, 1952.

124.  Junker, K. S. *The child in the glass ball.* New York: Abingdon, 1964.

125.  Rychman, D. B., and Henderson, R. A. The meaning of a retarded child for his parents: A focus for counselors. *Mental Retardation* 3 (1965): 4–7.

126.  Eaton and Weil, op. cit.

127.  Weingold, J. T., and Hormuth, R. P. Group guidance of parents of mentally retarded children. *Journal of Clinical Psychology* 9 (1953): 118–124.

## CHAPTER 11

128.  Scheerenberger, R. D. *Current trends and status of public residential services for the mentally retarded—1974.* Madison, Wisc.: National Association of Superintendents of Public Residential Facilities, 1975, pp. 4–7.

129.  Santiestevan, H. *Out of their beds and into the streets.* Washington: American Federation of State, County and Municipal Employees, 1975.

130.  Joint Commission on Accreditation of Hospitals/Accreditation Committee on Facilities for the Mentally Retarded. *Report of March 1975.* Chicago: American Hospital Association, 1975.

131.  Webster, T. G. Unique aspects of emotional development in mentally retarded children. In Menolascino, F. J., ed. *Psychiatric Approaches to Mental Retardation.* New York: Basic Books, 1970.

132.  Santiestevan, *op. cit.*

133.  Facts speak for themselves (Editorial). Mental Retardation Association of Utah (Salt Lake City), *Utah Beeline 4,* (1975): 4.

134.  Perske, R. *New Directions for parents of persons who are retarded.* Nashville: Abingdon Press, 1973, p. 36.

# CHAPTER 12

135.    President's Committee on Mental Retardation. *Mental Retardation: Trends in State Services.* Washington, D.C., U.S. Government Printing Office, 1976, pp. 31–32.

# INDEX